The Theorist's Mother

ANDREW PARKER

The Theorist's Mother

Duke University Press Durham and London 2012

© 2012 Duke University Press
All rights reserved
Printed in the United States of America
on acid-free paper ♾
Designed by C. H. Westmoreland
Typeset in Charis by Tseng Information
Systems, Inc.
Library of Congress Cataloging-in-
Publication Data appear on the last
printed page of this book.

Duke University Press gratefully
acknowledges the Amherst College
Language and Literature Fund for
assistance in the production of this book.

In memory of

Selma Blossom Cohen Parker

1926–1991

plus qu'une mère

A mother is only brought unlimited satisfaction by her relation to a son; this is altogether the most perfect, the most free from ambivalence of all human relationships.
—SIGMUND FREUD, "Femininity"

The writer is someone who plays with his mother's body . . . in order to glorify it, to embellish it, or in order to dismember it, to take it to the limit of what can be known about the body.
—ROLAND BARTHES, *The Pleasure of the Text*

Algernon: All women become like their mothers. That is their tragedy. No man does. That's his.
—OSCAR WILDE, *The Importance of Being Earnest*

"Why on earth should I feel called upon to write a book?" Ulrich objected. "I was born of my mother, after all, not an inkwell."
—ROBERT MUSIL, *The Man without Qualities*

Don't forget that it's almost as stupid to say of a book that "It's very intelligent" as to say "He was very fond of his mother." But that first proposition still needs proving.
—MARCEL PROUST, *Contre Saint-Beuve*

Wystan: I am *not* your father, I'm *your* mother.
Chester: You're *not* my mother! I'm *your* mother!
—RICHARD DAVENPORT-HINES, *Auden*

Salomé: He says terrible things about my mother, does he not!
2nd Soldier: We never understand what he says, Princess.
—OSCAR WILDE, *Salomé*

The sense I give to the name mother must be explained, and that is what will be done hereafter.
—JEAN-JACQUES ROUSSEAU, *Émile*

Contents

Preface and Acknowledgments

Here there is a kind of question, let us call it historical,
whose conception, formation, gestation and labor we are only
catching a glimpse of today.
—JACQUES DERRIDA, *Writing and Difference*

Every theorist is the child of a mother, but few have acknowledged this fact as *theoretically* significant. And why should they? Mothers, after all, may have helped to bring the philosopher into existence but not his or her philosophy. Mothers give birth and raise children but theorists think—a division of labor as old as the division of labor. That mothers work to make it possible for their philosopher-children to think never seems to affect what philosophers think, even if the language of philosophy leans heavily on maternity's imagery. We speak regularly of the birth of tragedy, say, or of the clinic, despite knowing that tragedies and clinics are neither born nor give birth. Indeed, our conception of generation "is so instinctive to us that the etymology of 'concept' goes largely unremarked."[1] We tell ourselves meanwhile that mothers, like the poor, are much too busy for theory.[2] Though both mothers and philosophers are educators, mothers do their work at home and not in public, teach by example rather than by argument, and are never made to stand for examinations or fulfill competency requirements of the sort that, since the nineteenth century, have made philosophy an academic profession. While women may now be philosophers, mothers qua mothers may not. And yet we theorists persist in describing our books as our children, perhaps the only time we do not derogate procreation as inferior to thought: "For anyone who looked at Homer and Hesiod and all the other great poets would envy them because of the kind of offspring they left behind them," says Diotima in Plato's *Symposium*. "They would rather be the parent of children like these, who have conferred on their progenitors immortal glory and fame, than of ordinary human children."[3]

Although in many ways Plato still defines how we think about thinking *and* mothers, the relationship between these terms has grown especially vexed during the past one hundred and fifty-odd years. Some of this turmoil is recent, stemming from the uncertain implications for philosophy of the proliferation of "assisted reproduction" technologies and the new family forms these technologies have helped create. But mother trouble is already legible in the theoretical traditions associated with Karl Marx and Sigmund Freud—Michel Foucault's twin "founders of discursivity"—given that these traditions uniquely pose the question of their own reproduction as an element of their theorization.[4] When, for example, Jacques Lacan pillories the psychoanalytic establishment for the inorganic way that it trains its future practitioners, he has recourse to an idiom that implicates as well the afterlife of his own thought: "In order to be passed on—and not having at its disposal the law of blood that implies generation or the law of adoption that presupposes marriage—it has at its disposal only the pathway of imaginary reproduction which, through a form of facsimile analogous to printing, allows it to print, as it were, a certain number of copies whereby the one [*l'unique*] becomes plural."[5] But can Marxism and psychoanalysis ever count on their reproduction when the one excludes mothers from its purview and the other has eyes mainly for fathers? Do we know, already with Marx and Freud as well as after them, who or what a mother may be? Where *do* theorists come from?

All subsequent theory—including feminist and queer varieties indebted (or not) to Marx and Freud—has had to grapple with these questions, and this book explores some of their disconcerting consequences. Maternal predicaments occupy center stage in three different ways in the book's central chapters, where the mother (dis)-appears in turn as an inassimilable body, a constitutive absence, and a foreign native tongue. Since I call philosophers to task for failing to consider their own mothers' pertinence for thinking, chapter 1—a rereading of "the body" in Lacanian teaching—includes reflection on my mother's form of psychosomatic pedagogy. In pondering the mother's near-total elision from Marxist thought, chapter 2 discerns in György Lukács's reading of Sir Walter Scott's *Waverley* a characteristic injunction to read fiction as history's parthenogenic child. Where the first two chapters treat Marxism and psychoanalysis separately, chapter 3 brings them together to consider what specifically in these traditions the mother can and cannot translate. At their con-

clusions all three chapters pass through the membrane that traditionally divides Writing from Life, as relations between particular
mothers and sons (my own, Lukács's, and Vladimir Medem's) enact
in a different register the argument that precedes them. The book's
introduction and coda explore more general questions concerning the
mother's troubling identity—more troubling now than ever, perhaps,
when even "her" gender may defy prediction.

Truth be told, *The Theorist's Mother* is an accidental book, but no less
beloved by me for that. Other books may begin at the beginning, but
this one came together belatedly with the surprising discovery that I
had already been writing about mothers—for years and years, in fact.
Have I ever written about anything else? Why, indeed, was I the last
to know? Perhaps, in structural terms, I am hardly the one to answer
these questions. In any case, Julia Kristeva's description of maternity
seems an apt characterization of this book's peculiar gestation—as
well as of the nature of writing more generally: "'It happens, but I'm
not there.' 'I cannot realize it, but it goes on.' Motherhood's impossible syllogism."[6] Maternity and writing will share many such traits
in the chapters that follow.
　A second surprise is that these pages turned out in some sense to
be "about" Jacques Derrida even though his work never occupies center stage for very long. Though I anticipated devoting a concluding
chapter to Derrida's abiding interest in maternity as an unmasterable
question for philosophy, it soon seemed clear to me that to do full
justice to this material—from *Of Grammatology* and "Khora" to *Glas*
and "Circumfession"—would require a book of its own. Given that
the impact of Derrida's thinking is nonetheless apparent throughout
this project, I sensed that a culminating chapter on his work could
also leave the impression that, here at last, is the maternal truth that
eluded all of his theorist predecessors. Nothing could be further from
the deconstructive point this book wants to make about maternity and
teleology, or, indeed, about maternity *as* teleology: that the mother's
identity has never been undivided, that our inability to recognize a
mother when we think we see one began well before the modern ad-
vent of technologically assisted conception. We will discover in what
follows that this point, moreover, is not simply Derrida's. The revital-

ized field of kinship studies, in grappling not only with the global impact of new reproductive technologies but also with sociosexual challenges to the definition of the family, will similarly conclude that there is always more than one mother. If Derrida retains some privilege here, it is in the hope that the terms he provides may help renew discussion within and between the fields of philosophy, ethnography, literary and media studies, linguistics, and feminist and queer studies—in short, in whatever remains today of Theory.

This book was inspired in a different way by the world-renowned artist Louise Bourgeois, whose *Blind Man's Buff* (1984) appears on the cover of the paperback. I read this highly tactile marble sculpture with its impossibly numerous breastlike protuberances mounted on a headless, phallic torso as a wry if unsettling take on what theorists want from their mothers. Bourgeois died in 2010 at the age of ninety-nine. Much of this book was written in the Manhattan neighborhood I "shared" with her (along with several hundred thousand others), and I am sorry not to have been able to make her a gift of it. Less tinctured by the Lacanian imaginary were the recent deaths of a number of other muses—friends and interlocutors I knew in different circumstances and at different moments of our sundry lives. I can recognize some of the places where Sean Holland, Barbara Johnson, Eve Kosofsky Sedgwick, Greta Slobin, and David Foster Wallace each left traces in the writing; perhaps others will emerge with the passage of time.

I have many happy debts to acknowledge as well. Françoise Meltzer and Stephen Melville may be reminded of conversations we had together in Chicago in the early 1980s. Colleagues and friends at Amherst College and in the Pioneer Valley—Michèle Barale, Anston Bosman, Greg Call, Jack Cameron, Jay Caplan, Jennifer Cayer, Cathy Ciepiela, Rhonda Cobham-Sander, John Drabinski, Tom Dumm, Judy Frank, Liz Garland, Deborah Gewertz, Heidi Gilpin, Margaret Groesbeck, Daniel Hall, Amelie Hastie, Nat Herold, Leah Hewitt, Marie-Hélène Huet, Nasser Hussain, Kannan Jagannathan, Michael Kasper, Sura Levine, Marisa Parham, Dale Peterson, Dennis Porter, Catherine Portugese, Ronald Rosbottom, Karen Sánchez-Eppler, Austin Sarat, Robert Schwarzwald, Adam Sitze, Kim Townsend, and Martha Merrill Umphrey—have fed my mind and stomach since 1982. My colleagues at Rutgers the past two years made me feel instantly at home; my thanks to Myriam Alami, Carole Allamand, César Braga-Pinto, Mathilde Bombart, François Cornilliat, Elin Diamond, Josephine Diamond, Uri Eisenzweig, Ann Fabian, Lynn Festa, Jerry Flieger, Sandy Flitterman-Lewis, Billy Galperin, Doug Greenberg, Myra Jehlen, John Kucich, Renée Larrier, Jorge Marcone, Susan Martin-Márquez, Yolanda Martínez-San Miguel, Michael McKeon, Richard Miller, Anna Pairet, Lorraine Piroux, Barry Qualls, Stéphane Robolin, Diane Sadoff, Evie Shockley, Derek Schilling, Richard Serrano, Mary Shaw, Jonah Siegel, Ben Sifuentes, Mary Speer, Jimmy Swenson, Henry Turner, Janet Walker, Steve Walker, Rebecca Walkowitz, Cheryl Wall, Alan Williams, and Carolyn Williams.

Jane Gallop, Marge Garber, and Bill Germano have kept me returning annually to the English Institute even when I no longer needed to. I am long beholden to Jonathan Arac, Ian Balfour, Geoff Bennington, Lauren Berlant, Judith Butler, Eduardo Cadava, Cathy Caruth, Cynthia Chase, Jonathan Culler, Penelope Deutscher, Shoshana Felman, Diana Fuss, Barbara Guetti, Michael Lucey, John Mowitt, Tim Murray, Yopie Prins, Bruce Robbins, Avital Ronell, and Gayatri Spivak for allowing me to feel like a fellow traveler. The cast and crew of the Leverett-Montague Players—among them Emily Apter, Lee Edelman, Jonathan Goldberg, Jay Grossman, Janet Halley, Lisa Henderson, Ann R. Jones, Joseph Litvak, Jeffrey Masten, Michael Moon, Hal Sedgwick, Peter Stallybrass, Tony Vidler, Daniel Warner, and Elizabeth Wingrove—have sworn that what happens onstage stays onstage, for which I am hugely grateful. Sean Belman, Brent Edwards, Yvette Christiansë, Mikhal Dekel, Stephen Engelmann, Lisa Gitelman, Stathis Gourgouris, Martin Harries, Virginia Jackson, Suvir Kaul, Ania Loomba, Tina Lupton, Daphne and Robert McGill, Sophia Mihic, Rosalind Morris, Neni Panourgia, Leslie Parker, Sarah Schulman, Michael Warner, and Nancy Yousef never once told me that they had heard enough already about mothers. Mary Russo argued with me every step of the way. I read the manuscript of Elissa Marder's *The Mother in the Age of Mechanical Reproduction* too late to profit from its stunning insights; I look forward to years of sharing the microphone with Marder on conference panels and daytime talk shows. I am delighted to have worked once again with the editors and staff of

Duke University Press—my special thanks to Ken Wissoker, Courtney Berger, and Leigh Barnwell, and to an anonymous reviewer of the manuscript. The index was prepared with the assistance of J. Naomi Linzer Indexing Services. A portion of chapter 1 appeared in *The Oxford Literary Review* 8, nos. 1–2 (1985), 96–104. Meredith McGill made this book necessary, as Yogi Berra would have said, and she is even happier than I am to see it in print. The book is dedicated to the memory of my mother, who taught me first about the limits of the possessive.

Jersey City, May 2011

Introduction
Philosophy's Mother Trouble

> . . . what is neither subject, nor object, nor figure, and which one can, provisionally and simplistically, call "the mother."
> —PHILIPPE LACOUE-LABARTHE AND JEAN-LUC NANCY, *Retreating the Political*

1.

The Theorist's Mother proposes that what unifies the otherwise disparate traditions of critical theory and philosophy from Karl Marx to Jacques Derrida is their troubled relation to maternity. This is a very large claim, to be sure, and perhaps also an obvious one: has anyone ever been spared a troubled relation to maternity? Even so, "mother trouble" has not typically been recognized as a defining feature of Theory (in its familiarly capacious sense) beyond the forms of its inherence in the work of particular theorists. The mother is seldom included among the customary topoi of philosophy, even as philosophers rely heavily in their discourse on the tropes of maternity. As a synonym for "beginning," the word *birth* appears in every conceivable context in the official histories of Western thought—except for parturition. Marx is in one respect an arbitrary origin for this project, given that he was hardly the first (nor will he be the last) to wish to do entirely without the mother. However much Sigmund Freud would have liked simply to follow suit, he invented his own procedures for making her disappear. Where Martin Heidegger assumed that *Dasein* has no gender, we may infer further that it had, for him, no mother either. Friedrich Nietzsche, Emmanuel Levinas, and Derrida were all unusual as philosophers in the explicit interest they took in maternity, though the various forms of their attention have irritated many of their feminist readers. And yet feminist philosophers and theorists have been no more immune to mother trouble than their canonical counterparts. Indeed, more than a generation after the first births by in vitro fertilization, we have been obliged by new developments in medical technology and by changing conceptions of kinship to think differently not only about the present and future of motherhood but also about its past. Clearly, as Jacqueline Rose has put it, thinking about mothers produces singular effects on the nature of thinking itself.[1] This book traces a number of such effects, primarily in the writings of Marx and Freud and their heirs, at a moment when philosophy and theory are confronting what may be their most perplexing challenge: a strangely queered, (im)possible maternity that—till now, at least—is not what we think. What is a mother when we cannot presuppose "her" gender? Were we ever able to?

I imagine the theorist of my title as a scholar working within and across the loose confederation of disciplines—primarily Continental philosophy, psychoanalysis, political theory, anthropology, and linguistics—that transformed literary and cultural analysis in the 1970s just as the "new reproductive technologies" began to change our understandings of conception, pregnancy, and birth. At the center of the book are the figures of Marx, Freud, György Lukács, and Jacques Lacan, with Derrida playing a significant though less direct role throughout. Heidegger, Roland Barthes, Levinas, J.-B. Pontalis, Walter Benjamin, Michel Foucault, and Alain Badiou all make appearances of varying length from supporting actor to cameo, and Nietzsche plays a prominent role in the coda. This book takes up, in other words, one plausible version of "the male theory canon," which, with few exceptions, earns its canonical status in part by not acknowledging itself *as* male.

Not to mention as maternal. One example will have to stand in here for others, many more of which will be discussed in detail in the chapters that follow. When Simon Critchley identifies as one of Continental philosophy's defining features an emphasis on the "thoroughly *contingent* or *created* character of human experience," we might have expected maternity—which, presumably, has something to say about the nature of contingency and creation—to count as part of that experience.[2] It does not. If Critchley had wanted philosophical precedent for *not* associating maternity with creativity, he could easily have turned to Simone de Beauvoir's *The Second Sex*, which argued that pregnancy is merely a bodily function and, as such, inherently uncreative.[3] But Critchley does not refer to that argument, or make any other, to justify maternity's omission, which thereby goes unremarked. The absence of reflection on maternity from his discussion of the "*created* character of human experience" thus has the effect of suggesting that motherhood is a kind of *in*human experience, alien to the forms of conceptual generality to which philosophy properly aspires.[4]

Yet philosophers seem to have no doubt as to where philosophers come from. The following is the first of the nine "stories" presented recently by Badiou as his "philosophical biography":

> My father was an alumnus of the *École Normale Superieure* and *agrégé* of mathematics: my mother an alumna of the *École Normale Supérieure* and *agrégée* of French literature. I am an alumnus of the *École Normale Supérieure* and *agrégé*, but *agrégé* of what, of philosophy, that is to say, probably, the only possible way to assume the double filiation and circulate freely between the literary maternity and the mathematical paternity. This is a lesson for philosophy itself: the language of philosophy always constructs its own space between the matheme and the poem, between the mother and the father, after all.[5]

Badiou is not, of course, simply recounting here his own origins as a philosopher whose distinctive interests include set theory as well as the writing of fiction and drama; he is telling us the genealogy of philosophy itself as the dialectical sublation of its literary and mathematical parentage. Philosophy is thus conceived by Badiou as an only child with no rivalrous siblings or cousins, queer aunts or uncles. Badiou's next biographical installment, "about mother and philosophy," carries this theme forward:

> My mother was very old and my father was not in Paris. I would take her out to eat in a restaurant. She would tell me on these occasions everything she had never told me. It was the final expressions of tenderness, which are so moving, that one has with one's very old parents. One evening, she told me that even before meeting my father, when she was teaching in Algeria, she had a passion, a gigantic passion, a devouring passion, for a philosophy teacher. This story is absolutely authentic. I listened to it, obviously, in the position you can imagine, and I said to myself: well, that's it, I have done nothing else except accomplish the desire of my mother, that the Algerian philosopher had neglected. He had gone

off with someone else and I had done what I could to be the consolation for my mother's terrible pain—which had subsisted underneath it all even until she was eighty-one.

You may be astonished (as I certainly was the first time I encountered this passage) at the speed with which Badiou transforms his mother's tale about her attachment to *a* philosopher into an "absolutely authentic" story about himself. Oedipally conflating the singular with the general, Badiou never pauses to consider the possibility that, rather than saying "on these occasions everything she had never told me," his mother may have been exercising her literary license, knowing well from her experience "the position" her auditor then asks *us* to imagine him in. She may have been playing with him, in short, knowing that he would take the bait—and that he could scarcely keep himself from turning her story into his tale of philosophical inheritance, a transformation that enables him to supplant his mother as the tale's protagonist: "The nature of philosophy is that something is eternally being bequeathed to it. It has the responsibility of this bequeathal. You are always treating the bequeathal itself, always taking one more step in the determination of what was thus bequeathed to you. As myself, in the most unconscious manner, I never did anything as a philosopher except respond to an appeal that I had not even heard." I am, indeed, willing to believe that this was an appeal he had not even heard.

Even while exploring the nature of creativity and the paths of philosophical vocation, Critchley and Badiou exemplify two of the prominent ways that the mother can be made to disappear—in the first instance as the *object* of Theory, and in the second as its *subject*. Critchley's omission of the mother from a discussion of human creativity bears on the question of whether her absence is contingent or constitutive: can there be a philosophy of the mother, a philosophy that includes maternity within its disciplinary purview? Badiou's replacement of his mother as the protagonist of a story about philosophical calling raises a different question: can mothers ever be philosophers? As we will observe often in the pages to come, this second question can occur in tandem with the first, though the two retain some formal independence from each other. Throughout his corpus, for instance, Derrida repeatedly frames maternity as an ineluctable problem for philosophy—as an incapacitation of its virile pretensions to transparent self-knowledge.[6] And yet Derrida was clearly flummoxed when asked the following in the recent documentary film that bears his name:

> *Question*: If you had a choice, what philosopher would you have liked to be your mother?
>
> *Derrida*: . . . I have no ready answer for this question. Let me . . . give me some time. [*Five-second pause*] My *mother*? [*Laughs*] A good question, it's a good question, in fact. [*Eighteen-second pause*] It's an interesting question, I'll try to tell you why I can't . . . It's *impossible* for me to have any philosopher as a mother, that's a problem. My mother, my mother *couldn't* be a philosopher. [*Switches to French*] A philosopher *couldn't* be my mother. That's a very important point. Because the figure of the philosopher, for me, is always a masculine figure. This is one of the reasons I undertook the deconstruction of philosophy. All the deconstruction of phallologocentrism is the deconstruction of what one calls philosophy, which since its inception has always been linked to a paternal figure. So a philosopher is a father, not a mother. So the philosopher that would be my mother would be a postdeconstructive philosopher, that is, myself, or my son. My mother as a philosopher would be my granddaughter, for example. An inheritor. A woman philosopher who would reaffirm the deconstruction. And consequently, would be a woman who thinks. Not a philosopher. I always distinguish thinking from philosophy. A thinking mother—it's what I both love and try to give birth to.[7]

It is fascinating to observe Derrida struggling here to respond to a question to which he had not previously given thought (an eighteen-second pause is an eternity of screen time). In replying finally that a philosopher could never have been his mother, he seems not to be affirming the classical prejudice that *women* are unfit for philosophy. Derrida is even willing to imagine himself as a mother who gives birth to himself, to his son, and to his granddaughter—but not to his mother. Indeed, as with Badiou's biographical sketches, philosophical inheritance proceeds generationally in one direction only, and the mother never receives her due when reckoned from the vantage of her son: "My mother *couldn't* be a philosopher. [*Switches to French*] A philosopher *couldn't* be my mother." Though strikingly similar in their syntax, these English and French phrases suggest rather differ-ent things: the first, that being "my mother" prevents a particular person from also being a philosopher; and the second, that being a philosopher prevents any one of a class of persons from also being "my mother." (I will soon have occasion to say more about such uses of the possessive pronoun, as well as the mother's peculiar relation to singularity and generality.)[8]

Of course, Derrida is scarcely unique in resisting the notion of the mother as philosopher—could philosophy exist without such resis-tance? Surprisingly, perhaps, a number of feminist philosophers have also found philosophy and maternity to be incompatible, though for different reasons than Derrida. Motherhood, Gail Weiss suggests, may be "so comprehensive" and consuming an identity as to "rule out the ability to simultaneously possess another identity, such as intellec-tual."[9] But philosophy is demanding too, as Robyn Ferrell pointedly recalls: "It is not only that it is not possible to do philosophy while being a mother; it is also not possible to do *anything else* while doing philosophy." As Ferrell explains,

> Motherhood is that part of being a woman that is least amenable to the demands of intellectual labor. This is not because a mother cannot think—it is not a case of the old gynecologists' lore that a woman "gives birth to her brain." Anyone who has had the care of a child, and has done it conscientiously, knows that there is no possibility of thinking sustained thought or losing oneself in concentration—care giving as a practice is extrovert in the extreme.
>
> Indeed, as styles of labor, maternal and intellectual labor are almost diametrically opposed: one demands extroversion and action, and is contingent on circumstances to a high degree; the other is solipsistic, autonomous, and sustained. Consequently, the fantasy of being able to write while the baby is asleep is just that.[10]

Ferrell's account of the differences between intellectual and ma-ternal labor clearly echoes Beauvoir's still notorious distinction be-tween genuine thought as a transcendental project and maternity as mere immanent repetitiveness. But Ferrell may have also been re-sponding to Sara Ruddick and her own complex response to Beauvoir. Recounting the genesis of her pathbreaking book *Maternal Thinking* (1989), Ruddick described a world in which motherhood and philosophy were irreconcilably at odds—the very world anatomized by *The Second Sex*:

> During most of the years that I was actively taking care of my children, mothering was said to be love and feminine duty rather than a thoughtful project. It was difficult for a woman of my class and time to believe that "as a mother" she thought at all, let alone that her "maternal thinking" was of value. Moreover, I had a graduate degree in philosophy; during these years of domestic responsibility and career confusion, I clung to the fragile identity of "philosopher." But Western philosophers had explicitly and metaphorically contrasted "rational" thinking with the kinds of particularity, passionate attachment, and bodily engagement expressed in mothering. Accordingly, "as a philosopher" I could imagine myself "thinking" only when I was not being "a mother" but was at "work"—teaching—or better still when I was trying to write about the transcendent objects and transcendental questions of philosophy.[11]

In an effort to break the grip of this opposition, Ruddick proposed not only that mothers *think* (a radical notion, then as now) but further that they think *distinctively*: "How might a mother, a person who thinks regularly and intently about children, think about 'the world'? What styles of cognition and perception might mothers develop? How, for example, might a mother, a person for whom maternal thinking was a significant part of her or his intellectual life, think about 'nature,' change, the self, and other such philosophical topics?"[12] Ruddick defined maternal thinking as a form of "practical consciousness"; she hoped that "maternal concepts," uniquely reflecting the experience of mothers, could make their way into larger "political and philosophical discussions" about the causes of war and the possibility of nonviolence. The subject of a recent volume of commemorative essays, *Maternal Thinking* has long since become a touchstone of feminist thought, but the breach that it discerned between maternity and philosophy remains today as wide as ever:

> The idea of "maternal thinking" posed questions about social construction, relativism, pragmatism, pluralism—but these are not questions posed by mothering. This is philosophy talking to itself. When you ask about mothering or motherhood inspiring philosophical reflection I think of issues of death, time passing, individuation and connection,

love and the sorrow it includes . . . subjects I talk about in the writing I am doing now. But neither the thinking that mothers engaged in nor the thinking about maternal thinking that I was doing twenty years ago were, in my view, philosophical. I was quite insistent on that point. I suspect now that I was afraid of appearing fraudulent or foolish if I pretended that I was doing philosophy. I published "Maternal Thinking" in *Feminist Studies*. I was enormously pleased that it was accepted there. That was my chosen audience.[13]

Ruddick seems to have no interest here in claiming maternal thinking *as* philosophy. I do not see her making a case for "philosophy in the nursery," or insisting, as Michèle Le Dœuff has done in a different context, that "philosophical work takes place in many more areas than that of mere professional philosophy."[14] Her concern, rather, is with an absence in feminist thought that no one had noticed before in these terms: "Neither I, nor the philosophers, feminists, and feminist psychoanalysts to whom I turned, represented mothers as thinking people. . . . feminist thinking was of limited use in forging a representation of mothers as thinkers."[15] Ruddick accounts for this absence by observing that the feminists of her generation tended to write from a daughter's perspective and were largely antipathetic to their mothers' concerns.[16] But another explanation may derive from feminist philosophy's claim that being a woman does not interfere with or otherwise disqualify one from pursuing philosophy. Against the crushing weight of the philosophical canon, which, to justify women's exclusion as both subject and object, elevates culture above nature, mind above body, and logic above emotion, feminist philosophers often respond with the argument that reason has no gender—an argument that is its own proof.[17] Yet if the claim is that women, like men, think with their minds and not with their bodies, then maternity can never register *philosophically* within these terms. While philosophy's exclusion of women may be contested by appealing to the universality of reason, such an appeal would fail were it made on behalf of mothers. For maternity is *not* the universal—certainly not for men, but also (though differently) not for women. All mothers (at least until recently) are women, but all women are not mothers, and the destabilizing, asymmetric difference between the two—neither simply a potential common to all women nor a synecdochic part of a

putative feminine whole—is enough to confound the project of maternal philosophy.[18] Moreover, unlike being a woman, being a mother
does interfere with or otherwise disqualify one from the practice of
philosophy, as Ferrell, among others, has suggested. Whatever else
Ruddick intended in developing her notion of maternal thinking, she
was not asserting a right to philosophize *as a mother*.[19]

In contrast to philosophy proper, which typically consigns maternity to its margins, feminist theory has understood this tension
between woman and mother to be central and irreducible. In fact,
latecomers to the field may wrongly conclude that motherhood has
always been its exclusive preoccupation. The first of several special
issues published by the journal *Hypatia* on motherhood as a feminist
problem dates only from 1986.[20] By 1992 Ann Snitow could describe
emerging "from a bout of reading, a wide eclectic sampling of what
this wave of US feminism has had to say about motherhood," her
own reader sensing the enormity of the task she had just completed.[21]
Eight years later, needing now to limit her survey to one decade, Terry
Arendell observed matter-of-factly that "mothering and motherhood
are the objects of a rapidly expanding body of literature."[22] To say
the least. It thus is shocking to recall Susan Griffin's words from 1974:
"On this subject—Feminism and Motherhood—very little has been
written. . . . I don't have a feminist theory of motherhood."[23] Ten
years after publishing *Of Woman Born*, Adrienne Rich explained that
"at the time I began it, in 1972, some four or five years into a new po-
liticization of women, there was virtually nothing being written on
motherhood as an issue."[24] At issue then for feminism was not maternity but its *prevention* as a basic right for women.[25] The chapter from
The Second Sex entitled "The Mother" thus began with a lengthy discussion of abortion and contraception:

> Contraception and legal abortion would permit woman to take her
> maternities in freedom. As things are, women's fecundity is decided in
> part voluntarily, in part by chance. Since artificial insemination has not
> come into common use at present, it may happen that a woman de-
> sires maternity without getting her wish—because she lacks contact
> with men, or because she is herself unable to conceive. And on the other
> hand, a woman often finds herself compelled to reproduce against her
> will.[26]

Paradoxically, second-wave feminism's very efforts to distinguish femininity from maternity helped to facilitate in the late 1970s a surge of feminist scholarship on motherhood and mothering that quickly turned into a deluge. Dorothy Dinnerstein's *The Mermaid and the Minotaur* (1976), Nancy Chodorow's *The Reproduction of Mothering* (1978), and Michele Wallace's *Black Macho and the Myth of the Superwoman* (1979) all questioned why women persisted as mothers even while affirming maternity as a woman's choice.[27] Chodorow's writing in particular kindled a new interest in maternally oriented object relations within psychoanalytic theory, which helped in turn to make the mother/daughter experience, perennially scanted by Freud, a major preoccupation for feminist critics.[28]

A decade later, Judith Butler could criticize such work—which now occupied "a hegemonic position within the emerging canon of feminist theory"—for ideologically reinforcing "the binary, heterosexist framework that carves up genders into masculine and feminine and forecloses an adequate description of the kinds of subversive and parodic convergences that characterize gay and lesbian cultures."[29] Teresa de Lauretis was even more emphatic: the supposition of a "maternal imaginary" common to all women reduces "female sexuality to maternity, and feminine identity to the mother," thereby rendering politically invisible lesbian and other nonprocreative sexualities.[30] Lesbian antipathy to the presumptive heterosexism of "maternal discourse" began to lessen in the mid- and late 1990s with the wider availability of assisted reproduction and the reality of procreation without sex.[31] Meanwhile, many of those whose views about maternity had become "hegemonic" began to change their minds— seemingly in all directions. "By giving birth," Julia Kristeva argued in an early essay, "the woman enters into contact with her mother; she becomes, she is her own mother; they are the same continuity differentiating itself."[32] But in her later, more traditionally psychoanalytic work, Kristeva stressed the mother's *dis*continuity with her offspring: "For man and for woman the loss of the mother is a biological and psychic necessity, the first step on the way to becoming autonomous. Matricide is our vital necessity, the sine-qua-non condition of our individuation."[33] Luce Irigaray's writings on the maternal oscillate in the opposite direction than Kristeva's—from an early emphasis on the chilly structural distance separating mother and daughter ("With your milk, Mother, I swallowed ice. And here I am now, my insides frozen") to the later "discovery" that "we are always mothers just by being women."[34] To observe such swings in alignment between woman and mother not only throughout second-wave theory but also in the careers of individual theorists is to recognize the maternal as both constitutive and destabilizing for feminist thought. The questions Snitow posed in her essay of 1992 remain today every bit as politically urgent—and just as undecidable: "Women have incorporated a great deal into their mothering, but one question for feminism should surely be: Do we want this presently capacious identity, mother, to expand or to contract? How special do we want mothering to be? In other words, what does feminism gain by the privileging of motherhood?"[35]

2.

Though not for lack of trying, the mother's destabilizing influence cannot be diminished through more precise definition; "her" resistance to univocal meaning suggests the opposite, in fact. Discussions of motherhood across the humanities, social sciences, and medical sciences often deliberately ask "what is a mother?"—a sign that the question is not as simple as it first may appear.[36] This question has always been complex—kinship theory has long recognized that "mater" and "genetrix" are analytically distinct categories—but more recently the mother's definition has passed from the complicated to the "impossible."[37] To ask "what is a . . . ?" is to inquire about the sense of a word—in Saussurean terms, about its function as a differential element within a closed lexical system. In this instance, *mother* is a kinship term whose sense is produced contrastively with respect to gender (= not father) and generation (= not child). On the other hand, to ask "*who* is a mother?" is to inquire extralinguistically about a word's referent, to wonder about the identity of a person. As will be noted frequently throughout this book, the relationship between sense and referent has never been straightforward where the mother is concerned. Indeed, their noncoincidence prepares the way not only for adoption, wet-nursing, and step-relations but for tragedy (*Oedipus Rex*) and comedy (*Tom Jones*) as well.

During the past several decades, however, the maternal "what" and "who" have undergone a kind of crisis unlike any experienced before. Today we tend to ask *both* who *and* what the mother is—often in consecutive sentences, as in the following two examples—hopeful that doing so may increase our chance of encountering a meaning (or a person) whose distinctness (or palpability) has somehow become elusive:

> Of whom do we speak when we speak of mothers and what do we denote when we refer to mothering, motherhood, maternal subjectivity, or the maternal more generally? What have the contours of these terms come to signify across different disciplinary domains, what are their genealogies, and where now may "a mother" begin and end?[38]

> What is a mother? Who is the mother of a child when one woman provides the ovum for fertilization and another carries the baby to term?[39]

The difficulty here may be that the mother—as usual, overextended—now covers so much semantic territory as to defeat any expectation of lexical cohesion:

> It is generally accepted that the maternal refers not only to the material and embodied experience of pregnancy, childbirth and lactation, but also to identities and meanings of mothering, the ongoing emotional and relational work of being with children and others, the daily material practices of childrearing, the social locations and structural contexts within which women mother: indeed, to the whole range of embodied, social and cultural meanings, practices and structures associated with reproduction and parenting.[40]

Scholars have attempted to constrain this polysemia of "meanings, practices, and structures" by filtering it through a series of binary oppositions; we will often find "mother" contrasted with "mothering" as an identity is said to differ from a practice, or as an impersonal institution stands to an individual's experience.[41] But the current crisis of maternal sense and reference seems to resist such strategies:

> For instance, it is evident that the identity of "mother" varies widely within and across cultures and time periods, as well as in different reli-

gious, social, and political contexts. Even if to be a mother, at the most minimal level, means to be a pubescent or post-pubescent female and to have and/or raise a child, this "bare" meaning is never all that is implied in a given society's or a given individual's respective understandings of this particular identity. Moreover, even this minimal definition is problematic because it is possible for a male-to-female transsexual to be a mother even though she isn't born female, and so this biologically based definition excludes some people who might identify themselves and/ or be identified by others as mothers. The meaning of being a mother is never just a matter of a "bare" definition in any case, since how any given individual understands the term is clearly influenced by the experience of being (or failing to be) mothered, having close (or distant) relations with mothers, social understandings of what it means to be a mother, and/or being a mother oneself.[42]

It is surely no accident that the very project of maternal definition is abandoned in this passage just at the point where the gender of the referent comes into question. Indeed, however complex the sense and reference of maternity may once have been, medical innovation has been producing of late unprecedented forms of lexical complexity— and Theory (of all kinds, feminist and queer included) has yet to catch up. As the anthropologist Janet Carsten has observed, "fundamental assumptions about familial connection" may have fallen permanently to the wayside since the introduction of "fertility treatments, genetic testing, posthumous conception, cloning, and the mapping of the human genome."[43] Many of these developments are not specific to the mother, and some concern only the father:

Artificial insemination by donor produces a clear distinction between the genetic father and the social father. Depending on the exact circumstances, *in vitro* fertilization might produce a situation in which neither social parent is the genetic parent (if both sperm and eggs are donated) or only one of them is (if there is only one donation). Surrogate motherhood can lead to an even more complicated situation, in which the social mother (that is, the commissioning mother) is one individual, the provider of the egg another, and the carrying mother a third. In addition, of course, the semen may be donated rather than coming from the social or commissioning father, involving five persons altogether.[44]

But the mother has received most of the publicity—scholarly and popular, lurid and dispassionate—in this age of technologically assisted reproduction. If a crisis exists today it concerns motherhood, not fatherhood: "A crisis precipitated to a great degree by the unforeseen destabilization of maternity and motherhood that we are witnessing in the early years of the twenty-first century. . . . What meaning do we make of the split between social, biological, and genetic mothers? How do we understand the spectrum from egg donors to surrogate, lesbian, adoptive, birth, and foster mothers? How does the distinction between bio- and non-biomoms come to have meaning?"[45] With maternal reference now fracturing along each of these bio-socio-legal dimensions, the identity of the mother cannot be disclosed through an act of perception, as we have long believed it must be. Whence the crisis—which, beyond the nature of maternity, concerns the evidentiary status of the senses. Where paternity in the West has traditionally been open to question, a matter of inference rather than observation, maternity has just as traditionally figured certitude itself: "Mama's Baby, Papa's Maybe," in Hortense Spillers's memorable phrase.[46] We think we know a mother when we see one, but the father's identity requires an interpretive judgment.[47] Freud tirelessly reiterated this distinction between maternity and paternity, which he considered foundational not only for psychoanalysis but for civilization itself on its long march from matriarchy to patriarchy:

> When the child realizes that "*pater semper incertus est*," while the mother is *certissima*, the family romance undergoes a curious curtailment: it contents itself with exalting the child's father, but no longer casts any doubts on his maternal origin, which is regarded as something unalterable.[48]

> As Lichtenberg says, "An astronomer knows whether the moon is inhabited or not with about as much certainty as he knows who was his father, but not with so much certainly as he knows who was his mother." A great advance was made in civilization when men decided to put their inferences upon a level with the testimony of their senses and to make the step from matriarchy to patriarchy.[49]

> But this turning from the mother to the father points in addition to a victory of intellectuality over sensuality—that is, an advance in civilization, since maternity is proved by the evidence of the senses while pater-

nity is a hypothesis, based on an inference and a premiss [*sic*]. Taking sides in this way with a thought-process in preference to a sense perception has proved to be a momentous step.[50]

We know better today, perhaps, why Freud's distinction between observation and contemplation is itself a tendentious "taking of sides." In a series of essays and interviews from the 1990s, Derrida suggested that the new reproductive technologies, by undermining maternity's grounding in sense perception, have compromised the terms of Freud's argument. But those same terms, Derrida added, have always been compromised, appearances indeed notwithstanding. If we can no longer identify a mother by sight—if a mother is now always potentially one of several people—then we may not be experiencing a crisis of maternity so much as recognizing one of its structural conditions:

> Today less than ever can we be sure that the mother herself is the woman we believe we saw giving birth. The mother is not only the genetrix since, as psychoanalysis (and not only psychoanalysis) has always taught us, another person can become or can have been "the" mother, one of the mothers. Now the most difficult thing to think, and first of all to desire, then to accept otherwise than as a monstrosity, is precisely this: more than one mother. Supplements of mothers, in an irreducible plurality. Today, the surrogate mother and the one who, properly speaking (as we improperly say), becomes the mother—that makes two people. Not to mention all the other mothers who step in to take over at different times. In other words, the identity of the mother (like her possible juridical identification) depends on a judgment that is just derived, and on an inference that is just as divorced from all immediate perception, as this "legal fiction" of a paternity conjectured through reason (to use a phrase from Joyce's *Ulysses* referring to paternity).[51]

For Derrida, the mother's "irreducible plurality" is, on the one hand, a relatively recent phenomenon, a singular event that has altered the ways we think about kinship, gender, sexuality, healthcare, capital, religion, the public, and the state. On the other hand, the structural possibility that the mother is more than one has altered our relation to the past (including our conception of what counts as an event) in enabling the recognition that the mother, in fact, has never been perceivable: "And when we realize that motherhood is not simply a matter of perception, we realize that it has never been so. The mother has always been a matter of interpretation, of social construction."[52] Pace Freud's commonsense insistence that "no one possesses more than one mother," Derrida claims that to be a mother is hence structurally—ineluctably—to be more than one, and what is truly news about this recognition is that it never should have been news: "Techno-scientific capabilities (artificial insemination, surrogate mothers, cloning, etc.) will no doubt accelerate a mutation in the father/mother relation in the future. But this will only be an acceleration, a *differance*, however spectacular or dreadful their effects may appear: the 'mother,' too, has always been a 'symbolic' or 'substitutable' mother, like the father, and the certainty acquired at the moment of giving birth was in my opinion an illusion."[53] Which suggests that, for Derrida, maternity also is a "legal fiction" and has always already been so:

> If today the unicity of the mother is no longer the sensible object of a perceptual certitude, if maternities do not transport us beyond the surrogate mother [*ne se réduisent plus a la portée de la mère porteuse*], if there can be, as it were, more than one mother [*plus d'une mère*], if "the" mother is the object of calculation and supposition, of projection and phantasm, if the "womb" is no longer outside all phantasm, the assured place of birth, this "new" situation simply illuminates in return an ageless truth. The mother was never only, never uniquely, never indubitably the one who gives birth—and whom one sees, with one's own eyes, give birth.[54]

Though Derrida's comments on the mother's plurality were occasional rather than systematically developed, they can take us far toward an appreciation of why maternity has been and remains a source of trouble for Theory—above all by confounding that notion of source. One consequence is that nobody will have ever seen a mother if the act of perception has always been structured by the possibility that the person viewed as "mother" is not the only one with a claim to maternity. This possibility defines the structure of maternity as such: the mother is, was, and will be "plus d'une mère"—not one, no longer one, more than one. In this sense, Sarah Kofman's childhood experience of multiple mothers would reflect maternity's rule rather than exception.[55] This rule would suggest, for example, that Adriana

Cavarero seriously undercounts the number of people structurally implicated in the act of giving birth when emphasizing that "in birth one is not alone but in a duo: the mother and the one who is born."[56] Insofar as we persist in speaking of "the mother" in the singular—"Allow me to take the mother's side," writes Kristeva, as if there is just one—Theory will find itself outpaced by a possibility of plurality that, paradoxically, has always defined the structure of maternity.[57]

A second consequence: if the mother is not a perception but an assumption or projection, then "she" cannot serve as "the last term of a regression," as meaning's ultimate bedrock.[58] Originally self-divided, maternity cannot ground any other account of origin—even (or especially) that of sexual difference. As will be noted at many points in the following chapters, this consequence will affect every version of history that conceives of itself as a genealogy (and which history does not?). It also will suggest why a revised ethics of motherhood, instead of seeking to protect or to recover the mother's identity, subjectivity, agency, or voice, will ask what it was that we thought we wanted from "her," and why.[59]

A third consequence: multiple from the outset, the mother exceeds her traditionally derogated role as the father's counterpart, unsettling the binary logic modeled on their relationship.[60] As a venerable nickname for *differance*, the mother (in Geoffrey Bennington's account) is "not in *opposition* to the father just as writing is not in opposition to voice":

> What was at stake in the thought of writing was not to rehabilitate writing in the common sense, but to see writing already at work in the voice: so that the point is not to promote a matriarchal power against a patriarchy, but to show that what has already been understood by "father" (or even by "power") is constituted only on the basis of an anteriority which can be called "mother" solely on condition of not confusing it with the habitual conception of mother.[61]

"As" this radical anteriority, the mother is neither subject nor object, not a person but rather (a) text that resists univocal definition less as a result of polysemic richness than of an unlimited capacity for dissemination—for "producing a nonfinite number of semantic effects [that] can be lead back neither to a present of simple origin . . . nor to an eschatological presence."[62] Aperceptual, non-self-identical, and highly allergic to the logic of the couple, this mother is never simply Theory's mother, however much it wants or claims to know "her." Indeed, despite the mother's centrality to a wide range of disciplines and interdisciplines—despite what Lisa Baraitser describes as "the vast and expanding research field of maternal practice, maternal relations, maternal embodiment and maternal representation, on the new technologies of birth and reproduction and their implications for women, and on the current rapid rate of change that family structures and parenting patterns are undergoing"—the mother troubles knowledge not simply by eluding its grasp (as if external to it) but by keeping knowledge from ever coinciding with itself.[63]

3.

With these consequences in mind, we will find the mother causing trouble along a number of conceptual axes not only in the materials considered in this book but everywhere "she" may be used, mentioned, or otherwise put to work theoretically. Which, indeed, is everywhere. In the first place, the mother is often invoked to regulate the distinction between the literal and the figural, a distinction that she undermines nonetheless and just as frequently. We speak regularly, for example, of "the literal birth act," "birth in its literality," and "the literal act of parturition"; we contrast "literal mothers" with "other women who function as surrogates."[64] We also insist that "maternity is not just a metaphor," and that it does not "refer in any simple way to the literal moment of giving birth," but it is the act of reference which can never be simple once the mother's identity is structurally uncertain.[65] Whenever canonical philosophy makes "more than a passing reference to birth," it does so catachrestically in casting parturition as "a metaphorical process of artistic or intellectual creation which is implicitly or explicitly coded as masculine."[66] And yet the mother is also the preeminent figure of the figural. Lynne Huffer thus distinguishes the "real mother" from "the mother as a powerful cultural symbol, a symbol so powerful that it shapes the dominant structures of Western thought. . . . In the Western tradition the mother is a symbol of beginnings; as the one who gives birth, she occupies the place of the origin. Metaphorically speaking, everything begins with the mother."[67] The mother-as-trope is so pervasive geographically and transhistorically—"the deep surrogacy of the sign 'mother'" so bottomless—that it may be impossible to recall the figure to anything like literality as a check against its possible (probable!) ideological abuse.[68] The mother of all metaphors is, of course, the maternal metaphor. As is the reverse.

Which suggests that, impossibly literal *and* figural, the mother may in fact be simply neither—or rather that maternity suspends our ability to discern the difference between the two. For if metaphor works by projecting the known qualities of the vehicle onto the unknown qualities of the tenor, this process loses its clarity when ("plus d'une mère") the maternal vehicle may always be unknown, thereby confounding itself with its tenor. How then can we distinguish between the literal and the metaphorical when "the mother" already may be both? The "port" of *mère porteuse* has the same root as metaphor's transport of sense. Freud may have learned this etymological lesson while chasing down another root:

> And, speaking of wood, it is hard to understand how that material came to represent what is maternal and female. But here comparative philology may come to our help. Our German word *Holz* seems to come from the same root as the Greek ὕλη [*hulē*], meaning "stuff" "raw material." This seems to be an instance of the not uncommon event of the general name of a material eventually coming to be reserved for some particular material. Now there is an island in the Atlantic named "Madeira." This name was given to it by the Portuguese when they discovered it, because at that time it was covered all over with woods. For in the Portuguese language *madeira* means "wood." You will notice, however, that *madeira* is only a slightly modified form of the Latin word *materia* which once more means "material" in general. But *"materia"* is derived from *mater* "mother": the material out of which anything is made is, as it were, a mother to it [*ist gleichsam sein mütterlicher Anteil*]. This ancient view of the thing survives, therefore, in the symbolic use of wood for "woman" or "mother."[69]

"As it were, a mother to it": that *gleichsam* "is" *mütterlich* seems to be all that holds together this unlikely proof of the archaic connection between mothers and . . . wood. Even as Freud translates doubtfully from term to term and from German to Portuguese to Latin, "mother" has been all along—tautologically—vehicle as well as tenor.

Levinas provides an even more impacted example of the instability of the literal/figural relation. In his late work *Otherwise Than Being*, Levinas suggests that the maternal body—at once host and hostage to an internal Other—is the universal model for ethical responsibility regardless of a person's gender:

> The one-for-the-other has the form of sensibility or vulnerability, pure passivity or susceptibility, passive to the point of becoming an inspiration, that is, alterity in the same, the trope of the body animated by the soul, psyche in the form of a hand that gives even the bread taken from its own mouth. Here the psyche is the maternal body [*Psychisme comme un corps maternel*].

> In proximity the absolutely other, the stranger whom I have "neither conceived nor given birth to," I already have on my arms, already hear, according to the Biblical formula, "in my breast as the nurse bears the nursling [*dans mon sein comme le nourricier porte le nourrisson*]." He has no other place, is not autochthonous, is uprooted, without a country, not an inhabitant, exposed to the cold and the heat of the seasons. To be reduced to having recourse to me is the homelessness or strangeness of the neighbor. It is incumbent on me.[70]

Since the mother's gender would appear to be at stake in this passage, Levinas's readers have been eager to know whether maternity is to be understood here literally or figuratively. Stella Sandford, for example, seems especially anxious as to which of these mothers is which:

> In a sense, the choice of the metaphor of maternity is an obvious one for Levinas. At the beginning of chapter 2, "the knot of subjectivity" is described as "the torsion of the Same and the Other . . . Intrigue of the Other-in-the-Same," which is or which accomplishes itself in proximity. More simply, "subjectivity is the Other-in-the-Same," and given these explanations, it is not difficult to see, in a rather literal way, how prenatal maternity could become the paradigm case of "the Other in the Same," or of passive (and perhaps unchosen) responsibility. References to "the gestation of the other in the same," used metaphorically but also as a description of maternity, reinforce such an interpretation. . . . Further-

more, the metaphor of maternity connects with, or is the archetype of, the idea of nourishment already introduced through the theme of mouth and bread. Again, pre- and postnatal maternity can provide very literal examples of nourishing the other with food that one has enjoyed, but maternity also carries the conventional symbolic signification attached, for example, to the figure of Demeter.[71]

Though "obvious" and employed in "a very literal way" as a model for the care of the internalized Other, maternity in Sandford's reading is also a metaphor with respect to its "conventional symbolic signification." But motherhood as ethical relation is as applicable to men as to women, which suggests finally, for Sandford, that Levinas "has confused the distinction between the literal and the metaphorical almost beyond repair."[72] Yet Levinas may have gone considerably beyond that point. Lisa Guenther recalls that the "Biblical formula" cited by Levinas is Numbers (11:12), where Moses complains to God about the Hebrews' constant complaining: "Did I conceive all these people? Did I give them birth? Why do you tell me to carry them in my arms, as a nurse carries an infant, to the land you promised on oath to their forefathers?" We grasp here that Moses *is* their mother, that he *did* give his people birth, even if the King James version prefers to think of him instead as "a nursing father [who] beareth the sucking child." But Guenther does not similarly shy away from the implications of the passage and from what Levinas may have implied in citing it: "The maternity of Moses and of God suggests that one is not born, but rather becomes like a mother. The biological fact of incarnation in a female body need not condemn me to a destiny of childbirth, nor does incarnation in a male body free me from the responsibility of bearing the Other 'like a maternal body.' If the literal and metaphorical dimensions of birth fail to remain separate here, then perhaps it is because the story of Moses disrupts the possibility of a strictly literal or metaphorical interpretation."[73] Indeed, in suggesting that the literal/figural distinction is impertinent if maternity is to function universally as an ethical injunction, Levinas broaches the question of male maternity that the present book will consider again in the coda.

Like the literal/figural distinction, the relation between singularity and generality is an especially rich node of mother trouble. Drawing on Hannah Arendt's conception of natality as a counterweight to Heidegger's being-toward-death, Cavarero understands birth not only as a singular event but as the very incarnation of singularity: "The first setting in which uniqueness and community meet each other is that of birth. Here the existent is found in its incarnated consciousness: this boy, this girl. The aspect of the community, on the other hand, is presupposed in the fact that this singular comes into the world, from the start, from and with another existent: the mother, this mother."[74] Cavarero's emphasis on "the mother, this mother" recalls Barthes's poignant distinction between the category "mother" and the person of his mother, whom he had recently lost: "And no more would I reduce my family to the Family, would I reduce my mother to the Mother. . . . For what I have lost is not a Figure (the Mother), but a being; and not a being but a quality (a soul); not the indispensable, but the irreplaceable. I could live without the Mother (as we all do, sooner or later); but what life remained would be absolutely and entirely unqualifiable (without quality)."[75]

For Cavarero as for Barthes, the mother's singularity can only be gestured at in writing; each resorts to repeated deixis and typographical convention in an effort to convey what exceeds writing's necessary generality. Indeed, Barthes famously declined reproducing in *Camera Lucida* the photographic image of his mother as a young girl, an image that he took to embody the essence of photography; to publish the photograph would have been to make the singular loss of his mother into the general Loss of the Mother. And yet, notes Derrida, this is what transpires in any case, in so far as the loss registers legibly for us *as* loss: "How else could we, without knowing her, be so deeply moved by what he said about his mother, who was not only the Mother, or a mother, but the only one she was and of whom such a photo was taken 'on that day'? How could this be poignant to us if a metonymic force, which yet cannot be mistaken for something that facilitates the movement of identification, were not at work?"[76] This "metonymic force" binds the Mother to the mother, publicity to privacy, generality to singularity. If each of us can say "*my* mother," then the mother is precisely never only mine. Perhaps this is what Freud's patient replied in protest when Freud insisted that he was dreaming of his mother: "It was *not* my mother," Freud recorded, convinced of his patient's denegation, but the emphasis in this sentence could easily have fallen on the *my* had Freud had the ears to entertain that possibility.[77]

The mother's uniqueness is similarly at stake in Pontalis's witty "Ersatz," a part of his collection of brief meditations on psychoanalytic terms:

> For those who knew the Occupation, *Ersatz* is rutabaga, margarine, Marmite, gasogene . . . Go ahead complain, it's better than nothing! Sinister Ersatz that the vanquished must be happy with. Ersatz due to defeat, humiliation, shame. The conqueror, the occupier gets hold of the goods, the food, our lives. He steals what we were thinking belonged to us—it goes without saying that it belonged to us—, and bestows on us some substitute products. What are we *to* him, if not the *Ersatz* of humankind?
>
> On this, I won't budge: that is *Ersatz*.
>
> Then Michel Gribinski reminds me that the word is found in Freud and doesn't always have the negative connotation that I give to it. He goes even further and claims that we are never dealing with anything besides *Ersatz*. I protest, refuse to let myself be convinced, particularly because the demonstration is convincing.
>
> I admit that our images are substitutes for presence. I have a hard time accepting the idea that throughout our lives we keep finding father substitutes who wouldn't be less than our own fathers.
>
> But are there mother substitutes? As unsatisfying as she had been, she was the only one. I tell myself that the only being who has no substitute, still less is interchangeable, who is perhaps immortal, is the (if not our) Mother, and I capitalize, I attribute a capital letter, to my tiny Mother.[78]

Artfully composed, "Ersatz" has the figural concision of a prose poem. It may take several readings until the realization sinks in that the territory described in its first paragraph is (also) the body of the mother, whose occupation by the father has expelled us into a world of imitative, second-rate pleasures. The admission that nothing, ultimately, distinguishes fathers from father substitutes would be the price happily paid by this narrator to defend the mother against any similar duplication—were it not for the fact that the very attribution of her uniqueness requires a capital letter that makes the mother everyone's in making her mine.[79]

A third kind of mother trouble erupts at the border between a theorist's life and writing. The life of a philosopher is usually thought to be extrinsic to the work because it embodies particularities foreign to the work's transcendental truths. The theorist's biography thus has no *philosophical* use or pertinence, at least as customarily understood. If we nonetheless retain an interest in theorists' lives, it tends to take the form of what Derrida described facetiously as "biographical novels" (he lists, among their many varieties, "the 'writer and his mother' series"), which suppose that "by following empirical procedures of the psychologistic—at times even psychoanalytic—historicist or sociological type, one can give an account of the genesis of the system."[80] But the border between life and work proves to be far less tractable than such procedures promise, and this will be especially the case in *The Theorist's Mother*, where the double genitive of the title positions the mother simultaneously inside and outside the theorist's work—inside as a philosopheme and outside as part of the theorist's life. These two mothers ("plus d'une mère" once again) often seem to communicate with each other, troubling in doing so our capacity to differentiate the immanent from the extrinsic, the necessary from the accidental.[81] We could ask, for example, whether Jean-Paul Sartre's mother Anne-Marie (who considered the happy years she lived with her son as her *troisième mariage*) left any traces in his philosophical work.[82] We could wonder, too, about Gayatri Chakravorty Spivak's frequent references to her mother in her many interviews and occasional writings—what functions might these moments possess beyond the "merely" anecdotal?[83]

Heidegger and his mother might offer us the most intriguing example to consider in this connection, since we know very little about Johanna Kempf Heidegger other than that she was pained by her son's growing irreligiousity. We know that when she died in 1927 Heidegger placed "an author's copy of the new published book [*Being and Time*] on his mother's deathbed," though none of his biographers has interpreted this act in any but the most admiring of ways.[84] We know, too, that maternity has never been one of his central preoccupations—in fact, he somehow managed not to take any notice of Augustine's mother Monica in his detailed reading of the *Confessions*.[85] What then should we make of the following (near the beginning of the fifth lecture of *What Is Called Thinking?*):

"You just wait—I'll teach you what we call obedience!" a mother might say to her boy who won't come home [*"Warte, ich werde dich lehren, was gehorchen heißt"—ruft die Mutter ihrem Buben nach, der nicht nach Hause will*]. Does she promise him a definition of obedience? No. Or is she going to give him a lecture? No again, if she is a proper mother [*Auch nicht, falls sie eine rechte Mutter ist*]. Rather, she will convey to him what obedience is [*Sie wird vielmehr dem Sohn das Gehorchen beibringen*]. Or better, the other way around: she will bring him to obey.[86]

Since Heidegger's writing is hardly famous for its representations of speech, we may wonder whether Heidegger himself had ever heard such a mother. This mother in any case takes center stage for once in philosophy, bringing her son to obey her command to return home (which is never a neutral word for Heidegger). But she does this, it seems, nonverbally, and not by defining her terms in advance or by lecturing.[87] These latter are the activities of a philosopher, and if she is a proper mother (*eine rechte Mutter*) she will leave those activities to others—perhaps to her son. But also to Nietzsche, whose unique manner of writing Heidegger turns to in the remainder of his lecture. Nietzsche, unlike a proper mother, did raise his voice: he "endured the agony of having to scream." But that dimension may be all that distinguishes a mother who transgresses the stage of philosophy from a philosopher who takes *himself* as his mother: "To put it in the form of a riddle, as my father I have already died, as my mother I am still alive and growing old."[88]

These three kinds of mother trouble—literal/figural, singular/general, life/work—will recur frequently in the following chapters, which commonly explore a further problem inherent to the practice of Theory: how to reproduce itself. I focus primarily on Marx and Freud, who, according to Foucault, "are unique in that they are not just the authors of their own works. They have produced something else: the possibilities and the rules for the formation of other texts."[89] As so-called founders of discursivity, Marx and Freud uniquely constrain their would-be heirs to "return to the origin"—to an engagement with the founders' texts—if this subsequent work is to count as a part of Marxist or Freudian tradition. "This return, which is part of the discursive field itself, never stops modifying it," Foucault added: "The return is not a historical supplement that would be added to the discursivity, or merely an ornament; on the contrary, it constitutes an effective and necessary task of transforming the discursive practice itself."[90]

This book puts many such "returns" on display: Lacan, famous for his "return to Freud," returns in chapter 1 to his own earlier work when he finds himself being read by others; Lukács returns to Marx in chapter 2 by reading Sir Walter Scott, Marx's favorite English-language novelist; new translations of Marx and Freud return us in chapter 3 not only to the texts of their originals but to previous translations of Marx and Freud. Each of these returns makes a place for later theorists by establishing new relations to the texts of a founder—precisely the process Foucault described in "What Is an Author?" But what Foucault neglected to emphasize is that such place-making inevitably turns Theory's history into a form of genealogy, an exchange between fathers and sons (and today, increasingly, daughters as well). Which means that the mother must somehow be involved in this family affair, even if (as in Marxism) she seems wholly absent, and even if (as in psychoanalysis) her contributions are discounted. While Theory may be incapable of imagining its past and its future other than in these procreative terms, it seems equally unable to imagine the mother as having much if anything to do with its own replication.[91]

Mothers do not take well to this treatment, needless to say. Lacanian pedagogy will founder on the mother's resistance to the model of somatic conversion. Scott's *Waverley* will show Lukács's sublation of the novel to be a fiction of reproduction. A new translation of Freud's book on jokes will help us understand why revolution for Marx requires the forgetting of the mother tongue—a forgetting we may not be fated to repeat.

I conclude with a brief coda that projects a different future for the theorist's mother, one that may already have arrived. "Other Maternities" briefly canvases the history of male writers portraying themselves as the mother of their literary and philosophical offspring. Feminist critics have decried this long-standing practice, calling out Nietzsche in particular but also Honoré de Balzac and many others for their "gyno-colonial" appropriation of maternity. But this critique assumes that women's maternity is not similarly an appropriation. It also assumes that men cannot give birth, which, *strictu sensu,* is no longer the case. On the brink of this brave new world, where biology is proving itself at least as plastic as culture, Shulamith Firestone's *Dialectic of Sex*, long rebarbative to many, has become newly readable in unexpected ways. What will become of Theory when we cannot presume its mother's gender?

1.

Mom, *Encore*

Rereading, Teaching, and

"Maternal Divination"

> With this title *Encore*, I wasn't sure, I must admit, that I was still in the field I've cleared for twenty years, since what it said was that it could still go on for a long time. Rereading the first transcription of this seminar, I found that it wasn't so bad.
>
> [Sous ce titre d'*Encore*, je n'étais pas sûr, je l'avoue, d'être toujours dans le champ que j'ai déblayé pendant vingt ans, puisque ce que ça disait, c'était que ça pouvait durer encore longtemps. A relire la première transcription de ce Séminaire, j'ai trouvé que c'était pas si mal.]—JACQUES LACAN, *Encore*

> Re-reading is here suggested at the outset, for it alone saves the text from repetition (those who fail to re-read are obliged to read the same story everywhere).
>
> [La relecture est ici proposée d'emblée, car elle seule sauve le texte de la répétition (ceux qui négligent de relire s'obligent à lire partout la même histoire).]—ROLAND BARTHES, *S/Z*

Beware the Crocodile!

First, a timeline for those who may have come in late.

In 1982 Juliet Mitchell and Jacqueline Rose published their landmark collection *Feminine Sexuality: Jacques Lacan and the École Freudienne*, which included texts by Lacan and members of his circle, nearly all of which had never appeared before in English.[1] Among the selections were two excerpts from Lacan's late seminar *Encore* (1972–73), which, enigmatic even by its author's standards, famously proclaimed that "~~Woman~~ cannot be said [*Ce La ne peut se dire*]."[2] Mitchell and Rose wrote long, separate introductions to the collection that contrasted Lacan's maverick views with previous psycho-analytic conceptions of femininity and that explained why, for Lacan, sexuality has everything to do with signs and nothing to do with anatomy. Challenging feminist as well as psychoanalytic tradition in its resolute and unfamiliar antinaturalism, *Feminine Sexuality* helped change the way its readers would henceforth think about "the body," a phrase that, in all the disciplines of the humanities throughout the ensuing three decades, has come to require little further qualification than an optional application of scare quotes.[3] The volume, in short, was an event. Lacan's death in 1981 had the effect of making it seem like a testament.

In 1985 I wrote a short essay called "Mom" that you will be hearing a lot about in what follows.

In 1998 Bruce Fink published a lavishly annotated translation of the entire *Encore* seminar, including all eleven original sessions, which appeared under the new title *On Feminine Sexuality: The Limits of Love and Knowledge*. For the first time, Anglophone readers were able to follow Lacan's argument as it developed over the course of the whole seminar; they learned that such puzzling axioms as "there's no such thing as a sexual relationship" (12/17) made much more sense in context. The translation was published by W. W. Norton, the same company that brought out Mitchell's and Rose's volume sixteen years before, though the complete *Encore* differed further from its prede-cessor in appearing as part of a standardized series: "The Seminar of Jacques Lacan, edited by Jacques-Alain Miller." Miller, the director of the department of psychoanalysis at Paris-VIII, is Lacan's son-in-law and, "by a notarized document dated November 13, 1980, the appointed executor of the oral and written work of Jacques Lacan."[4] Fink prefaced his translation with the reminder that *Encore* "was not a text at all originally, but rather a series of largely improvised talks given from notes. The French editor of the Seminar, Jacques-Alain Miller, had to work from a stenographer's faulty transcrip-tion of those talks, and was obliged to invent spellings for certain of Lacan's neologisms and condensations and new ways of punctuating for Lacan's idiosyncratic speech" (viii–ix).

More than a decade since appearing in English, *Encore* is now widely regarded as Lacan's most important account of the differential logic of "sexuation." The seminar's elaboration of a feminine form of *jouissance* that exists, as Lacan jokingly put it, "beyond the phallus" (74/69) continues to provoke controversy. But the seminar has also attracted of late another kind of commentary that seems eager to reclaim *Encore* from its initial auspices:

> Existing English-language scholarship on Seminar XX has been based, until quite recently, on the snapshot of the Seminar provided by partial translations of two chapters in *Feminine Sexuality*. Hence, its almost exclusive popularization as a text on sexual difference to the neglect of its other interventions into philosophy and science. With the advent of the recent translation of *Encore* by Bruce Fink, English-speaking audiences now have access to a complete translation of the Seminar. . . . Its complete version reveals as much concern on Lacan's part with the post-Cartesian status of the subject—and the implications of this status for the limits and possibilities of knowledge and jouissance—as it does with sexual difference, and it arguably represents the most sustained and sophisticated work on these themes in Lacan's oeuvre.[5]

What becomes of psychoanalysis (let alone Lacan's recasting of it) when sexuality has been redefined as merely *one* of its concerns? What could psychoanalysis possibly know that would be besides, or "beyond," whatever it knows about sexuality? What happens to psychoanalysis, and the possibility of its transmission, when the subject is said to be affected as much, or more, by "the limits and possibilities of knowledge and jouissance" as by sexual difference—as if, somehow, these domains were external to each other? When did *jouissance* stop being sexual?[6]

I ask these questions with some urgency since Lacan's legacy seems to me imperiled if sexuality is regarded as simply a subordinate or regional interest. Sexuality and knowledge have always been near synonyms in psychoanalysis, a conjunction that has never ceased troubling more traditional epistemologies, not to mention psychoanalysis itself. We need only recall Freud on the "sexual researches of children," his recognition that knowledge is erotic from the start, to grasp why psychoanalysis cannot free itself from its own discoveries. After decades of defending the notion that libido comes only in a single masculine flavor, Freud confessed at the end of his life that he still had no clue as to "Was Will das Weib?"—an admission that formally *in-completed* everything he previously thought about sexuality, that is, everything he thought.[7] Lacan's belated recognition of a feminine variety of *jouissance*—"something that one experiences and knows nothing about" (77/71)—was a far more avid embrace than Freud's of what keeps psychoanalytic knowledge from ever coinciding with itself. In *Encore*, indeed, Lacan pledged himself to "the side of the not-whole," to the kind of *jouissance* "that belongs to that 'she' [*elle*] that doesn't exist and doesn't signify anything" (74/69): "There are men who are just as good as women. It happens. And who also feel just fine about it. Despite—I won't say their phallus—despite what encumbers them that goes by that name, they get the idea or sense that there must be a jouissance that is beyond. Those are the ones we call mystics" (76/70). This would explain why Gianlorenzo Bernini's sculpture of Saint Teresa appears on the cover of the French edition of *Encore*: "She's coming. There's no doubt about that. What is she getting off on? It is clear that the essential testimony of the mystics consists in saying that they experience it, but know nothing about it" (76/70–71). We can certainly object here, as many frequently have, that any equation of mysticism with feminine *jouissance* risks re-inforcing the historical terms of women's subordination.[8] Some may object, too, that any wish to *devenir-femme* may go only so far—and hardly beyond the phallus.[9] Even so, it is important not to miss that Lacan aligned his own writing with that of Hadewijch d'Anvers and other "female" mystics (of both genders): "These mystical ejacula-tions are neither idle chatter nor empty verbiage; they provide, all in all, some of the best reading one can find—at the bottom of the page, drop a footnote, 'Add to that list Jacques Lacan's *Écrits*,' because it's of the same order" (76/71).

This is certainly not a list to which Freud would have wished to add *his* work. Indeed, we can sense Lacan's satisfaction in imagining himself able to see "everything that Freud expressly left aside. . . . That field is the one of all beings that take on the status of woman, assuming that being takes on anything whatsoever of her destiny" (80/75). And yet—this is the problem around which this chapter will pivot—feminine *jouissance* became conceivable for Lacan only at the expense of the mother, who is never *not* an object of routine psychoanalytic knowledge: "If there is a discourse that demonstrates that to you, it is certainly analytic discourse, because it brings into play the fact that woman will never be taken up except *quoad matrem*. Woman serves a function in the sexual relationship only qua mother" (35/36). Unlike ~~Woman~~, in other words, the mother in Lacan always lines up on this side of the phallus.[10] After inciting her child to be the phallus she wants, the mother then fulfills her role—or not—by making it clear to the child that her own desire has all the while been focused elsewhere, "attached to the father."[11] Everything therefore hinges on the quality of the mother's performance, but her desire, inherently erratic, is scary to behold:

> The mother's role is the mother's desire. That's fundamental. The mother's desire is not something that is bearable just like that, that you are indifferent to it. It will always wreak havoc. A huge crocodile in whose jaws you are—that's the mother. One never knows what might suddenly come over her and make her shut her trap. That's what the mother's desire is. . . . There is a roller, made out of stone of course, which is there, potentially, at the level of her trap, and it acts as a restraint, as a wedge. It's what is called the phallus. It's the roller that shelters you, if, all of a sudden, she closes it.[12]

Whatever phallic enjoyment the mother experiences in springing the trap of her desire, we now know that it falls far short of that truly excellent *jouissance* that most women (and some men) are capable of attaining. On the condition, of course, that they are not mothers. Lacan would seem to know how to tell the difference, though *Encore* itself refrains from doing so.

But: however much Lacan wants (to be) the woman rather than the mother, we ultimately will find him stymied by the task of reproducing his thought, a task that demands the teaching of what cannot be taught *psychoanalytically*: the noncoincidence of knowledge and experience. This task will require a version of the body, and a form of pedagogy, other than those conceivable within the institutions of Lacanianism—an impossible teaching body that functions not by the transmission of precepts but by what Lacan once described, elusively, as "maternal divination."

"Mom"

We will discover that Lacan tells this difference by *embodying* it, though to prepare the way for that conclusion I need first to revisit the essay I wrote in 1985.[13] "Mom" was a reflection on my efforts to understand the nature of my mother's psychosomatic illnesses (what today we might call "somatoform disorders"). Selma Parker was never happier than in the throes of a medical crisis, which meant that she was generally happy in her way: she suffered from migraine, lower back pain, high blood pressure, neuralgia, heart trouble, valium addiction, assorted digestive complaints, and even multiple menopauses—among other ailments and phobias. She was proud that photographs of her ovaries appeared, sadly uncredited, in a mid-1960s gynecology textbook. Lest you think I exaggerate the degree to which she turned illness into a vocation (if not an art), I can attest that she seemed to have contracted a rare tropical disease while never leaving New Jersey (she had read about the disease in a medical manual and simulated its symptoms).

I turned to psychoanalysis some twenty-five years ago in an effort to make sense of my mother's illnesses. It took me almost no time to conclude that she had "converted" psychic trauma into physical symptoms, her body offering itself as a compliant medium "for the symbolic expression of unconscious conflict" that would have gone otherwise unexpressed.[14] That this too is what my mothers' physicians concluded suggests the ubiquity within the medical profession, and within the culture at large, of a "psychoanalytic" understanding of illness as psychosomatic by definition.[15] This understanding has defined psychoanalytic knowledge as early as *The Psychopathology of Everyday Life* (1901), when Freud promulgated his credo: "I believe in external (real) chance, it is true, but not in internal (psychical) accidental events."[16] From that moment, people have died unluckily (in train wrecks, floods, etc.), but psychically they will always have been murdered. Though Freud later acknowledged great difficulty in distinguishing inner from outer causation, his heirs have seldom registered this problem as a problem.[17] To cite just one characteristic example: for the Lacanian analyst Juan-David Nasio, a client's cancerous tumor "is a formation of *objet a*, a toxic excess of jouissance."[18]

Can a tumor ever just be a tumor? Nasio pictures somatic conversion as the flow of phallic libido between the "connected vessels" of fantasy and body.[19] Do these vessels ever spring a leak? Are they always connected to each other? Can the flow between them ever be reversed?

My doubts were mounting, to say the least, about conversion's adequacy as a *reading* of the body given its constitutive dependence on a concept of representation in which meaning is transmitted from an unconscious source to its secondary and derivative delegate. As Monica Greco describes this model, "the bodily symptom of the hysteric . . . stood for something else that was fundamentally 'psychic'"; as a result, the hysteric's lesion "was only a *pseudo*lesion."[20] But the unconscious psyche seems ill-equipped to play the role of a delegator, for if its conflicts are understood dynamically as an antagonism between differential forces, then they lack by definition the punctuality required of an origin. As the secondary term, "the body" is no less problematic when depicted as a passive medium—"the great book," as Serge Leclaire put it, "on which is inscribed the possibility of pleasure."[21] Does this body ever do its own writing? Freud may have intended to challenge the body's traditional passivity in locating the drive (*Trieb*) both *at* the frontier between psyche and soma and *as* that frontier.[22] But he had recourse to no other language with which to imagine that *at/as* than through proliferating representations of representation: *psychische Repräsentanz, Triebrepräsäntanz, Vorstellungsrepräsentanz*, among other variants.[23] Even highly refined notions of an "erotogenic" body "situated elsewhere and otherwise than in the traditional opposition between the soul and the body" still conceive of the symptom as a representation of conflict whose origin is elsewhere. While Leclaire believes that psychoanalysis "puts into question the common and convenient distinction between a term of reality and its representation," he has difficulty describing the peculiar way that psychoanalysis nonetheless finds itself in representation—a difficulty that Leclaire seeks to remedy . . . with more representation:

> The division presupposed by the concept of representation would not be situated in psychoanalysis between, on the one hand, an objective reality and, on the other, its figuration in a meaning. Rather, it is situated

between, on the one side, a hallucinated reality, which is the mnemic image of a lost gratifying object, and, on the other, a substitute object, which may be a "formula-object" like the one that constitutes phantasms or an instrumental whatnot, such as a fetish. One could even envision situating the division of representation in a more radical way, between the presence of the hallucinated reality and the object of satisfaction, between the memory of the lost one-and-only-one and the attempt to find it again in a repeating staging.[24]

What Leclaire may be staging repeatedly in this passage is a distinction that psychoanalysis seems unable to do without, a "division of representation" that would be wholly intrapsychic even or especially when it relates to "the body."

Lacan's unique and still startling twist on this model of psychic delegation was his insistence that "there is nothing in the unconscious which accords with the body."[25] When this sentence first appeared in the Mitchell and Rose collection, it was truly shocking to an Anglo-American readership accustomed to thinking that psychoanalysis had something to do with sex and that sex had something to do with bodies. It was indeed Freud who looked forward to the day that the findings of psychoanalysis ultimately would be verified by the physical sciences, and whose writings are marked pervasively by a tendency toward naturalism (from the "exigencies of life" of the 1895 Project to the "life instinct" of his late work). But Lacan succeeded remarkably in drawing attention to a dimension in Freud's writing in which the sexual and the physiological appear fundamentally distinct. Here, for instance, is Freud complaining to his colleagues about a lack of doctrinal unanimity about women's sexuality: "I object to all of you to the extent that you do not distinguish more clearly and cleanly between what is psychic and what is biological, that you try to establish a neat parallelism between the two. . . . I would only like to emphasize that we must keep psychoanalysis separate from biology just as we have kept it separate from anatomy and physiology."[26]

This radical difference between the sexual and the biological, the psychical and the anatomical, was at the heart of Lacan's French revolution. Where the English translation of the *Standard Edition* failed to distinguish Freud's use of the terms instinct (*Instinkt*) and drive

(*Trieb*), Lacan stressed that this distinction founds psychoanalysis as a specifically human science—as a discipline that takes sexual drive rather than biological instinct, the lability of desire rather than the physiology of need, as its unique and proper object.[27] This distinction is clearly developed in Freud's *Three Essays on the Theory of Sexuality*, where sexuality is said to originate in a swerving from the body and its instinctual needs. It is this "anaclitic" deviation from the mother's milk and its replacement with the image of her breast—this excess of the fantasized object over and against any biologically determined need—that defines sexuality in its specifically Lacanian conception.[28] Born in and as its difference from the mother's body, sexuality for Lacan is thus unnatural from inception. Just as Ferdinand de Saussure suspended the relationship between sign and referent to inaugurate linguistics as a scientific discipline, so Lacan reconceived the unconscious as a semiotic order whose operations do not require prior tethering to a physical body. Far from preceding language, sexual difference is wholly the effect of signifiers that supplant the bodies of the child and the members of its family. The gender or even the number of these bodies matters little as long as all three positions in the Oedipal structure can find occupants, and as long as the child's relationship to the mother is thereby transformed by its recognition of a wider symbolic order. The law of the phallus, the paternal metaphor, the father's no/name do not refer here to any anatomical member or particular individual but signify instead the primordial separation of human beings from their desire. Anatomy, in this conception, is destiny no longer since neither subject, male or female, has the phallus that it wants.

With the psyche thereby conceived by Lacan as a kind of *langue*, it follows that "the body as an object in the real world has no place" and that anatomy "*only figures* (it is a sham)."[29] Something, of course, preexists the infant's recognition of the fact of the system to which it belongs, but this something does not count as such if it has not yet entered into the order of signifying relations (and it is only by way of being counted that the body counts for Lacan). What matters for analysis is not the child's "biological dependence" on its mother but "its dependence on love," where love is an intersubjectively intuited desire for the mother's phallic desire.[30] Thus in yet another sense "there is nothing in the unconscious which accords with the body," for there has never been an accord between the two. As Mitchell concluded: "For Freud it is of course never a question of arguing that anatomy or biology is irrelevant, it is a question of assigning them their place. He gave them a place—it was outside the field of psychoanalytic enquiry."[31]

But can the body stay in that place, wherever "outside the field of psychoanalytic enquiry" is supposed to exist? Mitchell says "of course," though we always seem to have trouble recalling that there is a world beyond that of psychoanalysis—a real that is not already classified as "the Real." Monique David-Ménard seeks to reassure us on that score:

> Freud proceeds to show with increasing clarity that in psychoanalysis, and especially in the investigation of hysteria, one cannot rely on the idea of a bodily sensorimotor system that would be independent of the history of the symbolization of the body. His essay on negation and Lacan's reading of it have taught us that the subject of desire maintains no immediate or natural relation with the real world. *It is not that that world does not exist* [*Non que ce monde n'existe*]; but the subject's relation to it is unverifiable, is not self-evident, notwithstanding psychology's claim that perception is the elementary act of psychic life.[32]

How remarkable that the italicized sentence—with its halting syntax and series of double negatives—is offered to us as a comforting clarification. David-Ménard's difficulty in limning this boundary between inside and outside indicates, despite Lacan's efforts, the intensity of the problem that the "outside" body constitutes for psychoanalysis. Which is perhaps why we are exhorted so often to distinguish clearly between reference and signification, penis and phallus, and told that we *must* not confuse them if Lacanian theory is to stand its chance. Rose warns us accordingly of "the relative ease with which [sexuality] can be used to collapse psychoanalysis into biology"; the drive "is so easily assimilated" into instinct, the father's metaphoric function "so easily confused" with the "idealized or imaginary father."[33] Why, Fredric Jameson laments, do we always confound "the penis as an organ of the body" with "the phallus as a signifier"?[34] Can we ever learn to tell them apart?

We cannot, I suggest, for if even Lacan jumbled them together, how could we do otherwise? The following is all that he said as justification in promoting the phallus to the signifier of signifiers: "One could say [*on peut dire*] that this signifier is chosen [*est choisi*] as the most salient aspect of what can be grasped in the real of sexual intercourse [*dans le réel de la copulation sexuelle*]. . . . One could also say that, by virtue of its turgidity, it is the image of the vital flow as it is transmitted in generation [*l'image du flux vital en tant qu'l passé dans la génération*]."[35] We might have expected that at this climactic moment Lacan would have avoided the conditional (*on peut dire*) and the impersonal (*est chosi*). And yet we learn only in these highly qualified terms that this supreme signifier stands out from all others in its turgid referentiality, "the most salient element in the real of sexual copulation." Reference to the outside therefore precedes and contaminates what should have remained a purely semiotic affair, which suggests why, in Jane Gallop's words, "it is nearly impossible to keep the distinction phallus/penis clear," and why every attempt to end this confusion seems only to produce more of it.[36]

Vigilance, in other words, will never be enough to prevent reference from contaminating sense, to keep the phallus/penis opposition from imploding (phenis/pallas, as it were). This would be Gallop's further point in her analysis of Irigaray's description of male genitality. Beginning in strict Lacanian fashion by reading Irigaray's text as if it were a "poetics," a self-contained system of signifiers, Gallop recognized that this approach failed when she was forced to refer to what Irigaray herself omitted—the testes, a part of male anatomy that exists outside of Irigaray's semiotic schema: "My triumphant entry into the poetic order *is itself made possible* through the stickiest of dealings with some extra-textual body." Concluding that semiosis is thereby conditioned by a castration of a reference, Gallop stressed that sexuality can be construed psychoanalytically only in its complex impurity, only along an inner fold where signification finds itself already entangled with bodily reference.[37] The body, in other words, cannot remain in the place where Mitchell would situate it—"outside the field of psychoanalytic enquiry"—for it always was inside that field not merely as an "image of the vital flow" but . . . as something else.

This "something else" conforms in many respects to what Kristeva defined as the *abject*, a heterogeneous component of the psyche that the superego seeks to expel in a failed effort to conserve its integrity. The abject, for Kristeva, is "radically excluded and draws me to the place where meaning collapses," where insides and outsides are no longer clearly distinguishable: "It lies outside, beyond the set, and does not seem to agree to the latter's rules of the game. And yet, from its place of banishment, the abject does not cease challenging its master." An internal exorbitance, an inassimilable excess that "constitutes [the] very being" of the superego, the abject is "a something which I do not recognize as a thing," "a reality which, if I acknowledge it, annihilates me."[38] Building on Kristeva's account, I think it possible that reference to an inassimilable body forms something like the abject of Lacanian theory, that very "something" that it cannot recognize as a thing while preserving its identity as a discipline. What if this body were not solely the mind's? What if it were, somehow, maternal?

Lacan's Two Bodies

That, more or less, is what I said in 1985 when I presented this material at two international conferences that July. The first, formally titled "Lacan's Legacy: Lessons of the Transference" but colloquially known as "Lacanference," took place at the University of Massachusetts, Amherst and featured Miller as a kind of roving master of ceremonies. Stephen Melville later described the event as a showdown between those who believed passionately that Lacan's legacy had something to do with mathemes—quasi-logical formulas, charts, and equations that distilled Lacan's topological thinking—and those whose more diffuse literary interests expressed themselves in a "resolute avoidance" of those mathemes.[39] I remember little today about that conference other than Miller having decided from the title of my talk that I advanced *la cause freudienne* in attacking Americans for turning their mothers into saints ("la 'Mumm,'" he would say, nodding approvingly whenever our paths crossed during that long weekend). I remember more about the following weekend's conference on sexual difference at the University of Southampton in the United

Kingdom, which brought together academics and activists from near and far at the height of the Thatcher era and in the early years of the AIDS pandemic. There were thousands of people, much reason to be serious, and little leeway for tonal nuance. My audience *and* copanelists hated "Mom," rising up as one to accuse me of having laughed at my mother, which, I learned, was not very feminist. The only person who came to my defense was Anthony Easthope, who, rest his soul, let it be known that my talk was not all bad, but that I really needed to stop making fun of my mother.

Crushed that my paper had failed to persuade either of my audiences of what I thought was obvious (Selma, *c'est moi!*), I was relieved, at least, that "Mom" generated no hate mail when it appeared in print. The exercise at least helped me appreciate what my mother had been teaching me all the while—that the very model of somatic conversion assumes forms of bodily transparence and passivity that run counter to the psychoanalytic insight that our knowledge and experience do not coincide. But the essay also produced little further discussion or debate about the body problem in Lacan. Indeed, in the quarter century that has elapsed since then, there has been little acknowledgment that a problem exists, and many new reminders not to confuse "the body as an organism, a biological entity governed by natural laws," with another body, inorganic, whose "physical symptoms have an 'Other' cause"—a body bound "not by the laws of nature, but by the laws of representation."[40] In this respect, Parveen Adam's influential essay from 1986, "Versions of the Body," seems today as contemporary as it did then. Acknowledging that "the body" has been a persistent issue for "those who try to develop a psychoanalytic account of women," Adams asked us to step back "from the problem a moment to ask what on earth the category of the body is": "Because in some sense it is obvious, perhaps it is also misleading. Perhaps because psychoanalysis is taken to be a theory of *psychical* mechanisms, it is all too easy to imagine that the body is what is external to it, some irreducible given system. This is made even more plausible when one considers that the body is also the object of clinical medicine, an organic domain subject to the laws of anatomy and physiology."[41] Adams follows Lacan here in locating the body at the limit between disciplinary insides and outsides. Though medicine and psychoanalysis both lay claim to the body, what they share is only the name and not the "thing": "The laws governing the workings of the body which is the object of clinical medicine assign a specific, distinct and stable place to bodily organs and their interconnections so as to explain the functioning of the parts and of the whole. This body is a given entity and follows the laws of anatomy and physiology."[42] But where the medical body is empirically available and inert, the psychoanalytic body is "something which is internal to the psyche" and, as such, actively constructed by the libido. Confusion ensues when even "much psychoanalytic writing" fails to take hold of that distinction:

> Obviously when Freud writes of hysterical paralysis he writes of a bodily symptom which is organised psychically. "Hysterical paralyses," Freud writes, "must be completely independent of the anatomy of the nervous system, since *in its paralyses and other manifestations hysteria behaves as though anatomy did not exist or as though it had no knowledge of it*" (1893). Just so. The problem is that what is true of hysterical paralysis is in some sense true of the experience of the body in general. We do not experience the body as if we had knowledge of the laws of anatomy and physiology.[43]

But why should *we* follow hysteria in behaving as though anatomy did not exist? Adams's frequent, unvarying repetition of the phrase "the laws of anatomy and physiology" (which recurs twice more in this brief essay) strikes me from today's perspective as the rote application of a formula, a placeholder for everything that Adams had no interest in then: an outer world whose "laws" are known in advance to have no effect on the *mind's* body (indeed, there is no other here). It strikes me also as today's *doxa*. Here, for example, is a passage from a fine recent book on Lacan by Charles Shepherdson — a passage notable among other things for the frequency with which "the body" appears as a shorthand:

> Lacan's topological formulations may seem esoteric, and many commentators have ridiculed them, denouncing his "pseudo-mathematical" interests as chicanery or mysticism or intellectual posing. But if one thinks for a moment about *the body* — about the peculiar structure of *the body*, and all the discussions in Freud about the limit of *the body*, the difficulty of containing *the body* within its skin, or of determining what

is inside and outside *the body* (the "relation to the object," the mechanisms of "projection" and "introjection," etc.), it becomes obvious that
the space of *the body* is not really elucidated by Euclidean geometry. *The
body* is not easily closed within itself, as a circle is closed with respect to
the outside. *The body* does not occupy space as a natural object does.[44]

I take what I think is Shepherdson's point about the need to grapple
with Lacan on his own terms. But I wonder whether the model for
his account of the difference between Lacanian and Euclidean spaces
will turn out to be, once more, the supposed difference between the
phallus and the penis—in which case, given what I sought to argue
in "Mom," these two spaces cannot be conceived as mutually extrinsic. To be a desiring subject is to experience both bodies or spaces
at once but not ever to know precisely which is which, because the
one is internal to the other as its inassimilable difference from itself.
Psychoanalysis is not easily closed within itself, as a circle is closed
with respect to the outside. Lacan's most intricate Borromean knots
would have difficulty modeling that.

My sense of the stubborn resistance to signification of a body that
would not always have been the mind's owes a great deal to Elizabeth A. Wilson's *Psychosomatic: Feminism and the Neurological Body*
(2004), which certainly has nothing orthodox about it. Wilson wonders why feminism—even forms of feminism hostile to psychoanalysis—has cared so much more about a cultural body composed purely
of signs than a natural body presumably incapable of signification:

> The cultural, social, linguistic, literary, and historical analyses that now
> dominate the scene of feminist theory typically seek to seal themselves
> off from—or constitute themselves against—the domain of the biologi-
> cal. Curiously enough, feminist theories of the body are often exem-
> plary in this regard. Despite the intensive scrutiny of the body in femi-
> nist theory and in the humanities in general over the past two decades,
> certain fundamental aspects of the body, biology, and materiality have
> been foreclosed. After all, how many feminist accounts of the anorexic
> body pay serious attention to the biological functions of the stomach,
> the mouth, or the digestive system? How many feminist analyses of the
> anxious body are informed and illuminated by neurological data? How
> many feminist discussions of the sexual body have been articulated
> through biochemistry? It is my argument that biology—the muscular

capacities of the body, the function of the internal organs, the biophysics of cellular metabolism, the micro-physiology of circulation, respiration, digestion, and excretion—needs to become a more significant contributor to feminist theories of the body.[45]

Hoping to persuade those working on hysteria that the neurophysiological body should be much more *grata* than *non*, and challenging in particular the feminist presupposition "that takes biology to be inert," Wilson wonders what would happen if the mind's "ideational content" no longer took exclusive pride of place in our thinking about psychosomatic experience. Despite our different disciplinary vocabularies, I draw from her critique of the unidirectional representationalism of neurological theory new ways of reengaging with what I wrote many years before in "Mom." The unfamiliar questions Wilson wishes us to ask seem much like those that motivated me inchoately in 1985 when I looked for help in thinking about my mother:

> Following Breuer and Freud, feminists have tended to retreat from the biology of hysteria and theorize hysteria as primarily ideational. It has been almost universally agreed among feminist commentators that what is most interesting politically and what is most important theoretically in hysteria is the complex condensation and displacement of ideational content that motivates hysterical attacks. The way these contorted ideational structures are then converted into bodily symptoms has attracted less attention than one might expect; oddly enough, it is the very mechanism of conversion (of psyche into soma) that has been the least explored aspect of conversion hysteria. We may be well equipped to answer why hysterics convert, but we appear to be collectively mute in response to the question of how they convert. Breuer and Freud's oft-quoted axiom that "hysterics suffer mainly from reminiscences" has been deployed perhaps too partially. Hysterics do indeed suffer from reminiscences; they also suffer from bodily symptoms: they are paralyzed, blinded, in physical pain, they cough incessantly, they have difficulty breathing. Perhaps the most obvious aspect of hysteria—the bodily disability—has been attenuated in feminist accounts of hysterical symptomology.[46]

How *was* Selma able to mimic the symptoms of a tropical disease she did not "have"? Her doctors never asked themselves this question. Neither did I.

Do Not Read

Inspired by Wilson's encouragement to think differently about the body, I return here once more to Lacan—to *Encore* (encore!) and to a few other late texts that have been published only recently—in search of what might remain of the mother in them, a mother different from the wholly knowable kind to which Lacan opposed feminine *jouissance*.[47] In light of these newly available works, we are in a better position today to appreciate both the nature and scale of the problem that *reading* had become for the later Lacan. As Melville intuited already in 1987 on the basis of much less published evidence, *Encore* marked the moment in Lacan's career at which he discovered himself being read, a strangely complex experience for someone whose preferred medium was the oral seminar and who had long been ambivalent about the *poubellication* of his *Écrits*.[48] People nonetheless were reading him, or were trying to, as the seminar began attracting throngs. Lacan responded in 1970 with some surprise (if uncertain satisfaction) to a Belgian radio interviewer's question: "You demonstrate that you've read my *Écrits*, something that others apparently don't think is necessary because they get to hear me."[49] It remains an open question whether he was thereby commending those who had read him or those who got him straight from the source. In *Encore*, at least, Lacan is less concerned with anonymous readers than with two very specific ones, Philippe Lacoue-Labarthe and Jean-Luc Nancy, who, in 1973, while the *Encore* seminar was still under way, published an informed but critical reading of Lacan's celebrated essay from 1957, "The Instance of the Letter in the Unconscious; or, Reason since Freud," one of the texts included in *Écrits* (1966).[50] Lacan ends up being angry at everyone in *Encore*—not only at the authors of *The Title of the Letter*, whose names he will not even utter since they have written their book "with the worst of intentions," but also at members of his circle for failing to read him as incisively as did his two critics: "I can say in a certain way that, if it is a question of reading, I have never been so well read—with so much love. . . . Let us simply say that it is a model of good reading, such good reading that I can safely say that I regret never having obtained anything like it from my closest associates" (65/62).[51] With friends like these, who needs readers?

It would appear in any case that Lacan had not reread "The Instance of the Letter" for some time when he was reminded of its existence by Lacoue-Labarthe and Nancy. *Encore* is full of remarks about and allusions to the then fifteen-year-old essay (see 34/35, 36/36), as if he suddenly remembered having written it. When he warns potential readers of *Écrits* to expect a hard time (26/29), he clearly is recalling the opening pages of "The Instance of the Letter," which explained his penchant for leaving "the reader no other way out than the way in, which I prefer to be difficult"—a place all the more difficult for being situated "between writing and speech."[52] Lacan allows himself in *Encore* to read himself encore, and this includes (as in the first epigraph to this chapter) informing his audience that he had just reviewed a transcript of the first session of the *Encore* seminar, and deemed it "pas si mal." To reread oneself here is not simply to acknowledge the passage of time between earlier and later editions of the same writerly self; it is to read (oneself) *as another*—which is hardly a pleasant experience:

> That is what I check when I look back, which I never do without trembling, at what I have proffered in the past. That always makes me awfully afraid, afraid of having said something stupid, in other words, something that, due to what I am now putting forward, I might consider not to hold up.
>
> Thanks to someone who is writing up this Seminar—the first year at the *École Normale* will be coming out soon—I was able to get the sense, which I encounter sometimes when put to the test, that what I put forward that year was not as stupid as all that, and at least wasn't so stupid as to have stopped me from putting forward other things that seem to me, because that's where I'm at now, to hold water.
>
> Nevertheless, this "rereading oneself" [*se relire*] represents a dimension that must be situated in relation to what is, with respect to analytic discourse, the function of that which is read [*ce qui se lit*]. (27/30)

Even with the interpolated announcement of the imminent publication of an earlier seminar, and with his acknowledgment of an unidentified "someone" for turning his current speech into writing, this is an extraordinary admission of vulnerability for Lacan to have made publicly, first orally to his seminar audience and then again in print. Rereading activates the superego, and it is never fun becoming the text when you thought you were its reader: "In your analytic discourse, you assume that the subject of the unconscious knows how to read" (37/38). We will henceforth reread exclusively for the purpose of quality control, and only as much as is necessary for the good of our legacy. In truth, any form of reading has little to recommend it. The supposition that animals cannot read, lacking unconsciousness (37/38), may be less an expression of chauvinism than of envy. Emblazoned on the back cover of the posthumous *Autres écrits* is thus a warning that could also be a legend: "PAS-À-LIRE. Définition lacanienne de l'écrit." For writing is posthumousness itself. With speech, at least, we know the speaker is alive when we hear him or her (30/32)—or, recalling that the 1960s introduced the portable tape recorder, had been. Today's seminar is being transcribed by stenographers but my voice is also being captured on tape. People will be able to hear it when they can no longer hear me: "This will be said after I'm dead, which will be the moment when I'll finally be heard [*l'on m'entendra*]"—not read, *heard*.[53]

But if Lacan merits by this distinction the charge of phonocentrism, his version of it is far from ordinary:

> What we need to know is what, in a discourse, is produced by the effect of the written. As you perhaps know—you know it in any case if you read what I write—the fact that linguistics has distinguished the signifier and the signified is not the whole story. Perhaps that seems self-evident to you. But it is precisely by considering things to be self-evident that we see nothing of what is right before our eyes, before our eyes concerning the written. Linguistics has not simply distinguished the signified from the signifier. If there a something that can introduce us to the dimension of the written as such, it is the realization that the signified has nothing to do with the ears, but only with reading—the reading of the signifiers we hear [*la lecture de ce qu'on entend de signifiant*]. What you hear is the signifier. The signified is the effect of the signifier. (33/34)[54]

This may be the high watermark of Lacan's self-proclaimed *linguisteries*. We know already from "The Instance of the Letter" that Lacan grants precedence to the signifier vis-à-vis the signified, but only in *Encore* does he align the signified with reading and the signifier with hearing. As if reading has not always been a part of hearing. Students of Saussure need no reminding that signifiers are never heard; *parole* and *langue* comprise different theoretical domains. But if we grant Lacan's point that reading "is" the signified, then reading "falls beneath the bar of repression," inaccessible to consciousness: "What is written is not to be understood" (33–34/34–35). In which case, what one reads—that is, writing—can never become the content of any teaching. But how, then, can *psychoanalysis* be taught? Where do analysts come from?

This was already no simple question for Freud, who considered it from several angles. Even though "the inclusion of psycho-analysis in the University curriculum would no doubt be regarded with satisfaction by every psycho-analyst," the analyst would get nothing by this:

> At the same time it is clear that the psycho-analyst can dispense entirely with the University without any loss to himself. For what he needs in the matter of theory can be obtained from the literature of the subject and, going more deeply, at the scientific meetings of the psycho-analytic societies as well as by personal contact with their more experienced members. As regards practical experience, apart from what he gains from his own personal analysis, he can acquire it by carrying out treatments, provided that he can get supervision and guidance from recognized psycho-analysts.

The university, on the other hand, stands to gain by bringing psychoanalysis under its aegis even if, as Freud warns, lectures about psychoanalysis "can only be given in a dogmatic and critical manner" without transmitting the experience of analysis, which can be acquired only *in* analysis. The psychoanalytic insight that knowledge and experience are hardly if ever coincident makes the teaching of psychoanalysis inherently vexed: Is its mission to deliver knowledge *or* to foster experience, since it cannot do both at once? University students who attend lectures may "learn something *about* psychoanalysis and something *from* it," but not at the same time.[55] Freud comes to no happier solution in *The Question of Lay Analysis* (1926):

> When we give our pupils theoretical instruction in psycho-analysis, we can see how little impression we are making on them to begin with. They take in the theories of analysis as coolly as other abstractions with which they are nourished. A few of them may perhaps wish to be convinced, but there is not a trace of their being so. But we also require that every-

one who wants to practise analysis on other people shall first himself submit to an analysis. It is only in the course of this "self-analysis" (as it is misleadingly termed), when they actually experience as affecting their own person—or rather, their own mind—the processes asserted by analysis, that they acquire the convictions by which they are later guided as analysts.

Thus, if lectures are to be included as part of the analyst's training at future "Institutes of Psychoanalysis," they will be welcomed only as supplements to a pedagogy that eschews the lecture format. Freud has no difficulty in imagining a "college of psycho-analysis" that would dispense with many of the subjects taught in medical schools and replace that material with "the history of civilization, mythology, the psychology of religion, and the science of literature." But such a college would not teach analysis per se, which is a supervised experience and not a "content" to be transmitted in lectures—or in seminars.[56]

In some sense, the turbulent institutional history of psychoanalysis is an effect of this pedagogical aporia—of possessing at its disciplinary core "something that one experiences and knows nothing about" (77/71). Lacan's "excommunication" from the International Psychoanalytical Association concerned his qualifications to practice analysis and to conduct his training seminar. Returning again to his teaching, Lacan concluded *The Four Fundamental Questions of Psychoanalysis* with the pointed question: "How can we be sure that we are not imposters?"[57] This is unanswerable, he concluded, given that there are no proficiency exams for analysts. But then "How can we teach what psychoanalysis teaches us?"[58] The inherently public nature of French university teaching makes it ill-suited as a site or medium for the production of psychoanalytic knowledge, which happens only behind closed doors and does not produce a "savoir" that can be transmitted impersonally: "It is only owing to the place of the Other that the analyst can receive the investiture of the transference that qualifies him to play his legitimate role in the subject's unconscious and to speak up there in interventions that are suited to a dialectic whose essential particularity is defined as the private realm."[59] Lacan was already suspicious of the university's anodyne, transference-free notion of "research," and he rejected any attempt to make psychoanalysis into an accepted "form of research."[60] Lecturing in any case was not his "style, because, every week for the last fifteen years, I have given something that is not a lecture, but what used to be called a seminar."[61] And yet his seminar as it expanded in the 1960s and 1970s included a new public of nonanalysts from the university community, and that audience was to grow even larger with his notorious appearance on French television, during which he insisted that "there's no difference between television and the public before whom I've spoken for a long time, a public known as my seminar."[62] Was he (still? ever?) teaching his seminar? Had he become instead a performer whose very body was essential to a spectacle? One can wonder in any case why Lacan held on so tightly to the public/private distinction, which seems incapable of withstanding the slightest psychoanalytic pressure (is analysis ever simply a private matter between two people?). The more pressing problem for Lacan was obviously how, and where, to teach his difficult *dire* when it lay "somewhere between speech and writing." Advancing in years, Lacan was thinking in *Encore* more and more intently about his work's afterlife, about how best to avoid prematurely "being summed up in three lines of a textbook," which will happen "when you have been dead long enough," and even if you are still alive.[63] If only his teaching could be . . . taught.

Years before, venting his rage at his excommunication, Lacan poked fun at the International Psychoanalytical Association for thinking it could reproduce itself simply by printing facsimiles: "In order to be passed on—and not having at its disposal the law of blood that implies generation or the law of adoption that presupposes marriage—it has at its disposal only the pathway of imaginary reproduction which, through a form of facsimile analogous to printing, allows it to print, as it were, a certain number of copies whereby the one [*l'unique*] becomes plural."[64] But by the time of *Encore*, Lacan found himself in the same position as his institutional nemesis, searching for ways to make his thought truly fecund. Lacan and Miller proposed three such ways: one had to do with the reproduction of analysts, the others with the transmission of Lacanian doctrine. None of them succeeded as intended. The first was "the pass," the moment at which an analysand could testify to the formal knowledge she or he had gained *about* analysis while undergoing analysis. If successfully "passed," the analysand would then be recognized by the community as an analyst. This was an ingenious attempt to remedy the teaching problem by attaching a savoir directly to the analytic process. It also proved hugely divisive, generating wholesale desertions from *la cause freudienne*.[65] But even on its own terms, the attached savoir failed to stick to its target, and a dispirited Lacan concluded that psychoanalytic knowledge and experience were as far apart from each other as ever:

> Now that I think of it, psychoanalysis is untransmittable. What a nuisance that each analyst is forced—since it really is necessary that he be forced—to reinvent psychoanalysis. . . . I must say that in the "pass" nothing attests to the [candidate's] knowing how to cure a neurosis. I am still waiting for someone to enlighten me on this. I would really love to know, from someone who would testify in the "pass," that a subject . . . is capable of doing more than what I would call plain old chattering. . . . How does it happen that, through the workings of the signifier, there are people who can cure? Despite everything I may have said on the topic, I know nothing about it. It's a question of trickery [*truquage*].[66]

The second attempt involved the codification of the text of the seminars, a task that Lacan left largely to Miller. This, too, proved controversial, as Elisabeth Roudinesco recounts:

> In 1972, Miller thus established the text of Lacan's seminar. He removed a number of asperities and ambiguities, regularized the oral inscription, eliminated redundancies, and invented from scratch a system of punctuation. The transcription was fine; it had the disadvantage of suppressing some of the improvisation and the advantage of desacralizing the stenographic record by supplementing it with a written version. In any event, it had the merit of making readable words which until then were not, since their delivery was intended to be listened to and gazed at. But through that "establishment," the seminar's author was no longer quite Lacan, without being completely Miller. In brief, the established text conveys the content of a doctrine which, although Lacanian, bears the trace of Millerism—that is, of a hyperrationalist tendency within Lacanianism.[67]

To be sure, not everyone has viewed Lacan's and Miller's corporate authorship as a catastrophe; Alexandre Leupin, for example, suggests that we owe Miller a great debt for taming Lacan's rebarbative "style":

> The primary internal cause of misunderstanding, in my opinion, re-sides in Lacan's style, which defies clear translation; his writing very often falls (on purpose) into a Mallarméan mannerism, the high and ob-scure style practiced by French doctors around the 1930s. On the other hand, if the Seminars, which are a reworked transcription of his oral teaching, appear more easily accessible, it is the result of Jacques-Alain Miller's work. His enormous effort in publishing his version of the tran-scription has been concerned with replacing the accent of Lacan's own, now vanished voice by emphasizing the logical underpinnings of the Seminars. All the signifying effects once carried by Lacan's voice, ges-tures, and body—reticences, emphases, silence, ironies that made his living discourse clear—have been substituted by the logical coherence of writing.[68]

This is, I think, a concise (and chilling) description of Lacan's great fear of finding himself embalmed in a textbook. Indeed, to eliminate the attributes of the voice for "logical coherence" is to betray Lacan's belief in "the only training that I can claim to transmit to those who follow me. It is called: a style."[69]

But Lacan also believed in the impersonal universality of logic, which he tried to reconcile with what was particular about *his* teach-ing. The tension between the two is palpable in *Encore*:

> Analytic discourse has a privilege in this regard. That is what I began from in what constitutes a crucial date for me in what I am teaching—it is perhaps not so much on the "I" that emphasis must be placed, namely, concerning what "I" can proffer, as on the "from" [*de*], in other words, on from whence comes the teaching of which I am the effect. Since then, I have grounded analytic discourse on the basis of a precise articulation, which can be written on the blackboard with four letters, two bars, and five lines that connect up each of the letters two by two. One of these lines—since there are four letters, there should be six lines—is missing. (27/30)

The impersonal "sexuation" chart to which he refers here is the far-thest remove from Lacan's "now vanished voice." Attempting to hold together the speaker's subjective "I" with the objective "I" produced by the system of speech, Lacan threw his lot in with the matheme in a third attempt to overcome teaching's aporia. In principle, Lacan and Miller reasoned, it should not matter in the slightest who devised or pronounces the formula $\forall\, x\, \Phi\, x \cdot \exists\, \Phi\, x$ (which holds that there must be at least one person who escapes subjection to the phallus), for this is a law with supposed universal applicability. Overcoming his former hostility to the university as a venue for the teaching of psychoanalysis, Lacan avowed that "the pure matheme" is "alone in being able to be taught"; that the content of his *dire* is "teachable only after I have mathematized it"; and that even the "non-teachable" could be made into a matheme of the nonteachable. The matheme in this sense constituted "life insurance" for his teaching.[70] Except that Lacan also refused to let the mathemes do their work without him — or his body:

> Mathematical formalization is our goal, our ideal. Why? Because it alone is matheme, in other words, it alone is capable of being integrally transmitted. Mathematical formalization consists of what is written, but it only subsists if I employ, in presenting it, the language [*langue*] I make use of. Therein lies the objection: no formalization of language is transmissible without the use of language itself. It is in the very act of speaking that I make this formalization, this ideal metalanguage, ex-ist. (119/108)

In trying, impossibly, to make the mathemes dependent on his living utterance, Lacan sought to recover the subjective "I" he seemed happy to have just relinquished. In doing so he admitted to the necessity of embodiment, but here the body speaks another language, not "the language I make use of": "Analysis can be distinguished from everything that was produced by discourse prior to analysis by the fact that it enunciates the following, which is the very backbone of my teaching — I speak without knowing it. I speak with my body and I do so unbeknownst to myself. Thus I always say more than I know [*plus que je n'en sais*]" (119/108).

That the body speaks has been from the start psychoanalysis's unique principle, but it has also proven to be an abiding problem for its own disciplinary integrity. For if the body is the "site" at which a subject's knowledge and experience fail to coincide, then psychoanalysis will find its own reproduction perpetually vexed. The hard lesson that psychoanalytic teaching requires a body it also cannot assimilate seems lost on Lacanian institutions that, in their subordination of sexual difference to "philosophy and science," conform despite themselves to the most traditional of pedagogic models. Derrida's account of "the teaching body," *le corps enseignant,* has particular resonance in this context:

> Teaching delivers signs. The teaching body produces (shows and puts forward) signs, or, more precisely, signifiers supposing the knowledge of a prior signified. In relation to this knowledge, the signifier is structurally second. Every university puts language in a position of belatedness or derivation in relation to meaning or truth. That the signifier—or rather, the signifier of signifiers—is now placed in the transcendental position in relation to the system changes nothing: the teaching structure of a language and the semiotic belatedness of didactics are reproduced insofar as they are given a second wind. Knowledge and power stay on the level of principles. The teaching body, as organon of repetition, is as old as the sign and has the history the sign. It lives from belief (what, then, is belief in this case and on the basis of this situation?) in the transcendental signified. It comes back to life, more and better than ever, with the authority of the signifier of signifiers, that of the transcendental phallus, for example.[71]

"For example": Derrida is thinking here again of Lacan. And of the "cadaverization" that befalls the body of the teacher, effaced in the service of transmitting what he or she thinks: in teaching, the body has "no life of its own but only a delegation of life."[72] By definition, then, the teaching body is psychosomatic. We teach what we know but do not experience, and what we experience but do not know.

Maternal Divination

This would not have been entirely news to Lacan, though he seldom made a spectacle of his body in his teaching. A notable exception is a passage in *The Four Fundamental Questions* that has attracted some of the best readers of my generation. Here, first, is the passage, which occurs in the context of a discussion of the *fort/da* game in Freud's *Beyond the Pleasure Principle,* in which the child throws and retrieves a spool that, according to Freud, "represents" the mother's absence and return:

I, too, have seen with my own eyes, opened by maternal divination [*la divination maternelle*], the child, traumatized by the fact that I was going away despite the appeal, precociously adumbrated in his voice, and henceforth more renewed for months at a time—long after, having picked up this child—I have seen him let his head fall on my shoulder and drop off to sleep, sleep alone being capable of giving him access to the living signifier that I had become since the date of the trauma.[73]

Whatever the phrase "maternal divination" may mean here, it is certainly not a standard Lacanian term, and this passage seems to be the only place it occurs in his published corpus. While we know that divination is a ritualized form of interpretive practice, Lacan never explains why or how "maternal" modifies this practice—whether, indeed, he is specifying *maternal* divination against all other possible kinds. This question, however, is deflected in Cathy Caruth's reading of this passage, which sees in it the awakening of a *father's* eyes, presumably Lacan's.[74] Nor is it posed directly by Michael Lucey, who seems more interested in the *child's* repose as an index of its relation to social trauma.[75] The most extensive treatment of the passage is by Carolyn Dever, who argues that Lacan herein "appropriates the voice of the mother in order to articulate the relationship among the mother, the symbolic, and the child-subject." After quoting the entire passage she continues:

> The Lacanian/maternal voice that narrates this passage describes the post-traumatic physical reconnection of "mother" and infant. The persistence of the voice over the head of the sleeping child makes a subtle equation between the maternal signifier and the language of the unconscious: the "mother" speaks while the child sleeps, and the "mother" speaks the child's anxieties, vulnerabilities, and phantasies, the maternal voice introjected and analogous to the dream. For the post-*fort-da*, post-Oedipal child, access to the "living signifier"—the lost object, the maternal absent presence—occurs only in sleep. For this child, sleep represents an abdication of agency, an abandonment of physical rigidity, and the emergence of the language of dreams; within the realm of the symbolic, the maternal voice subtends conscious discourse, lurking behind, beneath, below, above the signifier.[76]

Dever's scare quotes around *mother* may convey a sense that the position Lacan finds himself in vis-à-vis the child is not authentically his. Lacan "appropriates the voice of the mother" in speaking "over the head of the sleeping child"; "the 'mother' speaks while the child sleeps." And yet Lacan is not speaking these words over the head of a sleeping child but addressing the audience of his seminar. No one, in fact, seems to be speaking in the scene as narrated by Lacan. His own voice is absent from this other scene, which echoes instead with the narrated cries of the child. I read the embodied contact between Lacan and child as the scene's pedagogical center, but the nature of its pedagogy—what "maternal divination" seems to name—may not be what we think. We do not in any case know what Lacan was thinking here, other than what he told us his body displayed when he held the child, who perhaps encountered "Lacan" again but then only as a disembodied signifier and not as an embodied person. This complexly rendered scene of embodiment, narrated by a subject differently embodied on the stage of an auditorium, can supply an entire seminar with material on the noncoincidence of knowledge and experience. We know at least that we have no access here to the "meaning" of this subject's body, which has not compliantly sent us back as readers to an unconscious source. Eluding institutional transmission but not "maternal divination," this scene teaches us about a kind of teaching that requires a body other than the mind's. Lacan has not assumed here the role of "a mother," nor has he spoken in a "mother's voice." He becomes instead *text*—maternal only in that catachrestic sense— in staging himself as someone whose opened eyes testify, encore, to "something that one experiences and knows nothing about" (77/71).

Returning to "Mom" for this chapter after a wide span of years, I often recalled Lacan's description of the changes his body underwent when rereading his earlier work: "That is what I check when I look back, which I never do without trembling, at what I have proffered in the past." I developed a terrible case of psoriasis while rereading myself reading my mother. Unlike Barthes's more hopeful epigraph to this chapter, Lacanian rereading grants us no immunity from repetition.

History, Fiction, and "The Author of *Waverley*"; or, Fathers and Sons in Marxist Criticism

> When a young science is born, the family circle is always ready for astonishment, jubilation and baptism. For a long time, every child, even the foundling, has been reputed the son of a father, and when it is a prodigy, the fathers would fight at the gate if it were not for the mother and the respect due to her.
> —LOUIS ALTHUSSER, "Freud and Lacan"

> Dead Dad Reborn as Own Son—Widow Tells How They Planned It Together—Tabloid headline from *The Sun* (U.K., circa 1980)

Family Romances

Believing himself "unfitted" to his natural parents, a youth is adopted by a family whose social status surpasses his own and into whose circle he eventually will marry. A confessed romantic who consistently mistakes illusions for reality, he seeks a place for himself in the world only to find himself participating in revolutionary activities that threaten his very existence. Escaping from the authorities he awakens from his dreams, exchanges the fictions of his immaturity for the "manly" truths of history, and accommodates himself— though not without lingering regrets—to less colorful though more pragmatic pursuits.

Marx, in all likelihood, would have recognized this "family romance" as the basis for Sir Walter Scott's historical novel *Waverley* (1814).[1] We know, on the testimony of his daughter Eleanor and his son-in-law Paul Lafargue that Marx was "altogether an enthusiastic reader of Scott," that "Scott was an author to whom Marx again and again returned, whom he admired and knew as well as he did Balzac and Fielding." Though apparently never cited by Marx, Scott was one of a handful of "modern" novelists whose works Marx would read "two or three at a time." And while no record remains to verify which of Scott's novels (other than *Old Mortality*) Marx actually read, it seems probable he was familiar with the book that lent its title to almost all of Scott's subsequent fiction, the plots of which would play variations on the pattern Scott had established in the first of what became a lengthy series. Since we do in fact know that Marx's wife, Jenny, prided herself on her descent from Scottish nobility—that, after reading Scott, Eleanor jokingly confessed her "horror" that "she herself partly belonged to the detested clan of Campbell"—it is reasonable to infer that Marx would have been attracted especially to *Waverley*, one of the select group of novels in which Scott imaginatively recreated crucial moments in the history of Scotland.[2]

Yet Marx may have recognized this story of a "youth transformed" in another way as well—he may have viewed *himself* as its protagonist. For Marx's life (in his romantic telling) resembles curiously though closely the life of Scott's hero. Like Waverley, he was "adopted" by a family of superior social standing, the aristocratic von Westphalens, whose daughter he would marry;[3] like Waverley, he was sought across borders by governmental agents who would charge him with sedition. Above all, like Waverley, he glossed the pattern of his life as a passage from the romance of fiction to the reality of history, a passage Marx would replicate in forsaking juvenile literature for materialist science. What happens, however, to the authority of this science when, having staked its possibility on its difference from fiction, it can still recognize itself in the plot of a novel? What happens to that authority when the fiction in question is itself a *historical* novel, a work that not only portrays "historical" personages alongside "literary" characters but also explores within its fictional frame the relationship between fiction and history? What happens, finally, when this historical novel is also *about* the problem of authority, taking as its subject the circumstances surrounding the Scottish Jacobite Rebellion of 1745, events that raise the very issues of legitimacy and paternity that Marx would grapple with as well?

This chapter will explore such questions with regard to an immensely influential reading of Scott and his literary heritage, a reading that Fredric Jameson has called "perhaps the single most monumental realization of the varied program and promises of a Marxist and a dialectical literary criticism"—György (Georg) Lukács's *The Historical Novel*.[4] "A virtual introduction or handbook to dialectical thinking" through "its extensive quotations and references to both the Hegelian and Marxian philosophical traditions," *The Historical Novel* in Jameson's estimation "triumphantly fulfills the central mission of any Marxist criticism, which lies in the attempt to articulate what can very loosely be called the aesthetic text and its historical or social 'context'" (4, 1).[5] My goal in what follows is to demonstrate that if Lukács earns such centrality for this work, he does so by figuring Marx as his *ancestor*, by conceiving himself as the heir to a legacy whose conditions entail the rewriting of fiction as historical necessity. Since such legacies have a habit of engendering themselves as patrimonies, we will discover that *The Historical Novel* can secure its exemplary status only by inheriting questions of representation—questions, indeed, of the representation of inheritance—that surface at once in its theoretical principles and in the novels, *Waverley* first and foremost, that it reads. As a family romance that inevitably contaminates the purity of its genealogical origins, *Waverley* becomes an important text in the history of Marxist criticism paradoxically to the extent that its own history becomes problematic, that it both sanctions and resists the dialectical logic on which its figurations of inheritance depend.

The Prehistory of the Present

If it is commonplace today to describe the early nineteenth century as a period uniquely marked by "the emergence of history both as knowledge and as the mode of being of empiricity,"[6] it is no less customary to identify the appearance of *Waverley* as a decisive moment in that emergence. Most contemporary readers of Scott would agree that "the publication of *Waverley* was an event not only in the history of the novel, but in the development of the historical consciousness of Europe,"[7] that Scott's fiction transformed both the history of narrative in the West and the narrative of history. Scott (so this account proceeds) "did more than any professional historian to make mankind advance towards a true conception of history"; his fiction "did not merely make it possible to write novels about the Crusades" but also "made it possible to describe any society in its temporal dimensions."[8] Indeed, while it has long been accredited that "the modern historical novel arose as part of the rise of historicism," many now would argue for the opposite view as well—that historicism itself was, along with "the new masculinity" Scott imparted to the genre of the novel, the most significant effect of the power of his fiction.[9] Though he fell into disfavor early in the twentieth century, Scott should be acknowledged, as James Chandler has argued, with having created what "is arguably the most influential single body of literary work produced in English by any writer since Shakespeare. The Waverley novels, in other words, not only register how the modern historiographical operation produces its distinctive forms of meaning, they also, in their massive circulation and impact on the 'white mythologies' of national self-representation in the nineteenth century, play a significant role in the emergence of modern historiography itself."[10]

This revised assessment of Scott's importance may be dated with precision to the publication of *The Historical Novel*, Lukács having been the first to make the case that Scott's greatness consists in his "deeper, more genuine and differentiated sense of historical necessity [*historische Notwendigkeit*] than any writer before him" (58). There were, of course, earlier novelists who made use of historical settings, but their renderings of historical experience were vitiated, in Lukács's view, by their inability to portray the *process* of history, the fact that the past comprises "the concrete precondition of the present" (21). A constellation of unique historical circumstances enabled Scott to succeed in depicting this process where his predecessors had failed. He not only had to have lived during the period of "the French Revolution, the revolutionary wars and the rise and fall of Napoleon," events that "for the first time made history a *mass experience*" and that imparted an "awareness of the decisive role played in human progress by the struggle of classes in history" (23, 27). He needed to have been born an Englishman as well, for England alone could offer itself as "the practical, model example of the new style of historical interpretation," having "fought out its bourgeois revolution in the seventeenth century and . . . from then on experienced a peaceful upward development" (31–32). Even Scott's political con-

servatism uniquely fitted him to the requirements of his genre: notwithstanding the manifest disparity between his "directly political
views and his artistic world picture," Scott still could "portray objectively the ruination of past social formations despite all his sympathy
for, and artistic sensitivity to, the splendid human qualities which
they contained. Objectively, in a large historical and artistic sense: he
saw at one and the same time their outstanding qualities and the historical necessity of their decline" (54–55). Just as Balzac (in Engels's
often quoted formulation) was compelled as a novelist "to go against
his own class sympathies and political prejudices,"[11] Scott similarly
would transcend his ideological reservations and affirm the course
of progress in his writing—a progress *The Historical Novel* affirms as
well in tracing the vicissitudes of a genre that, at least in the hands of
its first great practitioner, "brings the past close to us and allows us
to experience its real and true being" (53).

At first glance, however, it is difficult to determine how these historical requisites function for Lukács as the basis for Scott's *political*
importance. For while Lukács seeks to demonstrate how "the historical novel in its origin, development, rise and decline follows inevitably upon the great social transformations of modern times," and
thus how "its problems of form are but artistic reflections of these
social-historical transformations" (17), it is remarkable to consider,
given its "monumental" status in the history of Marxist criticism,
just how narrowly the book construes what *counts* as the "social-
historical." In the first place, any analysis centered on the category
of *Praxis* or on the nature of the commodity form is almost entirely
absent from its pages; though we read a great deal about the political
interests and literary tastes of particular class formations, on capitalism as a specific mode of production Lukács has little here to say.
One can argue—as Jameson has done importantly following the lead
of Ronald L. Meek—that "Enlightenment Scotland was above all the
space of coexistence of radically distinct zones of production and culture," a space that was refracted in what might be called "the combined and uneven development" of Scott's fiction, its overlapping and
heterogeneous narrative modes . . . but this is not an argument that
Lukács makes.[12]

We might notice, too, that what would later attract the attention
of Scott's feminist critics is quickly glossed over by Lukács, who fol-

lows Balzac in observing blandly "that with very few exceptions all of Scott's heroines represent the same type of philistinely correct, normal English woman; that there is no room in these novels for the interesting and complex tragedies and comedies of love and marriage" (34).[13] Dispatching the need for any further reflection on the representation of gender, Lukács never considers, for example, how Scott typically contrasts his "light" and "dark" heroines, the latter possessing those sensual qualities the hero ultimately must reject for the domestic (and national) security embodied by the former. Neither does Lukács remark on the uncanny frequency with which these heroines appear in drag in an effort to transform their somnambulant male counterparts into less "feminized," passive specimens. Nor, finally, is he curious about the overwhelming homosociality of Scott's fiction—about the ways that the ostensibly binary "choice" between light and dark heroines may not in fact be a choice at all; that such apparent oppositions may screen an asymmetrical intensity that links Scott's heroes to their *male* "dark doubles."[14] In *Waverley*, for example, the first alluring description of Flora Mac-Ivor begins by stressing her "most striking resemblance to her brother Fergus" (*Waverley* 167). Fergus in due course will be executed and Flora sent to a convent so that the novel can conclude with Waverley's attachment to Rose Bradwardine, their marriage enshrining (as Flora accurately predicts) a rigidly hierarchical division between public man and private woman.[15] This properly Oedipal arrangement—the text makes a point of emphasizing how Rose's father stands "*in loco parentis*" to Waverley (*Waverley* 98)—thus seems infinitely preferable to the possibility that "incorrect" object choices might lead history astray.

What is, however, more disturbing than his limited interest in Scott's treatment of gender is Lukács's tendency to diminish the costs entailed by his vision of historical necessity. Offering itself as a contribution to the Popular Front (17), the antifascist coalition whose rhetoric sought to transcend sectarian differences, *The Historical Novel* generally discounts the historical experiences of groups who had little to gain from such imagined unity. Lukács describes, for example, how Scott's fiction often takes as its subject the "liquidation" of the clans, those "remnants of feudalism" who formed a "surplus population" unable to "maintain themselves on the basis of their primitive economy" (25, 58). "Scott can do this," Lukács explains, because "the inability of the clans to defend their common interests against nobility or bourgeoisie and the dissipation of their energies in the local insularity of such petty struggles are an inevitable result of the basis of clan life" (57). If Lukács hardly regrets this "dissipation"—if he seems rather indifferent to the social and economic devastation that the semifeudal Highlands suffered in the wake of the union with England—such sacrifices would appear to be the price necessarily exacted if a dialectically united kingdom is to proceed on its path from feudalism through capitalism to socialism. Committed implicitly to the *Communist Manifesto*'s conception of capitalism as a stage "through which precapitalist peoples must pass in order to be reprogrammed and retrained, transformed and developed,"[16] Lukács never wonders whether Scott's famous "nostalgia" may have been the kind of luxury that belongs to victors, or whether his "progressive" account of history may have helped legitimate a present state of affairs by demonstrating that the conflicts of the past could not, after all, have been differently resolved. Though one may justly characterize Scott as a kind of Highlands "Orientalist," a codifier not only of folklore but also of the image of a sublime (because just recently depopulated) landscape, Lukács, once more, does not.[17]

Wholly uninterested, then, in the kinds of issues that have dominated contemporary criticism, Lukács ascribes a political importance to Scott's works solely for the ways that they instantiate a critical moment in the coming-to-consciousness of history. Scott embodies his awareness of this process through the development of "characters who, in their psychology and destiny, always represent social trends and historical forces" (34). As "historical-social types [*historisch-soziale Typen*]" whose role is to "present the totality of certain transitional stages of history," Scott's heroes "bring the extremes whose struggle fills the novel, whose clash expresses artistically a great crisis in society, into contact with one another" (35, 36). Though "never mere representatives of historical movements, ideas etc.," these types are depicted "in such a way that certain, purely individual traits of character, quite peculiar to them, are brought into a very complex, live relationship with the age in which they live" (47). Lukács singles out *Waverley*'s hero as one such example of the exemplary, a living synthesis of the individual with the world-historical:

> Waverley is an English country squire from a family which is pro-Stuart,
> but which does no more than quietly sympathize in a politically ineffec-
> tive fashion. During his stay in Scotland as an English officer, Waverley,
> as a result of personal friendships and love entanglements, enters the
> camp of the rebellious Stuart supporters. As a result of his old family
> connections and the uncertain nature of his participation in the uprising,
> which allows him to fight bravely, but never to become fanatically par-
> tisan, his relations with the Hanoverian side are sustained. In this way
> Waverley's fortunes create a plot which not only gives us a pragmatic
> picture of the struggle on both sides, but brings us humanly close to the
> important representatives of either side. (37)

Waverley thus is a figure who recapitulates internally a range of historical experiences, a type who reconciles dialectically not only the
conflict between Stuarts and Hanoverians but a larger discrepancy
between the personal and the social. In mediating between these
categories, Waverley's character would share a lineage with Hegel's
conception of the "concrete universal," for it is the function of each to
form totalities that unify previously distinct antinomies, "so negating
[themselves] as infinite and universal as to become finitude and particularity, and in nevertheless cancelling this negation in turn and so
re-establishing the universal and the infinite in the finite and the particular." Indeed, if, for Hegel, "art's vocation is to unveil the *truth* in
the form of sensuous artistic configuration, to set forth the reconciled
opposition just mentioned," this would be, for Lukács, the vocation
of Scott's hero as well, forming in miniature an image of the totality
of the work he inhabits.[18]

Lukács, in fact, stresses these similarities between novelist and philosopher: "Scott's manner of composition here shows a very interesting parallel to Hegel's philosophy of history" (39). Just as Hegel
regards "'the present in general as a consequence of those events
in whose chain the characters or deeds represented constitute an
essential link,'" Scott similarly brings "the past to life as the prehistory of the present [*als Vorgeschichte der Gegenwart*]," a "process full
of contradictions, the driving force and material basis of which is
the living contradiction between conflicting historical forces, the
antagonisms of classes and nations" (53). Qualifying this dialectic
as decidedly "English"—Scott "finds in English history the consola-

tion that the most violent vicissitudes of class struggle have always finally calmed down into a glorious 'middle way'" (32)—Lukács also acknowledges that there are limits to the terms of his comparison, that "Scott had no knowledge of Hegel's philosophy and had he come across it would probably not have understood a word" (30). The parallel nevertheless stands, for Lukács, to the extent that the teleology of Scott's fiction reflects the progress of Hegel's World Spirit, whereby "the Idea creates that illusion, by setting an antithesis to confront it; and its action consists in getting rid of the illusion which it has created. Only out of this error does the truth arise."[19]

That Lukács can read this lesson in Scott's *novels*—that it is through fiction that the historical spirit first properly comes to consciousness—is not, however, a problem Lukács considers at all, for Scott's works would themselves be about this progressive overcoming of their heroes' illusions, fiction standing to history within them as error to truth, childhood to maturity. Scott's importance resides precisely, for Lukács, in the way his novels illustrate this becoming-history of fiction, the literary inexorably growing (up) into its heir. But Scott *as a novelist* could not possibly know that this was his most significant achievement: "For in the field of theory and historiography only historical materialism is capable of intellectually unearthing this basis of history, of showing what the childhood of mankind [*die Kindheitsperiode der Menschheit*] was really like. But what in [Lewis Henry] Morgan, Marx and Engels was worked out and proved with theoretical and historical clarity, lives, moves, and has its being poetically in the best historical novels of Scott" (56). For Lukács, in other words, Marxism is the *science* of maturation, of the present's inheritance of the past: just as Freud claimed not to have discovered the unconscious but simply systematized the intuitions of the poets who preceded him, so does Marxism, for Lukács, repeat Scott's insights with a difference—where romance was there shall history and theory be.[20] Not only are Scott's novels said to dramatize this pattern of transmission, the growth of their heroes from youth to adulthood, but Marxism stands to this body of work in an identical manner as well, as the destined overcoming of an illusory precondition: Scott will grow up to become Marx, from whom, in turn, Lukács will inherit an understanding of this process of inheritance. The genre of historical fiction is thus in no sense an oxymoron, its "literariness" sublating itself in the dialectical movement of time. For where Hegel's Spirit "in its highest form eludes the sensuous medium of art,"[21] history (as Lukács adapts this argument) similarly comes into its own at the moment it surpasses the medium of fiction.

Lukács's reading is unquestionably powerful, resolving at one stroke, for example, the long-standing critical problem of Scott's so-called ambivalence. The binary oppositions one frequently encounters in *Waverley* and its successors—the two heroes (Waverley and Fergus) and the two heroines (Flora and Rose); the private plot (Waverley's "awakening") and the public plot (the Jacobites' defeat); the extended thematic contrasts between past and present, tradition and progress, emotion and reason, Tory and Whig, aristocracy and bourgeoisie, the House of Stuart and the House of Hanover, Scotland and England, the Lowlands and the Highlands, Kirk and Church, *Gemeinschaft* and *Gesellschaft*, romance and history, fiction and truth— all these antitheses can now be grasped dialectically as the narrative projection of Scott's "divided" allegiances. Even when it refrains from directly recording its debt to Lukács, subsequent criticism on Scott remains dominated by his argument that the *Waverley* novels reconcile in fiction the historically conditioned dualisms of their author:

> Intellectually he endorsed and upheld the Scotland of his own day; it possessed the stability and order essential for Improvement—the economic, commercial development and cultural advance which Scott respected. But, in comparison with the past, the present was dull and prudential, perhaps even mean-spirited and materialistic, devoid of colour and excitement. Scott's best fiction utilizes and explores this ambivalence; it dramatically juxtaposes the values, attitudes, habits of mind and behaviour, of old world and new.[22]

Such a reading is certainly an advance over earlier and less comprehensive approaches, its dialectic making it possible "to see both sides of Scott," "to come closer to seeing him whole." The "Author of *Waverley*" may thus be recovered with a sense of balance restored "between fact and fiction, between the real world and the world of the imagination, the two worlds of the *Waverley* novels."[23] And since, following Lukács, it is history on which this synthesis is held to depend—it is history that produces both Scott's ambivalence and its narrative resolution—*Waverley* can be considered today "an immensely readable novel," its legibility a function of its historical being.[24]

Yet this newly consensual reading of *Waverley* participates in a decidedly venerable tradition, one that dictates (in Avrom Fleishman's version) that fiction "retells history in order to make a truer story than has been written by historians, prophets, or other artists. The story is not truer to facts . . . but is 'intellectually more acceptable'— suggesting a universal implication of the historical particulars."[25] This implicitly Lukácsian formulation not only assumes unquestioningly the derivation of fiction from history; it suggests above all (as Derrida puts it in another context) that it is "through fiction [that] truth properly declares itself," a truth that would be at once historical and mimetic: "Truth governs the fictional element of its manifestation, which permits it to be or to become what it is, to declare itself. Truth governs this element from its origin or its telos, which finally coordinates this concept of literary fiction with a highly classical interpretation of *mimesis*: a detour toward the truth, more truth in the fictive representation than in reality, increased fidelity, 'superior realism.'"[26] It is history, in other words, that obligingly allows fiction on occasion to be truer than itself, permitting itself to stray from itself on the condition of its eventual homecoming. Paving the way for this mimetic interpretation, fiction conforms here to its traditional conception as "a teleological and totalizing dialectics that at a given moment, however far off, must permit the reassemblage of the totality of a text into the truth of its meaning, constituting the text as *expression*, as *illustration*."[27] Each of these terms plays a role, we have seen, in Lukács's reading of Scott: fiction as its own self-transcendence, as a detour from the conditions of its production to its reappropriation as history; history as a sending, a transmission from a punctual origin to its destiny in truth; truth as the synthetic expression of the totality of a work, its teleology underwriting the possibility of its dialectical recovery. Yet for this recovery to take place, a whole family of metaphors—the metaphor of family—typically comes into play to ensure that "the claim to understanding is incorporate with the claim to transmissibility."[28] History consistently will figure itself as a trusting father who bequeaths an inheritance to his faithful, fictional son—a son who must not be a prodigal (or, much worse, a parricide) but simply return to the fold when his wanderings are done. If mothers play no discernible role in this process and daughters are merely trafficked in exchange—if the circuit from history through fiction to history thus begins to betray a singular gender—such an exclusion seems to be required if the improved capital is to return, safely, to its putatively undivided source: "The scene would be acted out, if such were possible, between father and son alone: autoinsemination, homoinsemination, reinsemination."[29]

In view of this drama it seems easy to grasp why paternity becomes "a dominant issue within the great tradition of the nineteenth-century novel (extending well into the twentieth century), a principal embodiment of its concern with authority, legitimacy, the conflict of generations, and the transmission of wisdom."[30] But paternity remains a dominant issue within the Marxist tradition as well: indeed, as Jon Elster recalls, to be a Marxist has never required one to subscribe to *all* "the beliefs Marx thought were his most important ideas"; one need only "trace the *ancestry* of [one's] most important beliefs back to Marx," thereby locating oneself patrilineally as the heir to a theoretical legacy.[31] The question to be asked of Lukács's reading, then, is whether Scott's novels simply enact this process of inheritance, whether history relates to fiction within them only as indulgent father to devoted son. In the following sections I will reexamine *Waverley*'s genealogical patterns with just this question in mind. Assessing the degree to which Scott's fiction achieves the dialectical synthesis it seems patently to desire, I shall also seek to discover what in it—and with what consequences for Lukács's patrimony—fails to "return to the father."

The History of the Father

Scott not only helped create a new genre of historical fiction; he precipitated the crisis of its theory as well. Denounced as an "immoral, irrational, hybrid form, combining novel with history, false and true," the historical novel seemed for many in the nineteenth century to threaten all distinction between fact and invention.[32] As Alessandro Manzoni explained in an important early essay on the subject, "the historical novel counterfeits and corrupts, namely history. . . . Though we know it is a work in which history and fable must figure, we cannot determine or even estimate their proper measure or relation." Failing, on the one hand, to "give a faithful representation of history," and, on the other, to maintain "the unity that is the vital condition of this or any other work of art," the historical novel was condemned by Manzoni as "a work impossible to achieve satisfactorily, because its premises are inherently contradictory."[33] Though Manzoni himself had written an influential historical novel (*The Betrothed*, 1827), the impurity he found endemic to the genre led him ultimately to repudiate its practice.

Scott, typically, was bemused by these reactions: rather than purposely seeking to degrade the historical, he claimed to have done nothing but respect its priority, putting his works at the service of a properly nonfictional truth. In his "Essay on Romance," for example, Scott expressed his disdain for "the character of mere fictions," books devised solely "to beguile the leisure of those who have time enough to read and attend to them." Scott censured these productions for their tendency to efface their "common origin" with "real history"—a history that tellingly grounds itself in the authority of a male ancestor:

> The father of an isolated family, destined one day to rise into a tribe, and in further progress of time to expand into a nation, may, indeed, narrate to his descendants the circumstances which detached him from the society of his brethren, and drove him to form a solitary settlement in the wilderness, with no other deviation from truth, on the part of the narrator, than arises from the infidelity of memory, or the exaggerations of vanity. But when the tale of the patriarch is related by his children, and again by his descendants of the third and fourth generation, the facts it contains are apt to assume a very different aspect.

Unfaithful to the memory of the patriarch, these distorted replications compel us finally "to renounce all hope of deriving serious or authentic information from the materials upon which the compounders of fiction have been so long at work, from one generation to another." The meager "realities" such works contain are simply

> the few grains of wheat in the bushel of chaff, incapable of being winnowed out, or cleared from the mass of fiction with which each new romancer had in his turn overwhelmed them. So that Romance, though

certainly deriving its first original form from the pure font of History, is supplied, during the course of a very few generations, with so many tributes from the Imagination, that at length the very name comes to be used to distinguish works of pure fiction.[34]

Scott's "Essay on Romance" would imply, however, that fiction need not be fated to such infidelity, leaving open the possibility of a more obedient relation to history. Just as Hegel contrasted two kinds of writing—"a bad writing [*une mauvaise écriture*], secondary, artificial, cryptic or hieroglyphic, voiceless, [which] intervenes to obscure good writing [*la bonne écriture*]"—Scott similarly distinguished bad fiction from good, reversing this process of generational decay by developing a kind of novel uniquely suited to preserving what was rapidly fading from memory: a novel, in short, that would respect its patriarchal origins.[35] Though he acknowledged that a latter-day romancer could not avoid entirely what *Waverley* describes as the "tincturing" of historical fact with a "romantic tone and colouring," Scott professed that this very novel was intended wholly "for the purpose of preserving some idea of the ancient manners of which I have witnessed the almost total extinction" (*Waverley* 55, 492). If the "worst evil to be apprehended from the perusal of novels is, that the habit is like to generate an indisposition to real history, and useful literature,"[36] Scott did all that he could to counter this tendency: he "embodied in imaginary scenes, and ascribed to fictitious characters, a part of the incidents which I then received from those who were actors in them. Indeed the most romantic parts of [*Waverley*] are precisely those that have a foundation in fact" (493). That fiction for Scott can support rather than hinder history in this work of preservation is a lesson Waverley learns as well from his uncle's "oft-repeated tale of narrative old age":

> Family tradition and genealogical history, upon which much of Sir Everard's discourse turned, is the very reverse of amber, which, itself a valuable substance, usually includes flies, straw, and other trifles; whereas these studies, being themselves very insignificant and trifling, do nevertheless serve to perpetuate a great deal of what is rare and valuable in ancient manners, and to record many curious and minute facts, which could have been preserved and conveyed through no other medium. (*Waverley* 51)

"Insignificant and trifling" in itself, fiction still may be valued as an *aide mémoire* for its ability to fill in "the cold, dry, hard outlines" of history: the romance as a kind of fortunate fall "which gives light and life to the actors and speakers in the drama of past ages" (*Waverley* 109). Unwilling, however, to allow invention free rein—distinguishing his novels from those "written and read merely on account of the exercise they afford to the imagination"—Scott praises himself (in an anonymous review of his own work) for simply having "collected and brought out with accuracy and effect, incidents and manners which might otherwise have slept in oblivion."[37] Even William Hazlitt (who was not, to be sure, one of Scott's great admirers) viewed as remarkable the care Scott expended to separate the properly from the merely fictional, the loyal son from the faithless prodigal: "He has conversed with the living and the dead and let them tell their story in their own way. . . . He is only the amanuensis of truth and history."[38] Hence two kinds of fiction, corresponding to two ways of relating to historical origins: the one disloyal to the memory of its father, the other ever mindful of its filial obligations.

Most critics would agree that *Waverley* explores in detail the nature of these differences between fiction-as-invention and fiction-as-history, differences that its hero gradually learns to *read*. At the outset, for example, Waverley is described as "warm in his feelings, wild and romantic in his ideas and in his taste for reading, with a strong disposition for poetry" (108)—an inclination fostered by "a vague and unsatisfactory course of reading" that permits him "to learn as he pleased, what he pleased, and when he pleased" (45, 73). Unchecked by parental authority—his mother, no surprise to us, is dead (49)[39]—Waverley tends to "read rather to awaken the imagination than to benefit the understanding," thereby acquiring "that wavering and unsettled habit of mind which is most averse to study and riveted attention" (49, 73). Each of the many "mistakes" Waverley will commit in the course of the novel—his infatuation with Flora, his desertion of his regiment, his taking arms with Fergus, his inability to guess that Rose has been his secret benefactor—all of these errors are directly attributable to a "common aberration from sound judgment" that treats a "variety of incidents" as occasions for "the exercise of a romantic imagination" (55, 73, 138).

It is only when, in the midst of the rebellion, Waverley's "Reason asked, was it worthwhile to disturb a government so long settled and established, and to plunge a kingdom into all the miseries of civil war" (*Waverley* 222), that our hero learns to read in a less purely imaginative way, ultimately obtaining "a more complete mastery of a spirit tamed by adversity than his former experience had given him; and he felt himself entitled to say firmly, though perhaps with a sigh, that the romance of his life was ended, and that its real history had now commenced" (415). No longer "tincturing" events with his own powers of invention, Waverley has progressed from illusion to reality, from youth to maturity, from mere romance to historical necessity, achieving at the end of this transition what one critic has called an entirely "unambiguous present."[40] If, as we have seen, fiction for Scott can relate to history either faithfully or disloyally, Waverley has discovered at the completion of the novel what kind of a son he was destined to become, proving himself worthy of his patrimony by spurning the temptations of romance.

The struggle Waverley undergoes in learning to discern the limits of the "merely" fictional is echoed, of course, by the novel's portrayal of a larger historical conflict concerning the nature of sovereign authority: the Stuarts' defense of Charles's hereditary right to the throne against the Hanoverians' more distant but legally supported claims. Indeed, *Waverley*'s plot works to persuade that these questions of royal legitimacy are structurally identical to those its hero must resolve, that the lesson of fidelity through deviation is one that every subject of the realm is required to master. The Shakespearian motto "Under Which King?" that the novel takes as its epigraph can itself be rewritten as "Under Which Fiction?": though Scott would concede that the claims of both houses are, at bottom, equally fictitious (how, after all, did the Stuarts become kings?), his narrative suggests that only the house with the Act of Settlement and the Bill of Rights in its safekeeping can lead beyond its fictional status to affirm history's just authority. For what *Waverley* appears to ratify is less the supposed naturalness of the paternal origin than the collectively agreed-on conventions that render it authoritative—less, in short, the reality of any particular Father than the place-holding function his patronym performs. Thus, Colonel Talbot's formal observance of the fictions of the law will discredit as entirely romantic Fergus's defense of his hereditary prerogatives; and while it is Richard who is Waverley's "natural" father, the novel will dismiss him as a "placeman" (*Waverley* 43) to justify, by contrast, Everard's foster paternity as British destiny: fiction in the service of national truth.[41]

These public and private concerns coalesce in a single detail at the end of the novel when the Baron of Bradwardine—the figure who, we recall, stands "*in loco parentis*" to Waverley (*Waverley* 98)—recovers the antique drinking cup he had lost in the course of the rebellion. "Supposed in old and Catholic times to be invested with certain properties of a mystical and supernatural quality" (92–93), the cup (along with the Baron's manor, Tully-Veolan) is restored legally in the new dispensation to its formerly hereditary proprietor (490–91), thereby becoming "a magical symbol" of "achieved reconciliation" and "entire restitution."[42] Presenting itself as a *figure* for this process of loss and recovery, of what Derrida has called "departure-returning itself, in other words the presentation of itself of re-presentation, the return to-itself of returning," the cup thus inscribes by its narrative motion the path that leads back to the place (if not the person) of the Father.[43] Honoring the fiction of its paternal origin—transforming loss into gain, deviation into destiny, detours into homecomings, the Baron's private good fortune into national inheritance—the cup asks to be read as the very image of history, dramatizing in its itinerary the trajectory of necessity itself.

Uniting particulars with universals in this circular chain, *Waverley* thus would conform to the dialectic that Lukács finds operative throughout Scott's corpus. History's returning to itself through the detour of fiction; the past's becoming present through the bonds of filial devotion; Waverley's reconciling within himself the dialectical antimonies of his age—these are the fictional elements Lukács reads as the "immaturity" Marx will sublate in time. In undertaking this reading, of course, Lukács would prove himself faithful to Marx's memory, receiving from his paternal ancestor the dialectical knowledge that history remains destined to transcend its preconditions. The difficulty, however, is that Lukács can demonstrate his loyalty to Marx only by refusing the letter of this patrimony, by effacing the critical distance between his own text and Scott's. For just as Marx may have recognized his life in *Waverley*'s fiction, Lukács similarly finds himself absorbed in the novel, repeating in his reading what was already staged in the text he reads. Comprehending in its plot its subsequent analysis, *Waverley* places Lukács in the position of its hero, directing him to do precisely what Waverley had done—exchange error for truth, fiction for history—an exchange that thereby repeats, transferentially, the novel's own structures of transference.[44] Though this mise-en-scène of *The Historical Novel* within a historical novel may not suffice to make the dialectic waver, *Waverley* will trouble in many other ways as well the progressive sublation of fiction on which the father's authority depends. The following section examines a number of such obstacles to family harmony—what Judith Wilt has called "curious hitches, catches, and reversals in this apparently smooth passage from romance to real history"[45]—generational conflicts that do not lend themselves to the assurance of a dialectical resolution. We will discover that if Scott had indeed "not . . . understood a word" of Hegel's philosophy, this would have had much less to do with Scott's apparent ignorance of Hegel or with his supposed philosophical incapacity than with the novel's resistance to the (paternal) structure of dialectical reason.

Fictions: Of Paternity

Waverley's generation gap can be discerned above all in the distance, both spatial and temporal, that separates two of the novel's voices (the "combined and uneven" discourses mentioned earlier). For although the book appeared originally in 1814 without any other explanatory apparatus than that already included in the first and last chapters, Scott appended over the course of the following fifteen years an "Advertisement," a general preface, several appendices to the general preface, a separate preface to the third edition, an introduction, a dedication, extensive editorial notes, and even a glossary. Typically, the self-consciously "fictional" mode of the original edition will conflict with the kind of "historical" claims made by these subsequent materials, forcing the question of how we are to make sense of a text which grew so intractably divided from itself.

The voice of the notes and prefaces attempts repeatedly to document the novel's foundation in historical fact: it will seek to verify, for example, that one of the characters in the narrative is based on an actual acquaintance of the author (*Waverley* 569), or that a certain poem cited within the text is not itself an "original" invention but "a genuine ancient fragment, with some alteration in the last two lines" (82n). This is the Scott of whom F. A. Pottle remarked that "no other English author . . . has ever taken such delight in exposing his *sources*,"[46] the Scott who constantly obtrudes to signal both where his fiction adheres to its origins and where it deviates all the better to return:

> The Author has sometimes been accused of confounding fiction with reality. He therefore thinks it necessary to state, that the circumstances of the hunting described in the text as prepatory to the insurrection of 1745, is, so far as he knows, entirely imaginary. But it is well known that such a great hunting was held in the Forest of Braemar, under the auspices of the Earl of Mar, as prepatory to the Rebellion of 1715; and most of the Highland Chieftains who afterwards engaged in this civil commotion were present on this occasion. (192n)

Located spatially on the outer margins of the narrative, such notes would provide the historical information on the basis of which the internal fiction should be read, presenting the reader with all "the various legends, family traditions, or obscure historical facts, which have formed the ground-work" (518). It is as if, on rereading the first published version of *Waverley*, Scott determined that the novel alone did not adequately reflect his conception of historical fiction, that it required a historical supplement to ensure its proper filial behavior.

This historical voice is contested, however, by one rejecting claims that the novel's value depends ultimately on its conformity to documented fact. Operating within the confines of the story as such, this "fictional" narrator stresses instead the rather arbitrary nature of its own functioning:

> Shall this be a long or a short chapter?—This is a question in which you, gentle reader, have no vote, however much you may be interested in the consequences; just as you may (like myself) probably have nothing to do with the imposing a new tax, excepting the trifling circumstance of being obliged to pay it. More happy surely in the present case,

since, though it lies within my arbitrary power to extend my materials as I think proper, I cannot call you into Exchequer if you do not think it proper to read my narrative. (*Waverley* 186)

This is the kind of passage that George Levine has described as insufficiently "serious,"[47] one that suggests that the narrative is less responding to historical exigencies than taxing its readers with another kind of necessity. Merely one of *Waverley*'s many self-referential asides—the metaphor of the novel as "post-chaise" that Scott borrows from Henry Fielding (63) would belong to this category as well—such passages do not refer extratextually to historical fact but mime only the process of their fictional construction. Deriving from a history that is thus already "literary," this narrative mode fails to heed its obligation to return to historical origins, to a fatherly source that precedes and directs its subsequent elaboration:

But before entering upon a subject of proverbial delay, I must remind my reader of the progress of a stone rolled down hill by an idle truant boy (a pastime at which I was myself expert in my more juvenile years): it moves at first slowly, avoiding by inflection every obstacle of the least importance; but when it has attained its full impulse, and draws near the conclusion of its career, it smokes and thunders down, taking a rood at every spring, clearing hedge and ditch like a Yorkshire huntsman, and becoming most furiously rapid in its course when it is nearest to being consigned to rest forever. Even such is the course of a narrative like that which you are perusing. (480)

That this is a voice that has not grown up is one of the inferences to be drawn from its self-reflexive rhythms: still writing fiction after all these years, imitating only the conditions of its narrative production, it identifies itself not with the good son but the truant, not with the cadences of historical becoming but with fiction's "proverbial delay."

Where the Baron's drinking cup traces in its loss and recovery the novel's historical self-understanding, *Waverley*'s many portrait scenes offer instead only instances of fictional truancy.[48] Early in the novel, for example, Waverley beholds a painting of Sir Hildebrand, a warlike male ancestor whose "features were almost entirely hidden by the knight's profusion of curled hair, and the Bucephalus which he bestrode concealed by the voluminous robes of the Bath with which he was decorated" (*Waverley* 64). And later on, when Waverley is brought to meet Charles Edward, he enters a gallery "hung with pictures, affirmed to be the portraits of kings, who, if they ever flourished at all, lived several hundred years before the invention of painting in oil colours" (292). Not only do these paintings cast doubt on their fidelity to their fathers—not only do they suggest, indeed, that there may never have been originals at all—they also parody Hegel's conception of portraiture as a historically progressive art form, a "concrete universal" that renders synthetically the spiritual through the particular:

> The portrait-painter . . . *must* flatter, in the sense that all the externals in shape and expression, in form, colour, features, the purely natural side of imperfect existence, little hairs, pores, little scars, warts, all these he must let go, and grasp and reproduce the subject in his universal character and enduring personality. It is one thing for the artist simply to imitate the face of the sitter, its surface and external form, confronting him in repose, and quite another to be able to portray the true features which express the inmost soul of the subject. For it is throughout necessary for the Ideal that the outer form should explicitly correspond with the soul.[49]

Scott's portraits, however, would seem to have rewritten Hegel as follows: it is one thing for the artist simply to imitate the face of the father, and quite another to deface him entirely. For rather than harmonizing the inner with the outer, the personal with the universal, the paintings that Waverley views consist of nothing but externalized particulars, nothing that could possibly lend themselves to a dialectical Ideal.[50] By calling into question the primacy traditionally accorded to the object represented over its derivative representation, Scott's portraits challenge the genealogical priority of the father to his son, the assumption that an origin should remain different in kind from what, in principle, descends from it.

It is thus with much suspicion that we greet the last of the portraits that the novel describes, a gift from Waverley to his father-in-law, which will hang in the restored Tully-Veolan:

> It was a large and spirited painting, representing Fergus Mac-Ivor and Waverley in their Highland dress; the scene a wild, rocky, mountainous

pass, down which the clan were descending in the background. It was taken from a spirited sketch, drawn when they were in Edinburgh by a young man of high genius, and had been painted on a full-length scale by an eminent London artist. Raeburn himself (whose Highland chiefs do all but walk out of the canvas) could not have done more justice to the subject; and the ardent, fiery, and impetuous character of the unfortunate Chief of Glennaquoich was finely contrasted with the contemplative, fanciful, and enthusiastic expression of his happier friend. Beside this painting hung the arms which Waverley had borne in the unfortunate civil war. The whole piece was beheld with admiration, and with deeper feelings. (489)

Though he has just been executed for his role in the rebellion, Fergus reappears here framed with his erstwhile companion; seemingly poised to "walk out of the canvas," his image lives on in the minds of the beholders through the "deeper feelings" the scene invokes. While Levine decries this resolution as an aestheticization of the historical ("The fact is there, but the practical force of the fact is transformed in art. Action becomes image"[51]), the problem is that the action does not *become* an image but was one from the start. For rather than memorializing an event originally set in the Highlands, the portrait was first sketched in Edinburgh and then drawn to life scale by yet another (and tellingly English) hand. At least twice removed from a never present origin, the painting thus raises for one final time the question of fidelity that *Waverley* never simply puts to rest.

No wonder that, faced with this question, *Waverley*'s readers have often sought to reaffirm "a complementary relationship between the real world and the world of the imagination."[52] In practice, however, complementarity almost invariably gives way to hierarchy, for just as Lukács conceives fiction as the negation of the truth from which it both derives and returns, so have the critics tended to assign final authority to history, to the Scott presumed to speak from the margins in his own "authentic" voice. Yet this distinction between external prefaces and internal story begins to break down as *Waverley* blurs the lines between the "fiction" as such and the "history" that surrounds it. Since the appendices to the general preface actually include fragments of Scott's "earliest attempts" at writing fiction (534–66), we already can identify one such transgression of generic limits. For by

including explicitly fictional materials in an account of historical origins, the prefaces no longer simply stand opposed to fiction but incorporate the latter, translating what should have remained internal
to the novel into its putatively nonfictional exterior. But *Waverley*'s
"outside" breaches the borders of its "inside" as well, as the narrative includes passages that are less clearly fictional in mode than
overtly historical and theoretical: the novel's first chapter summa-
rizes Scott's principles for the writing of historical fiction (33–36),
while the final chapter describes the historical changes undergone by
Scotland "within the last half a century" (491–94). If such were not
enough "to confuse the march of a whole history,"[53] *Waverley*'s last
chapter—titled "A Postscript Which Should Have Been a Preface"—
introduces yet another "violation of form" (492):

> This should have been a prefatory chapter, but for two reasons:—First,
> that most novel readers, as my own conscience reminds me, are apt to
> be guilty of the sin of omission respecting the same matter of prefaces;—
> Secondly, that it is a general custom of that class of students, to begin
> with the last chapter of a work; so that, after all, these remarks, being
> introduced last in order, have the best chance to be read in their proper
> place. (492)

The very possibility of a "proper place"—of an unwavering distinction between a before and an after, an inside and an outside—is ex-
posed in this passage as a fiction, indeed as the "bad" kind of fiction that, far from performing its filial obligations, "disorganizes all
the oppositions to which the teleology of the book ought violently to
have subordinated it."[54] Rather than accomplishing what it should
have done, vouching for the truth of the novel from an anterior position of knowledge, Scott's postscript feigns any final resolution by
underlining the impropriety of its placement. We might well be in-
clined to think that Scott *had* read and was commenting on the preface to Hegel's *Phenomenology*, setting out playfully to unsettle its self-
confidence. For if Scott's readers tend to skip right to the fiction,[55] they
are not the only ones guilty of this "sin of omission"—it was Hegel, of
course, who contended that prefatory matter should be both super-
fluous and extrinsic, completely different in kind (particular, anecdotal, idiomatic) from the philosophical text that it brackets. Scott
confounds this argument by emphasizing the belated location and

timing of his chapter, describing it not only as necessary and intrinsic but also as incapable of properly laying out in advance the rules by which the fiction needed to be read. If, in other words, one first must read the novel to determine how one is to read it, then the "true" preface to the historical novel is itself the historical novel, the child the father to the man. Conforming less to a logic of dialectical development than to the Freudian notion of deferred action—*Nachtrag*, as Derrida recalls, "has a precise meaning in the world of letters: appendix, codicil, postscript"—Scott's postface functions neither simply as an origin nor as an end but remains undecidably both, perforating the teleological pattern on which dialectical progress depends:

> While pretending to turn around and look backward, one is also in fact starting over again, adding an extra text, complicating the scene, opening up within the labyrinth a supplementary digression, which is also a false mirror that pushes the labyrinth's infinity back forever in mimed—that is, endless—speculation. It is the textual *restance* of an operation, which can neither be opposed nor reduced to the so-called "principal" body of a book, to the supposed referent of the postface, nor even to its own semantic tenor.[56]

Given the proliferation of these structural anomalies, we no longer can say exactly where the story begins and where it ends, for the novel's historical exterior is now both inside and out, its fictional interior both outside and in. Indeed, though *Waverley*'s notes and prefaces seem to offer themselves as a privileged site for the disclosure of the novel's historical truth—though they would play the traditional role "of a father assisting and admiring his son, losing his breath in sustaining, retaining, idealizing, reinternalizing, and mastering his seed"[57]—their imputed authority remains compromised by an offspring already turned prodigal, by a fiction that does not return to the father but divides all such origins from the start.

"The Author of *Waverley*"

If *Waverley* thus can be said to contest the genealogical authority it also endorses, if the novel "progressively" seems to undermine its commitment to historical progress, one thing at least has seemed certain to Scott's readers: that he *authorized* such an intractably divided text, that while its internal consistency may be doubted, the integrity of its own origin is not. For even as *Waverley* fails to cohere dialectically, the possibility remains for grasping such failure in dialectical terms; programmed in advance by Lukács's understanding of Scott's ambivalence, such an approach still allows us to take *Waverley* as Scott's wayward son, his text as an authoritative if ironic expression of his own divided loyalties. The problem with this solution, however, is that it simply displaces onto "Scott" as historical subject the valued homogeneity that the novel does not sustain, thereby reducing the text's internal conflicts by grounding them in what is presumed to be a self-identical source. In his essay "What Is an Author?" Michel Foucault analyzed the presuppositions underlying this traditional critical procedure:

> Modern literary criticism, even when—as is now customary—it is not concerned with questions of authentication, still defines the author in the same way: the author provides the basis for explaining not only the presence of certain events in a work, but also their transformations, distortions, and diverse modifications (through his biography, the determination of his individual perspective, the analysis of his social position, and the revelation of his basic design). The author also serves to neutralize the contradictions that may emerge in a series of texts: there must be—at a certain level of thought or desire, of his consciousness or unconscious—a point where the contradictions are resolved, where incompatible elements are at last tied together or organized around a fundamental or originating contradiction. . . . And if a text should be discovered in a state of anonymity—whether as a consequence of an accident or the author's explicit wish—the game becomes one of rediscovering the author.[58]

I cite Foucault's work here at length not only because it raises crucial issues that Lukács omitted but also because it poses, and with uncanny precision, the question Scott had to confront throughout the strangely protracted period of his anonymity: was he, indeed, "the Author of *Waverley*"?[59] The answer to this question carries more weight than might be expected, since not only *The Historical Novel* but also the history of analytic philosophy depend equally on its successful resolution, Bertrand Russell having based his theory of definite descriptions on an analysis of the proposition "Scott was the author of *Waverley*."[60] Yet Scott—the Great Unknown—was never wholly certain that he was:

> [In] sober reality, writing good verse seems to depend upon something separate from the volition of the author. I sometimes think my fingers set up for themselves, independent of my head.[61]

> I have repeatedly laid down my future work to scale, divided it into volumes and chapters, and endeavoured to construct a story which I meant should evolve itself gradually and strikingly, maintain suspense, and stimulate curiosity; and which, finally, should terminate in a striking catastrophe. But I think there is a demon who seats himself on the feather of my pen when I begin to write, and leads it astray from the purpose.[62]

Giving the unconscious its due in these passages, Scott hesitates to identify his fictions simply as his own; he may have *written* the novels that were formerly anonymous—their manuscripts (most of them, anyway) betray the sign of his own "hand" (*Waverley* 532)—but whether he can claim to be their *author* is another question entirely. After itemizing in *Waverley*'s general preface the many factors that may have contributed to the prolongation of his anonymity, he reaches a similar conclusion:

> If I am asked further reasons for the conduct I have long observed, I can only resort to the explanation suggested by a critic as friendly as he is intelligent; namely, that the mental organization of the Novelist must be characterised, to speak craniologically, by an extra-ordinary development of the passion for delitescency. I the rather suspect some natural disposition of this kind; for, from the instant I perceived the extreme curiosity manifested on this subject, I felt a secret satisfaction in baffling it, for which, when its importance is considered, I do not know well how to account. (*Waverley* 528)

"I do not know well how to account"—as if writing and a knowledge of origins were mutually interfering; as if some anxiety still remained as to whether Scott were, in fact, the father of the novels that now would bear his name: "The question was not so much whether I should be generally acknowledged to be the author, as whether even my own avowal of the works, if such be made, would be sufficient to put me in undisputed possession of that character" (529). Even his final statement on this question is hedged with these same doubts: "The volumes, therefore, to which the present pages form a preface, are entirely the composition of the Author by whom they are now acknowledged, with the exception, always, of avowed quotations, and such unpremeditated and involuntary plagiarisms as can scarce be guarded against by anyone who has read and written a great deal" (532).[63]

To acknowledge one's works as one's own, then, is to admit the possibility that they always may not be. This potential remains haunting for Scott, as *Waverley*'s first chapter can make a place for itself only by invoking the shades of its literary ancestors, only as its origin already is marked by generational conflict: "'A Tale of Other Days,' 'A Romance from the German,' 'A Sentimental Tale,' 'A Tale of the Times'—all of these formulas stand ready to kidnap his own *Waverley*."[64] Scott rejects such narrative possibilities in order to father *himself*, anticipating that future day when he will call his fictions home, reassert his "parental control" (*Waverley* 517), and reestablish his genuine "paternity" (532). When he finally acknowledges his authorship, however, something curious occurs, for Scott speaks ultimately not in the voice of a satisfied father but as "a spoiled child" who "has sometimes abused or trifled with the indulgence of the public" (533). If the questions of authority at stake in the prefaces thus begin to resemble those that the fiction explores—if, indeed, Scott will confess that his own early education mirrors that of his wavering hero (521)—we may begin to wonder what happened to the father who seemed clearly to know his own difference from his son. Scott wondered, too, acting at times as though he were on trial for his murder:

> I do not recollect any of these novels in which I have transgressed so widely as in the first of the series. (525)

> And yet I ought to stand exculpated from the charge of ungracious or unbecoming indifference to public applause. (527)

> I may perhaps be thought guilty of affectation should I allege as one reason of my silence, a secret dislike to enter on personal discussions concerning my own literary labours. (528)

> I therefore considered myself entitled, like an accused person put on
> trial, to refuse giving my own evidence to my own conviction, and flatly
> to deny all that could not be proved against me. (529)

Scott's language is of interest here not simply because it reflects the
preoccupations "of a lawyer of thirty years' standing" (529) but also
for the way it can help illuminate a possibility that the novel itself
periodically entertains: "Edward felt as if he were about to see a parricide committed in his presence" (334); "'Good God!' exclaimed
Waverley, 'am I then a parricide?'" (417). Is *Waverley* imagining
. . . the death of the author? Few axioms of contemporary theory
have been as thoroughly misunderstood as this one; beginning with
Barthes's famous essay on the subject, the death in question has too
often been construed as simply a predicate of modernist literature,
an event that many date to the end of the nineteenth century.[65] But if
the author's demise is not a singular occurrence but a properly structural relation—a non-self-presence intrinsic to the practice of writing more generally—then part of *Waverley*'s topical interest derives
from its capacity to stage this relation at the moment that the author function was still undergoing its modern consolidation: "Texts,
books, and discourses really began to have authors . . . to the extent
that authors became subject to punishment, that is, to the extent that
discourses could be transgressive."[66]

No one, of course, knew better than Lukács the extent to which
authors could become subject to punishment. In his 1962 preface to
The Theory of the Novel (1920), Lukács distanced himself from the
"romantic" anticapitalism of this early pre-Marxist work by refusing, explicitly, all claims to have been its author. The mature Lukács
did not write this book, his rhetoric consistently maintained; it was
written instead by an entirely different person long since dead and
buried, "the author of *The Theory of the Novel*"—an apotropaic formulation that recurs throughout the preface:

> But the author of *The Theory of the Novel* sticks so obstinately to the
> schema of *L'Education sentimentale* that all he can find here is "a nurs-
> ery atmosphere where all passion has been spent," "more melancholy
> than the ending of the most problematic of novels of disillusionment."
> Any number of such examples could be supplied. Suffice it to point out

that novelists such as Defoe, Fielding and Stendhal found no place in this schematic pattern, that the arbitrary "synthetic" method of the author of *The Theory of the Novel* leads him to a completely upside-down view of Balzac and Flaubert or of Tolstoy and Dostoevsky, etc., etc. . . .

The author of *The Theory of the Novel* did not go so far as that. He was looking for a general dialectic of literary *genres* that was based upon the essential nature of aesthetic categories and literary forms, and aspiring to a more intimate connection between category and history than he found in Hegel himself; he strove towards intellectual comprehension of permanence within change and of inner change within the enduring validity of the essence. But his method remains extremely abstract in many respects, including certain matters of great importance; it is cut off from concrete socio-historical realities.[67]

Looked at in retrospect, these faults, belonging to "the author of *The Theory of the Novel*," would not yet have been properly Lukács's, a syntactic and pronominal distinction that the latter adopted to clarify the "somewhat grotesque situation" of the 1930s "in which Ernst Bloch invoked *The Theory of the Novel* in his polemic against the Marxist, Georg Lukács" (clearly, Bloch had mistaken the identity of his addressee).[68] Indeed, though Lukács contends that *The Theory of the Novel* should now be justly criticized for its "highly naïve and totally unfounded utopianism," it is the author of *that* book rather than the mature Lukács "himself" who is responsible for such youthful errors—a "he" who will not have fully grown into the "I" of the preface until "a decade and a half later" when, "on Marxist ground," Lukács "succeeded in finding a way towards . . . a genuine historico-systematic method."[69]

That this ground may always prove less than firm, however, is a possibility with which Marx was surely familiar, his own practice as a writer conditioned by the kinds of self-division that *Waverley* inscribes without ultimately resolving. As suggested by his fascination with the Waverley novels, Marx would share with Scott aspects of a common predicament: each sought to frame fiction with history, only to discover that the origin had been framed by what it would frame, that fiction is less the corruption of history than its limiting, internal condition. Each would become the "amanuensis of truth and history," only to produce a kind of writing no longer entirely "justified" by the dialectical norms of "reason and philosophy" (*Waverley* 415) that *Waverley* both invokes and contests. The issue that both jointly faced, then, is not (a phrase often heard today) that history is merely a species of fiction, but that an origin cannot be thought outside of or prior to its constitutive heterogeneity, that a father is a father only to the extent that he is also not purely himself.[70] If, from Scott to Marx to Lukács through the present chapter and beyond, *Waverley* will have secured for itself a privileged place in the history of Marxist criticism, its very centrality keeps the question alive of what it means for that criticism to inherit that history—to inherit inheritance as its distinctive and recurring dilemma.

Not just anyone can qualify to be an heir, however, as Christine Delphy's work on the gendered economics of patrimony reminds us: "In my research I discovered what a huge quantity of goods change hands without passing through the market. These goods change hands through the family—as gifts or inheritance."[71] Marx's legacy comes to us through such exchanges, as indeed it came to him: "I have fallen out with my family," Marx wrote to Arnold Ruge in 1843, "and as long as my mother lives I have no right to my inheritance."[72] Proving himself worthy of his patrimony, Lukács wrote the following in a sketch of his early life:

> All this: very poor relationship with my mother. Clever and—what used to be called cultured in our circle of acquaintances (later observation), without any interest in the way things are in reality, what needs are genuine. That is to say, entirely conventional, and since she was able to live according to the rules of polite behavior very competently, even with flair, she was highly respected. My father too (as a self-made man) revered her greatly; I felt a measure of respect for him as a child (his work and his intelligence), but was indignant about his reverence for my mother, and sometimes despised him for it (his blindness). We only found ourselves on better terms when, perhaps under pressure from me on occasion, he began to view my mother more critically.[73]

Though this particular foreclosure of the maternal cannot begin to account for all that divides gender- from class-based analyses, it might help explain why such differences will never be resolved satisfactorily through a *synthesis*: "Mediation: the return (close) by self that overcomes the division and the loss. The relief of the two in(to) the three, unity's self-return. The father divides himself, goes out of himself into his son, and finds himself again, recounts himself in his revenue."[74]

Or as the second epigraph to this chapter has it: "Dead Dad Reborn as Own Son—Widow Tells How They Planned It Together." Which is to say that Scott's fiction determines Lukács's relation to Marx in a peculiar if exemplary way: loyal and disloyal to both his father and himself, Lukács defines for his own readers and heirs the possibilities—and the attendant limits—of filial love.

Translating Revolution

Freud, Marx, and the *Mameloshn*

They want to call "das Es" "the Id." I said I thought everyone
would say the "Yidd." So [Ernest] Jones said there was no such
word in English: "There's 'Yiddish,' you know. And in German
'Jude.' But there is no such word as 'Yidd.'" — "Pardon me, doctor. Yidd is a current slang word for a Jew." — "Ah! A slang expression. It cannot be in very widespread use then." — Simply
because that l[ittle] b[east] hasn't ever heard of it.
— JAMES STRACHEY TO ALIX STRACHEY, 9 October 1924

It is not my language that is maternal,
it is my mother who is a language.

[Ce n'est pas ma langue qui est maternelle,
c'est la mère qui est une langue.]
— GILLES DELEUZE, "Louis Wolfson; or, The Procedure"

The Mother of Language

If busy mothers, at times, have wished themselves cloned, then why
could they be said to resist translation?

Derrida may have asked himself this unlikely question in gloss-
ing a famous passage from Heidegger's "Letter on Humanism" (1947),
where Heidegger tried to clarify what he meant when declaring in
previous writings that "thinking builds upon the house of Being [*Das
Denken baut am Haus des Seins*]." The clarification concerned the rhetorical status of the latter phrase, which Heidegger insisted was no
mere figure of speech. *Dwelling* and its cognate terms, he emphasized,
are indispensable for the thinking of Being, and we should not take
them simply to be metaphors:

> The reference in *Being and Time* to "being-in" as "dwelling" is not some
> etymological play. The same reference in the 1936 essay on Hölderlin's

word, "Full of merit, yet poetically, man dwells upon this earth," is not the adornment of a thinking that rescues itself from science by means of poetry. The talk about the house of being is not the transfer of the image "house" onto Being [*ist keine Übertragung des Bildes vom »Haus« auf das Sein*]. But one day we will, by thinking the essence of Being in a way appropriate to its matter [*sondern am dem sachgemäß gedachten Wesen des Seins*], more readily be able to think what "house" and "dwelling" are [*was »Haus« und »wohnen« sind*].[1]

Derrida responded to this passage in his essay "The *Retrait* of Metaphor" as part of a larger argument about the nature of figural language in philosophical discourse. Though he might have mounted a challenge to Heidegger's derogation of rhetorical "adornment," Derrida instead agreed with him that the phrase "house of Being" resists conforming to our traditional sense of metaphor, which he then described in the following terms:

> This current and cursive sense—I understand it also in the sense of direction—transports a familiar predicate (and here nothing is more familiar, familial, known, domestic, and economic, or so it is thought than the house) toward a less familiar, more remote, *unheimlich* subject, which it would be a question of better appropriating for oneself, knowing, understanding, and which one thus designates by the indirect detour of what is nearest: the house.[2]

Derrida quickly noted, however, that nothing about the *Haus des Seins* example agrees with this model of metaphoric transference, for rather than illuminating the still unfamiliar "Being" by way of an already familiar "house," the phrase's vehicle and tenor seem to trade places and identities in mid-course. The house, chiasmically, is now what *Being* would illuminate—or would succeed in doing "one day," when we will have learned better how to think "the essence of being appropriate to its matter." Derrida described this "tropical inversion in the relations between predicate and subject" as a "bizarre *Übertragung*," a translation gone strangely awry: "Being has not become the essence of this supposedly known, familiar, nearby being, which is what one believed the house to be in the common metaphor. And if the house has become a bit *unheimlich*, this is not because it has been replaced by 'Being' in the role of what is nearest" (69). Whatever else it may be, then, *Haus des Seins* is something other than a metaphor.

Just prior to this analysis of the "house of Being" passage, Derrida discussed a different text by Heidegger—his lecture "Sprache und Heimat" (1960) on the dialect poet Johann Peter Hebbel—in which Heidegger once again explored the limits of translation in its "traditional and ideal sense, that is, the sense of the transport of an intact signified into the vehicle of another language" (62–63). "Sprache und Heimat" also introduced a "character" whose appearance in this context we might have been expecting all along.[3] For whose task will it be to superintend the domestic economy of Being? Who does the upkeep in this *oikos*?

> Heidegger says that *das Sprachwesen*, the essence or being of language, is rooted in the "dialect" (another word for *Mundart*), in the idiom, and if the idiom is the mother's language, then also rooted there is "das Heimische des Zuhaus, die Heimat." And he adds, "Die Mundart ist nicht nur die Sprache der Mutter, sondern zugleich und zuvor die Mutter der Sprache," the idiom is not only the language of the mother, but is at the same time and above all the mother of language. According to a movement whose law we will analyze, this reversal would lead us to think that not only the *idion* of the *idiom*, the proper of the dialect, is the mother of language, but that, far from knowing before this what a mother is, such a reversal alone allows us perhaps to approach the essence of maternity. A mother tongue would not be a metaphor for determining the sense of language, but the essential turn that must be taken to understand what mother means. (61–62)[4]

Heidegger prized the *Mundart* because, unlike *Sprache*, it resists translation: dialect would be the local, sensual, accented voice of the *Heimat* conceived as a maternal bulwark against a universalized, deracinated Language of exchange reduced to its sheer instrumental functioning ("die Sprache gibt es nicht").[5] Dialect is what the mother speaks to (and teaches) her child; archaic if not wholly originary, it not only precedes but generates Language as its offspring. It may thus seem by analogy that the first of these mothers, "die Sprache der Mutter," is the literal one from which "die Mutter der Sprache" would be the derived figure. But the very distinction between literal and figural is what the chiasmus takes away: which of these mothers is now the vehicle and which the tenor? Which, indeed, precedes the other? How can one tell the mother from . . . the mother? If the identity of the mother suspends itself between (or among) these questions, then we truly cannot presume to have known what maternity "is"—as if this were a question that language could ever elucidate: "A mother tongue would not be a metaphor for determining the sense of language, but the essential turn that must be taken to understand what mother means."

I take Derrida's characterization of these two "bizarre *Übertragungen*" as an inducement to ask more generally about the mother's relation to translation—beyond, that is, the resistant role "she" plays in Heidegger's *Heimat*. At a minimum, we might test the assumption that translation and maternity have *something* to do with each other—something the remainder of this chapter will explore in shifting its attention to Freud and Marx on the occasion of the recent publication of new English translations of their work. What might these historic translations tell us about mothers? What might mothers tell us about translation? How might these versions of Freud and Marx make the familial newly *unheimlich*? What kinds of politics might they constrain and/or make possible?

The Translator's Hand(s)

If it is rare enough for stories about translation to make the headlines, then it was news indeed in 2003 when the *New York Times Sunday Magazine* profiled Adam Phillips, the prolific author, psychoanalyst, and general editor of the New Penguin Freud series that had just made its North American debut.[6] The first new English translations of Freud to have appeared in some forty years, the Penguin series seeks to offer, as Phillips told the *New York Times*, a "literary Freud" where James Strachey's magisterial *Standard Edition*—also known as the King James Version—fostered the impression that psychoanalysis is instead a science. Complaints about the translation of the *Standard Edition* began mounting even before its ink had dried. As Bruno Bettelheim and others argued, Strachey's rendering of Freud's colloquial *das Ich*, *das Es*, and *das Überich* as "ego," "id," and "super-ego" was just one instance of a systematic (if inherently defensive) effort to make Freud's language sound rigorous to Anglophone ears, which, presumably, would find a Latinate *parapraxis* easier to credit as scientific than the vernacular *slip of the tongue*.[7] Freud's familiar *besetzen* found itself transformed somehow via Greek into the neologism *to cathect*, an infinitive that few English speakers have since managed to invest with libido. A more serious charge was that, in translating both *Instinkt* and *Trieb* as "instinct," Strachey obscured a distinction on which the specificity of psychoanalysis depends: where animals may have mating instincts, human sexuality—much more plastic than any imperative to reproduce the species—is predicated rather on "drives," a noun form that the *Standard Edition* only rarely employed.[8] Strachey failed to perceive, moreover, that certain of Freud's recurrent lexical choices were in fact psychoanalytic concepts: for example, *Nachträglichkeit*—rendered variously by Strachey as "deferred action," "aftereffect," "deferred effect," and (giving up entirely) "later"—was used consistently by Freud during the length of his career to name a uniquely psychoanalytic conception of temporality and causality that has itself become legible only "after the fact" of the *Standard Edition*.[9]

In light of these and other deficiencies, and taking advantage of the expiration of the Strachey copyrights, the New Penguin translations seek to dispense with the obscurantism of scientific-sounding jargon, constructing in its place a Freud who now can be read, Phillips suggests, "as you would any great novelist."[10] To that end, the sixteen volumes that comprise the new series have appeared without any prefatory statement of common editorial policy and also without a standardized vocabulary—a virtue that may have been born of necessity, some have inferred, given that Phillips is reported not to know German.[11] Where Strachey thought it preferable "if a single hand were responsible for the whole text" of Freud, Phillips has promoted instead a multihanded diversity in an effort to desacralize Freud's language: his original plan called for as many translators as texts in the series, with each translator responsible for just one book. Chosen not from the ranks of the psychoanalytic establishment but mainly from British faculty in German studies "who had previously translated literary texts, and need not have previously read Freud," the translators were set to work independently from one another and instructed by Phillips simply to "follow their noses."[12] Envisioning in this way "a more various Freud, less consistent in idiom and terminology than even Freud himself was able to be," Phillips hoped that the new translations would show us Freud "as the writer he wanted to be, and is"—a writer who, differing from himself from volume to volume, would take his rightful place at last among the (Penguin) modern classics.[13]

Now complete, the New Penguin Freud series is as fascinating in its resemblances to the text of the *Standard Edition* as in its differences. Though some changes immediately stand out—will the flattening title "Drives and Their Fates" ever replace the familiar cadences of "Instincts and Their Vicissitudes"?—most readers will agree with Michael Woods that "the main impression left by the comparison, surely, is the lack of important differences."[14] This is truly a remarkable outcome given that the translators worked in isolation. All of them seem to have decided on their own to translate *Trieb* as "drive," with one preface explaining that "the word 'drive' in this [psychoanalytic] sense has developed a life of its own, independent of Strachey, and can now safely be considered an English word."[15] The translators split roughly down the middle on whether to render *Besetzung* as "investment" or "charge," though one of them was unable to decide either on a single equivalent or, indeed, on whether readers would ever recognize the term purged of its attachment to Strachey's Latin ("an idea is cathected—that is, charged, invested and occupied").[16] Not surprisingly, the trio ego-id-superego presented the most vexing problems. The translator of the new *Studies in Hysteria* rendered *das Ich* as "Self" rather than as "ego" on recalling what Strachey did not—that Freud in 1893 had not yet developed his tripartite schema. Other volumes had no choice but to translate *ego* and *id* as "I" and "it" because these were the very texts in which Freud explained his preference for "plain pronouns rather than adopt some more fancy Greek or Latin terms." One translator despaired of a solution and simply left the three terms in German. Most, however, retained *ego*, *id*, and *superego* for the simple reason that "these Latin terms have now irretrievably passed into standard modern English—not least by dint of Freud's own enormous impact on twentieth-century consciousness."[17] This impact had to have been felt by *all* the series' translators, even those who, somehow, previously avoided reading Freud in English, which may help explain why, with a major exception to be discussed below, there is finally little to distinguish the *Standard Edition* from the New Penguin Freud, the One from the Many, except for the latter's more useful thematic grouping of texts and more attractive book design.[18]

If this is granted, then there is little reason to imagine a "literary," many-handed translation project as inherently more diverse than a single scientific one.[19] Indeed, if variety were its own reward, Phillips might have looked no further for a model than the English-language *Collected Works* of Marx and Engels, newly completed in 2005 with the publication of its fiftieth volume.[20] Conceived in the late 1960s at the Institute for Marxism-Leninism in Moscow with initial funding from the Central Committee of the Communist Party of the Soviet Union, the *Collected Works* was a joint venture supported by three different publishing entities: Lawrence and Wishart of London, International Publishers of New York, and Progress Publishers of Moscow. No single editor oversaw the whole project. As befits a collective and decentralized endeavor, each publishing enclave operated with its own editorial committee, whose decisions were then subject to the other two committees' approval.[21] Given the unwieldiness of these procedures, and all the political upheavals during the past generation that made funding anything but secure, it is nothing short of a miracle that this enterprise met its goal of bringing into existence what had never before been attempted: a critical edition in English of all the major works of Marx and Engels.[22] Relatively little of Marx's work was published in his lifetime, and still less of it had been translated into English. The *Collected Works* absorbs or supersedes some of the earliest canonical translations by, among others, Eleanor Marx-Aveling and Samuel Moore; it incorporates the work of such iconic figures as C. P. Dutt, Martin Milligan, and Dirk J. Struik, known in the 1930s and after for their English editions of individual texts; it employs Russian translators almost exclusively in the pedestrian final volumes. Though the series also contains much anonymous translation, this must have been partly a programmatic decision: what, after all, is a communist translator if not someone who distrusts single-handed individuality as a matter of political principle? While for Phillips a diversity of translations functions as the antidote to science, the *Collected Works* suggests that diversity is, instead, science's very medium.

Of course, the scientific status of Marx's writing is no more settled than Freud's. As I have argued elsewhere, Marx appeals often *to* literature as a way of distinguishing his work *from* literature. To read him, for instance, in the act of disavowing his literary juvenilia is to recognize what Jacques Rancière described in another context as "the set of literary procedures by which a discourse escapes literature, gives itself the status of science, and signifies this status."[23] I will say more below about the relation between literature and science, and between the one and the many, as they bear on each other and on the topic of translation. In the next sections, however, I use the occasion of the new Freud and Marx translations as an opportunity to explore in some detail the status of translation *in* Freud and Marx. Significantly, if again not unexpectedly, the mother will play crucial roles in both instances—as though Freud and Marx could not conceive translation without some form of maternal involvement.

Philosophies of Translation

Marxism and psychoanalysis are each bound intrinsically to translation; indeed, their very possibility and fates can be said to depend on it. I do not mean this only in the sense that both are international, indeed, global in their reach (if not their grasp); translation into what is now a vast multitude of print languages—North and South, East and West—has itself become evidence in support of their universalizing truth claims.[24] Nor is translation necessary only in the sense that, for Marx as for Freud, English-language editions of their collected works preceded—and in different ways formed the model for—the publication of their comparable German editions, a paradoxical confirmation of the deconstructive axiom that origins are derived.[25] Even more crucially, translation is fundamental to Marxism and psychoanalysis in that both imagine themselves inherently as *philosophies* of translation. As Derrida has argued,

> . . . the philosophical operation, if it has an originality and specificity, defines itself as a project of translation. More precisely, it defines itself

as the fixation of a certain concept and project of translation. . . . What matters is truth and meaning, and since meaning is before and beyond language, it follows that it is translatable. Meaning has the commanding role, and consequently must be able to fix its univocality or, in any case, to master its polyvocality. . . . If this plurivocality can be mastered, then translation, understood as the transport of a semantic content into another signifying form, is possible. There is no philosophy unless translation in this latter sense is possible.[26]

Despite their common insistence that they should be classified as science rather than philosophy, psychoanalysis and Marxism are philosophical in precisely Derrida's terms—as translation practices sharing a commitment to the work of reason (to work as reason, to reason as work); to the hermeneutic deciphering of a prelinguistic truth that may resist positivity but never meaningfulness; to the conveyance of "a sense whose secret is only the hidden secret, the dissimulated meaning, the veiling truth: to be interpreted, analyzed, made explicit, explained."[27] Moving *behind* the veil or *around* or *through* it, Marxism and psychoanalysis commonly translate backward (*zurück-übersetzen* is the repeated verb form) from copy to original, symptom to source, superstructure to base, consciousness to life, the manifest to the latent, literary fiction to scientific truth. By definition, all such translations always succeed—sense in this model never fails to reach its destination—which poses the question of whether *mis*translation can ever pertain to styles of reading in which errors make as much sense as sense.

Take, for instance, the famous case of Freud's text on Leonardo, marred by his reliance on an inaccurate German translation of the species of bird that visited Leonardo in his childhood dream. Does the confusion of the kite's tail feathers for those of a very different looking vulture invalidate Freud's analysis? Or does it validate psychoanalysis even more by making legible the psychoanalytic logic of Freud's own unconscious investments? Thus Alan Bass can read "Freud's mistranslation" as "itself a fetish: Freud has continued to maintain that he sees what was never there—the vulture—for motivated reasons, that is, because it fits in too well" with his theories of infantile sexuality.[28] Or take a tiny sentence from a letter Marx wrote to Engels explaining why, in the political depths of 1853, imagining revolution was out of the question: "Alles bürgerlich," he sighed, rendered in the French edition as the unexceptional though equally damning "Tout est bourgeois." In the English of the *Collected Works*, however, this sentence appears as "It's day-to-day routine."[29] While it is not simply wrong to translate *bürgerlich* as "day-to-day routine"— the German does convey a suggestion of quotidian civil society— voiding Marx's phrase of its class resonance is also not exactly being faithful to the context. If we suspect that Marx's political despair was so intolerably bleak to the translators that they had to render it otherwise, we would be crediting their decision with a motivation that sustains a political truth, indeed the very notion that truth is political. When infidelities thus become recuperable as *illustrations*, by what standard can translations of Freud and Marx ever be found wanting? Strachey's *Standard Edition* may truly be inaccurate, but its very inaccuracy thus becomes, paradoxically, the sign of its fidelity.[30] *Traduttore traditore* would seem to make neither Marxist nor psychoanalytic sense.

Except, that is, whenever Marx and Freud betray these same hermeneutic impulses, which also happens in relation to translation (in other words, all the time). For Nicolas Abraham, what makes psychoanalysis distinctive, indeed peculiar, as a practice is "the radical semantic change" it confers on language: after Freud we speak regularly of pleasure that is never experienced as pleasure, of pleasure that would be felt as a kind of suffering, and of pain that would be pleasure—all the while conserving the word *pleasure*, allowing it to resonate in its semantic difference from itself, as if the single word were translating itself to itself, "so that between the translated text and the translating text nothing apparently will have changed and yet between them will only be relations of homonymy."[31] Abraham calls this capacity for homonymic self-difference "anasemic translation" and hails it as the defining achievement of psychoanalysis—a perverse form of knowing that reproduces in itself the properties of its unconscious object.[32] We might recognize the same perverse capacity in the "radical semantic change" that Marx, too, brought to language. Indeed, just as "sexuality" after Freud "goes lower and also higher than the popular sense of the word"[33]—just as consciousness, forgetting, analysis, and resistance mean both what they mean in ordinary language and what they have come to mean psychoanalytically—so may we describe as anasemic the way Marx has redefined such words as *critique*, *worker*, and *value*, words whose significance now depends, as with Freud, on an intralinguistic difference that is neither strictly paraphrase nor polysemia. Thus *critique* both is and is not the practice that Marx shares with Kant; the *worker* is both an identity and the abolition of that identity; *value*, as something other than an inherent property of things, becomes with Marx something other than itself as well.[34]

Along with *translation*, *science* would be of course another candidate for anasemic redescription, especially sciences like Marxism and psychoanalysis that no longer conform to any hermeneutic concept of translation when they find themselves speaking more than one language at once. In "What Is an Author?" Foucault tried to account for their common anomalousness by assigning them to a nonce category somewhere between science and literature—a strangely dialectical solution from a thinker characteristically averse to dialectical thinking. To make Marx and Freud into "founders of discursivity" not only slights their conception of themselves as scientists; it also leaves the categories of literature and science intact and strictly opposed to each other—and unaffected by the perversities of Marx and Freud. Even so, Foucault is surely right in proposing that the founder's proper name plays a uniquely regulative role in Marxist and psychoanalytic discourse.[35] Derrida is never more implicitly Foucaultian than when he calls psychoanalysis

> an institution that can't get along without Freud's name, a practical and theoretical science which for once must come to terms and explain itself with its author's name. Unlike every other science, it cannot set aside or dispense with its founder's name. Mathematics, physics, etc., might on occasion celebrate the name of a great physicist or great mathematician, but the proper name is not a structural part of the corpus of the science or the scientific institution. Psychoanalysis, on the other hand, has been inherited from Freud and accounts for itself with the structure of this inheritance.[36]

Derrida could have said the very same about Marxism.[37] Just as proper names do not translate as a rule—they should remain outside the language system per se, exhausting themselves wholly in acts of reference—so "normal" science requires the exteriority of its founder's life to its practice. But psychoanalysis and Marxism are in this respect anything but normal: unable to do without patronyms, they translate them into the heart of their systems, incorporating them in ways that violate received canons of scientificity. This common aberration never ceases to produce discomfort among those who wish that these sciences would act more like sciences. Even Freud disliked "Freudianism," and Marx may well have asserted that he was not a Marxist. Some today still prefer "dialectical materialism" rather than admit to the possibility that Marx's insights happen to be related to someone named Marx. But the introjected name can become the occasion for new interpretive possibilities, among them a reimagination of the autobiographical as a relation internal to science, an exteriority inside its inside.

Forgetting the Mother Tongue

Hermeneutic, anasemic, and autobiographic: these, then, are three kinds of translation practiced in the writings of Marx and Freud. If it constitutes an abuse of its literal meaning to call *any* of the three "translation," it may be that the difference between the figural and the literal is especially hard to determine when translation is itself a noted figure for figure, which makes translation a translation of translation: "It is no mere play of words," Paul de Man reminds us, "that 'translate' is translated in German as *übersetzen*, which itself translates the Greek *meta phorein* or metaphor."[38] Inherently catachrestic, anasemic in relation to itself, translation exploits maximally the indissociability of concept and metaphor. It is in any case useless to try disentangling these many strands in Freud: the trope of translation is ubiquitous in his work, most famously in the modeling of the dream-thoughts and dream-content "as two different versions of the same subject-matter in two different languages"; the analyst compares "the original and the translation" in reading the one as the "transcript" of the other.[39] This is hardly an isolated example, however, for Freud describes as translation just about *everything* that might have any psychic content—from "hysterical, phobic, and obsessional symptoms" to "recollections, parapraxes, the choice of the means of suicide, the choice of fetish, the analyst's interpretations, and the transpositions of unconscious material to consciousness."[40] If repression is conspicuously absent from this list, this is only because Freud had already defined it elsewhere as "a failure of translation."[41] Translation is, as Phillips puts it, so apt an analogy for "what goes on in psychoanalysis" that we may wonder if there was anything Freud did not think of comparing to it.[42]

But the same cannot be said for Marx, who hardly ever thinks explicitly through the trope of translation. This may seem at first surprising given that Freud and Marx are equally polyglot (besides German they share Latin, Greek, English, French, Italian, and Spanish—Marx will add Russian late in his life). Both quote their sources exclusively in the original languages, assuming their readers to be as linguistically competent as they.[43] Marx also writes often and with ease in English and French. But Marx always finds something in language to distrust: "We do not set out from what men say, imagine, conceive, nor from men as narrated, thought of, imagined, conceived, in order to arrive at men in the flesh."[44] In "descending" instead "from language to life," the materialist method assumes as a given the ontological secondariness of representations, *Vorstellungen*—which is to say that Marxism is no *talking* cure.[45] The instances in which Marx employs translation as a model are thus few in number (I have counted all of three), and each of these is rather perplexing. I consider here briefly the two more notable examples, the first of them a celebrated passage from *The Eighteenth Brumaire*:

> Men make their own history, but they do not make it just as they please; they do not make it under circumstances chosen by themselves, but under circumstances directly encountered, given and transmitted [*überlieferten*] from the past. The tradition of all the dead generations weighs like a nightmare on the brain of the living. And just when they seem engaged in revolutionising themselves and things, in creating something that has never yet existed, precisely in such periods of revolutionary crisis they anxiously conjure up the spirits of the past to their service and borrow from them names, battle cries and costumes in order to present the new scene of world history in this time-honoured disguise and this

borrowed language. Thus Luther donned the mask of the Apostle Paul, the Revolution of 1789 to 1814 draped itself alternately as the Roman republic and the Roman empire, and the Revolution of 1848 knew nothing better to do than to parody, now 1789, now the revolutionary tradition of 1793 to 1795. In a like manner a beginner who has learnt a new language always translates it back into his mother tongue [*So übersetzt der Anfänger, der eine neue Sprache erlernt hat, sie immer zurück in seine Muttersprache*], but he has assimilated the spirit of the new language [*den Geist der neuen Sprache*] and can express himself freely in it only when he finds his way in it without recalling the old and forgets his native tongue in the use of the new [*sobald er sich ohne Rückerinnerung in ihr bewegt und die ihm angestammte Sprache in ihr vergißt*].[46]

This entire passage is of course a bravura performance, especially striking in the self-confidence with which it makes its way through the densest thickets of comparison. With translation the vehicle and revolution the tenor, the paragraph proceeds to liken the relation between mother tongue and second language to a host of other binary contrasts, among them past and present, the dead and the living, theater and history, parody and authentic action, form and spirit, the old and the new, the familiar and the foreign. This would be the hermeneutic version of translation to the nth degree, with translation making itself obsolete in a revolutionary future that will henceforth do without it. Unlike Heidegger's maternal *Mundart* (which, in giving birth to *Sprache*, will henceforth be recalled in the most pious terms), Marx's *Muttersprache* gives way to a new language that forgets where it came from. But is this an accurate rendering of language learning? *Does* one forget the old language in learning the new? If that were so, language systems would be discretely self-identical, differing only between each other rather than also in themselves, and anasemia would perforce become impossible. Why does revolution depend on the forgetting of the mother tongue—and what in this context does "forgetting" mean? Would "remembering" be its opposite? Who, or what, would be the subject of this forgetting? Does one mourn the loss of what is here forgotten? Can one inherit what one forgets? And if the mother tongue truly can be forgotten, will there have been translation at all? "Totally translatable," notes Derrida, "[a text] disappears as a text, as writing, as a body of language."[47]

Marx revisited these questions five years later in the *Grundrisse* when, with the failure of revolution in France and elsewhere, he prepared himself for the writing of *Capital*:

> (To compare money with blood—the term circulation gave occasion for this—is about as correct as Menenius Agrippa's comparison between the patricians and the stomach.) (To compare money with language is not less erroneous [*ist nicht minder falsch*]. Ideas are not transformed in language [*Die Ideen werden nicht in die Sprache verwandelt*] with their particularity dissolved in it and their social character existing alongside, like prices alongside commodities. Ideas do not exist separately from language. Ideas which first have to be translated out of their mother tongue into a foreign language [*Ideen, die aus ihrer Muttersprache erst in eine fremde Sprache übersetzt werden müssen*] in order to circulate, in order to become exchangeable [*austauschbar*], offer a somewhat better analogy; but the analogy then lies not in language, but in their foreignness [*nicht in der Sprache, sondern in ihrer Fremdeit*].)[48]

This passage, please be warned, has been known to produce migraines, one cause of which is its own resistance to translation: the two published English versions are both so undone by Marx's text that they seem to enact the breakdown in analogy that the passage itself analogizes through the trope of translation. The metaphor that compares money with blood on the basis of resemblance is no more truthful, Marx says, than the well-worn synecdoche falsely totalizing the body politic. Comparing money with language "is not less erroneous" than the claims made by both of these tropes, for while prices are simply extrinsic to commodities, ideas are embodied in a language from which they also stand apart. (Marx will say later in *Capital* that "value is independent of the particular use-value by which it is borne, but it must be embodied in a use-value of some kind."[49]) Would translation, then, offer a better analogy to money? A qualified yes, so long as we recall that it is not language per se but ideas becoming foreign as the condition of their circulation that forms the basis of the comparison with the circulation of money in exchange. Translation is thus exchange, and exchange translation. What could be clearer? Well, Marx might have wondered what makes ideas foreign in this sense, and whether *all* ideas therefore need translation if they are to circulate successfully—in which case the mother tongue would be peculiarly empty of ideas (as in Heidegger's *Mundart*), and perhaps not even or not yet a language. Why is this mother tongue once more politically insufficient, and why again must it be consigned to the past?

In certain ways, Marx's wish to leave the mother tongue behind may call to mind Louis Wolfson's far more elaborate attempts to dispense with it. In a remarkable 250-page treatise that caught the attention of Gilles Deleuze in the late 1960s, Wolfson, a schizophrenic New Yorker, explained in French prose how he "systematically sought not to listen to his mother tongue," specifically his mother's Yiddish-inflected English, the sound of which had become intolerable.[50] He did this by converting his mother's English words as quickly as he could into French, German, Russian, and Hebrew cognates that sounded close enough to their originals while preserving some degree of their sense—a radical experiment in translation, in short: "A kind of foreign language is extracted from the maternal language, on the condition that the sounds or phonemes always remain similar."[51] Referring to himself exclusively in the third person as "the student of schizophrenic language," Wolfson hoped that his method would spare him from the pain of having to hear again his mother's English. In practice, however, he discovered that he needed to keep recollecting the mother tongue precisely to efface its effects: "Forcing himself never to forget to forget his mother tongue, he obliged himself always to remember to remember it."[52] Marx, of course, was in no sense "a schizophrenic student of language," and Wolfson never formulated his need to forget the mother tongue as a revolutionary imperative. And yet, notwithstanding the many differences in situation and scale, the goal for both is an act of translation that would also be an act of forgetting. Would Marx never forget to forget the mother tongue, or would he, like Wolfson, inevitably remember to remember it?

The *Mameloshn*

One of the New Penguin Freud translations may help us with these questions in the example it provides of "a comic unmasking" from Freud's meditation on humor, *Der Witz*. Here, first, is how Strachey presents the passage:

"The doctor, who had been asked to look after the Baroness at her con-
finement, pronounced that the moment had not come, and suggested
to the Baron that in the meantime they should have a game of cards in
the next room. After a while a cry of pain from the Baroness struck the
ears of the two men: 'Ah, mon Dieu, que je souffre!' Her husband sprang
up, but the doctor signed to him to sit down: 'It's nothing. Let's go on
with the game!' A little later there were again sounds from the pregnant woman: 'Mein Gott, mein Gott, what terrible pains!'—'Aren't you
going in, Professor?' asked the Baron.—'No, no. It's not time yet.'—At
last there came from next door an unmistakable cry of 'Aa-ee, aa-ee, aa-
ee!' The doctor threw down his cards and exclaimed: '*Now* it's time.'"

This successful joke demonstrates two things from the example of the
way in which the cries of pain uttered by an aristocratic lady in childbirth changed their character little by little. It shows how pain causes
primitive nature to break through all the layers of education, and how
an important decision can be properly made to depend on an apparently
trivial phenomenon.[53]

Freud's example depends for its comic punch on its implicit model
of translation—the notion that the "same thing" is being said each
time by the woman giving birth even while the different languages
she cycles through unmask her multiple fluencies as imposture. The
joke seems to confirm a long tradition in which translation and childbirth come to figure each other; Derrida, indeed, highlights the word
"*laborious* to announce several words in *tr* and to indicate that the
motif of *labor* [*travail*], the *tr*avail of childbirth, but also the *tr*ansfer-
ential and *tr*ansformational *tr*avail, in all possible codes and not only
that of psychoanalysis, will enter into competition with the apparently more neutral motif of *tr*anslation, as *tr*ansaction and as *tr*ans-
fer."[54] But Freud's joke gives this tradition a particular spin: behold
the woman, it suggests, progressively denuded of genteel artifice as
she is translated into her true nature, which *is* nature—that is to say,
the primitive "Aa-ee, aa-ee, aa-ee!" of a cry too absorbed in the act of
giving birth to care much for consonants. The misogyny is of course
recognizably Freudian, as is the familiar cast of characters—two men
and a woman—that make this, in psychoanalytic terms, an exemplary comic scene.[55]

But in the New Penguin translation this passage reveals something different about the original, something that English-language readers might never have noticed otherwise:

> The doctor who has been requested to attend the Baroness at her confinement declares that the moment has not yet arrived, and suggests to the Baron that meantime they play a game of cards in the next room. After a while the Frau Baronin's cry of pain reaches the ears of the two men: "*Ah mon Dieu, que je souffre.*" The husband leaps up, but the doctor detains him: "It's nothing. Let's carry on playing." A while later they hear her crying out in labour: "*Mein Gott, mein Gott, was für Schmerzen!* [lit.: "My God, my God, how it hurts!"]—"Won't you go in, Professor?" asks the Baron. "No, no, it's still not time."—Finally, from the next room they hear an unmistakable cry of "*Ai, waih, waih*" [equivs: "O weh," "Oy vay"]; then the doctor throws away his cards and says: "It's time."
>
> How pain will allow the original nature to break through all the layers of education, and how an important decision is—rightly—made dependent upon a seemingly unimportant utterance—both are displayed by this good joke in the example of the stage-by-stage transformations in the lamentations of the noble lady in labour.[56]

This new version is certainly less fluid than Strachey's, and it emphasizes much more the fact of its multilingualism by inserting italics and square brackets. But the revelation here is that Strachey fudged Freud's punch line, which turns out to have been Yiddish all along rather than a non- or a prelinguistic cry.[57] While retaining its misogyny, the joke takes aim at the class aspirations of assimilating Ashkenazi Jews: look in the cosmopolite's closet and you will be sure to find a babushka. Strachey was hardly alone in being unable to identify Yiddish. In its own version of "kettle logic," the nineteenth century wondered all at once whether Yiddish was even a language *and* whether it was more than one—a hybridized German written in a Hebrew alphabet with ancient Semitic and modern Slavic elements: "Yiddish was referred to contemptuously as 'jargon,' as a patchwork of various languages. Critics said it was not a language at all, since it has no grammar; it is only corrupt German, it is merely a dialect of German."[58] *Plus d'une langue*, in short. Insofar as it counted as a Germanic language, Yiddish was thought to be an anomalous, anachronistic, and corrupt survival from the Middle High period, in essence a living dinosaur. This diagnosis was in fact shared by German Jews anxious to put behind them what they considered a degraded image of their past. The Jewish version of the Enlightenment known as the *Haskalah* would thus divide western and eastern European Jewry on the basis of language: German Jews now spoke German, the *Ostjuden* Yiddish.[59]

Whether or not Strachey was capable of recognizing Yiddish, we know that Freud surely was, for he puns elaborately on it in his joke on the birth of the mother's tongue.[60] If Yiddish can be *this* mother's tongue it is because it is, preeminently, *the* mother's tongue: the *Mameloshn*, the everyday language of eastern European Jewish women and men, rather than Hebrew, the *Loshn-koydesh* or holy language of prayer and study reserved exclusively for men. This structural dimorphism pertaining both to language and gender was so pervasive an element in Yiddish culture that it remains naturalized even in the work of contemporary linguists like Benjamin Harshav, for whom the *Mameloshn* connotes "the warmth of the Jewish family, as symbolized by mama and her language, embracing and counteracting the father's awesome, learned Holy Tongue."[61] As a consequence of this division, as Naomi Seidman points out, Jewish men who were illiterate in Hebrew were effectively effeminized; she quotes an early homiletic work "written in Yiddish for women and men who are like women in not being able to learn much."[62]

Restored in the New Penguin translation, Freud's joke depends on the reader's ability to grasp that the mother's tongue "is" the mother's tongue; inextricably literal *and* figural without simply being either, the *Mameloshn* is an anaseme (and thus no metaphor, as Heidegger might have said in the unlikely event that he thought about Yiddish). Freud's joke thus comes at the expense of the hermeneutic model of translation that he seemed initially to validate; rather than transporting "the same thing" across different languages, the *Mameloshn* routes linguistic difference in and through itself. Marx may have gotten this same joke, too, for if a mother's tongue had to be forgotten, this may have been because of its familiarity. We have long known that Marx descended from many generations of rabbis on both his father's and mother's sides; we have known that his father's given name was Heschel (or Hirschl), which he changed to Heinrich when he converted to Lutheranism after the Prussian authorities refused to rescind laws blocking Jews from practicing professions. We have known that Heinrich was nonetheless a Prussian patriot, a German-speaking product of the *Haskalah* who believed in assimilation as the solution to the Jewish Question. We have known, too, that Karl was converted to Christianity as a six-year-old (which means that he must already have been circumcised), and that Marx's mother Henriette Pressburg, the daughter of a Dutch rabbi, delayed her own conversion until her father's death. Henriette was largely uneducated, and nearly all of Marx's biographers point with disdain to an unpunctuated letter she wrote to young Karl at university. Marx, of course, would grow up to be the author of *On the Jewish Question*, which looks forward to the disappearance of Jewish particularity figured as the quintessence of capitalism. What we have never fully comprehended, however, is that Henriette's own mother tongue was Yiddish. Though lately settled in Holland, the Pressburgs were a Hungarian family originally from Pressburg, now Bratislava, the capital of Slovakia. As Sander Gilman reports, Henriette "never acquired a native command of German." "Literate in neither Yiddish nor Dutch," she spoke Yiddish in her parents' house and wrote "a Yiddish-tinged German." Young Karl—or Carel, as his mother would have called him in her mother tongue—thus grew up in a family divided as much by language as by gender, or, indeed, by language *as* gender: the distinction between German and Yiddish reflected "the contrast between the integrated world of his father's family and the image of his mother's family as intruders from the East. When one turns to Marx's discussions of his family, it is not surprising that his mother seems to vanish from his perceptions."[63]

Was Henriette, then, "forgotten"? Will we have understood what forgetting means here?

All the biographical sources agree that Marx grew to detest his mother; he had little contact with her after his father's death except concerning the money he thought was due to him: "I have fallen out with my family, and as long as my mother lives I have no right to my inheritance."[64] When Engels's domestic partner Mary Burns died, Marx sent his condolences by wishing it were his own mother who had died instead.[65] Unsurprisingly, psychobiography has had a field day here, with some wishing that Marx could have been nicer to his mother and others deciding that she was not in any way worthy of his love.[66] It would help, once more, if we knew what it was that we wanted from her: "The mother," writes Derrida, "would present for analysis the term of a regression, a signified of the last instance, only if you knew what the mother names or means (to say), that with which she is pregnant."[67] The question for us to ponder in this context is not what it was that made Marx hate his mother, but what revolution might be if it can be figured as a question of translation—a question whose answer entails, for Marx, the forgetting of the *Mameloshn*. To pursue that problem systematically would be to inquire about traces of Yiddish in Marx's writings more generally: if, as Marx joked in *Capital*, "the language of commodities has, besides Hebrew, many other more or less correct dialects," can we be sure that Yiddish was not one of his own?[68] Did Marx write *only* in German when he wrote in German? To my knowledge this subject has never been broached in these terms, perhaps because to pursue it would undermine the notion that the language of science is "an empirical accident and not an experience tied to the exercise of thought."[69] Much of course depends on preserving the autobiographical as extrinsic and detachable, as if we knew clearly and in advance where life leaves off and where life's work begins, where proper names adhere to texts and where they do not—as if, in short, we knew always and absolutely the difference between literature and science, the many and the one. Where Strachey and Phillips commonly construe that assumed difference as an opposition in their respective demotions and promotions of a literary Freud, Marxist theory does the same in conceiving science and ideology as mutually exclusive categories. But what if, in its anasemic non-self-identity, the *Mameloshn* displaces these too-symmetrical oppositions? What if it divides science and literature from themselves? What if, far from being inimical to revolution, the *Mameloshn* could be enlisted as one of its resources?

What if Yiddish were the language of Marxism?

Yiddish once, at least, was *a* language of Marxism. Little known today, Vladimir Medem was a major theoretician of the Bund (Algemeyner Yidisher Arbeter Bund in Lite, Poyln un Rusland), the Jewish socialist organization founded in 1897 in Vilnius (located in Paris, the Bibliotèque Medem, named for him, is today the largest Yiddish-language library in Europe). One of the founding members of the Russian Social Democratic Labor Party (from which the Bolsheviks and Mensheviks later sprang), the Bund staked out a combination of political and cultural positions that were as unprecedented in the history of the Jewish Question as they were in that of socialism. For one thing, it refused to count itself as pro- or anti-assimilation: secularist and antimessianic, the Bund was not in the historical prediction business. Inspired by Austro-Marxism's emphasis on cultural autonomy, the Bund organized around nationality even while resisting nationalism—especially when the latter took the form of Zionism, which became the Bund's bitter adversary. Lenin decried the Bund as a "nationalist deviation," but its sense of the national seems to have been utterly anasemic: "The principal task today in the field of cultural creation," Medem wrote, "is the consolidation of the position of the mother tongue"—by which he meant, of course, the *Mameloshn* (which was not, in fact, *his* own: Medem was born to an assimilated, Russified family and raised in the Orthodox Church). The Bund refused further to generalize its program, to project its conception of multicultural socialism as a universal model, to think that it could offer "the key for the solution of the Jewish problem on a worldwide scale." For the Bund, indeed, Yiddish was simply one among the many languages of the disintegrating Tsarist Empire, which meant that Yiddish-speakers in the Pale were thought to have more in common culturally and politically with speakers of, say, Armenian, Finnish, and Tajik than with the partisans of modern Hebrew.[70] And yet Medem remembered hating Yiddish when he first heard it as a child:

> Both of Vladimir's parents converted [from Judaism], as had most of his aunts and uncles. The older children were baptized into the Lutheran Church and Vladimir, the youngest, into the orthodox Russian Church. His childhood was happy, but there was a pervasive shame about the family's Jewish origins and the use of Yiddish. When an old Jewish woman Leykeh spoke to his mother in Yiddish, the six-year-old Vladimir was sickened and upset by his mother's replies in Yiddish.[71]

All the rest was not exactly history, if history is what belongs to the victors. Medem died in 1924 on a fund-raising tour to the United

States at the age of forty-four and was buried in Brooklyn, near the grave of the great Yiddish writer Sholem Aleichem. In that decade and after, both Zionism and Leninism overtook the Bund. But perhaps the recollected shame of a six-year-old boy points to a possible future for revolution that does not, for once, require the forgetting of the *Mameloshn*.

Coda
Other Maternities

[Status confusion.] For months I have been her mother. It is as if I had lost my daughter (a greater grief than that? It had never occurred to me.). —ROLAND BARTHES, *Mourning Journal*

I sometimes think that, "fundamentally," in a human being, what makes the difference, *his* or *her* difference, is the mother. Who the mother was, how she left her mark. At times I tell myself that we ought to set down the invisible meridian not between men and women, but between vengeance and patience, between the insatiable and the nourisher. —HÉLÈNE CIXOUS, *Stigmata: Escaping Texts*

Science seems to have as its always possible outcome an escaping of sexual difference, not a reinforcement of it, so that what seems like a biological invariant can be gotten around. That, in fact, is one of the aims of science, and perhaps also what makes science seem like a not entirely benign force (Frankenstein: "I thought that I held the corpse of my dead mother in my arms"). —BARBARA JOHNSON, *Mother Tongues*

I claimed in the foregoing that, beyond the kinds of trouble it causes generally for Theory, maternity constitutes a special conundrum for Marxism and psychoanalysis, theories distinguished by their peculiar conditions of reproducibility. If, as Foucault suggested in "What Is an Author?," a proposition counts as Marxist or Freudian only "in relation to the work of the founders," then Marx and Freud are "not just the authors of their own works" but also the producers of "something else: the possibilities and the rules of the formation of other texts."[1] Pregnant with this unique potential for continuity as well as deviation, Marxism and psychoanalysis thus seem to reproduce themselves without a trace of maternal involvement. Whether each theory retains sufficient genetic variation to produce a healthy population of descendents is another question entirely, of course.

While this is not, per se, Foucault's own understanding of the implications of his "founders of discursivity" paradigm, he may have been tending in that direction nonetheless. Two years before writing "What Is an Author?" Foucault celebrated Nietzsche, Freud, and Marx as a trio whose writings "changed the nature of the sign."[2] But in the later essay Nietzsche is conspicuously absent, which suggests that he failed to make the grade as a founder of discursivity even though Foucault thought of himself as writing "with the aid of Nietzsche's texts—but also with anti-Nietzschean theses (which are nevertheless Nietzschean!)."[3] Perhaps Nietzsche was omitted because of his enduring preoccupation with (his own) pregnancy as the condition of philosophy. Despite or because of his animosity toward his mother, Franziska ("When I look for my profoundest opposite, ineradicable vulgarity of the instincts, I always find my mother and sister"), Nietzsche opened *Ecce Homo* with a riddle for his readers: "As my father I have already died, as my mother I am still alive and growing old."[4] Nietzsche's maternal identification seems here as much a commandment as a biographical oddity:

> We philosophers are not free to separate soul from body as the common people do; we are even less free to separate soul from spirit. We are no thinking frogs, no objectifying and registering devices with frozen innards—we must constantly give birth to our thoughts out of our pain and maternally endow them [*und mütterlich ihnen alles mitgeben*] with all that we have of blood, heart, fire, pleasure, passion, agony, conscience, fate, and disaster. Life—to us, that means constantly transforming all that we are into light and flame, and also all that wounds us; we simply can do no other.[5]

For once, Nietzsche insists, philosophers are philosophers only insofar as they are mothers:

> *Mothers.*—Animals think differently about females than humans do; they consider the female to be the productive being. There is no paternal love among them, only something like love for the children of a beloved and a getting used to them. In their children females have a satisfaction of their desire to dominate, a possession, an occupation, something that

is totally intelligible to them and can be prattled with: all this taken together is motherly love—it is to be compared to the love of an artist for his work. Pregnancy has made women gentler, more patient, more timid, more pleased to submit; and just so does spiritual pregnancy [*die geistige Schwangerschaft*] produce the character of the contemplative type, to which the female character is related: these are male mothers [*die männlichen Mütter*].—Among animals the male sex is considered the beautiful one.[6]

Though Nietzsche's idiom is certainly distinctive, his conceit is hardly new. The notion of "spiritual pregnancy" is at least as old as the *Symposium*—"All human beings are pregnant in body and in soul," Diotima tells Socrates (206c)—and the trope's male offspring includes, among countless examples from the entire Western canon, Sir Philip Sidney's description of Astrophel as "great with childe" in composing a sonnet, as well as Honoré de Balzac's much less decorous homage to the *maternité cérébrale* of authorship:

He who can describe his plan in words is already deemed to be an extraordinary man. All writers and artists have this ability. But to produce! To bring to birth [*accoucher*]! To work hard at rearing the child [*élever laborieusement l'enfant*], to put it to bed every night well-fed with milk [*gorgé de lait*], to kiss it every morning with the inexhaustible love of a mother [*avec la cœur inépuisé de la mère*], to lick it clean, to dress it a hundred times in the prettiest of jackets which it tears again and again.[7]

But even if Nietzsche's *männlichen Mütter* are far from novel, they may yet be unique in the degree of their persistence. As one of his recent critics notes,

From his first book, *The Birth of Tragedy*—in which Apollo and Dionysus "continually incite each other to new and more *powerful births*"—to his last book, *Nietzsche contra Wagner*—in which "the Dionysian god and man, can afford not only the sight of the terrible and the questionable, but even the terrible deed and luxury of destruction, decomposition, and negation . . . because of an *excess of procreating*, restoring powers which can yet turn every desert into luxurious farm land"—and nearly every book in between, Nietzsche's Dionysian spirit usurps the powers of procreation, pregnancy, and birth.[8]

That Nietzsche has *usurped* these "powers of procreation, pregnancy, and birth" is the contention of many of his feminist readers,
who charge that his mothers eliminate "women altogether via the appropriation of her one useful capacity—pregnancy and childbirth—
for men. . . . This desire to appropriate the birthing capacity for himself and other male creators suggests that Nietzsche prefers a world
that does not really include women at all."[9] Indeed, if to imagine
(male) philosophers as mothers is to assume "both the appropriation and the disavowal of woman's ability to reproduce life," it is also
to assume that women have nothing of their own to contribute to
culture—neither writing nor children.[10] It certainly takes concerted
effort not to notice these assumptions at work in Nietzsche's writing.

But in protesting Nietzsche's use of the metaphor of childbirth, his
critics may be objecting in fact to his use of metaphor more generally. For to decry "male writers' metaphoric appropriations of the
female process of birth-giving" is to open the possibility that what
is objectionable here has less to do with the appropriation "itself"
than with its rhetorical status.[11] The charge of usurpation is in this
sense an accusation of catachresis, the misuse of language. Susan
Stanford Friedman's important essay "Creativity and the Childbirth
Metaphor" seems as much at war with figurative language as it is
with gendered inequality. Poems are not babies, she reminds us, and
to compare the one creation with the other is to blind ourselves to
"the metaphor's literal falsehood." When male writers use the childbirth metaphor, they require their readers to forget or overcome "the
literally false equation of books and babies," as well as "the biological impossibility of men birthing both books and babies." These two
impossibilities would seem to be the same one.[12]

It may be argued in response that the distinction between the literal and the figural is as difficult to maintain in this context as we
discovered it to be throughout this book. And Nietzsche provides us
with little guidance for deciding whether his *männlichen Mütter* are
figurative or not. But in any case it is no longer technically true that
men cannot give birth. Thomas Beatie is currently the most famous of
several transgendered men who legally may be called male mothers.[13]
I do not take Beatie's experience as the basis for imagining a tendentious equivalence or symmetry between "male" and "female" births,

but rather to see the former as no longer simply fantasy . . . or as a catachresis. Like *heterosexuality*, invented after the coining of *homosexuality*, we find ourselves newly belonging to an era of "female maternity," and we have yet to take its theoretical measure.

Shulamith Firestone's manifesto of 1970, *The Dialectic of Sex*, imagined that liberation for all would be achieved only through the development of artificial wombs—ectogenesis—thereby overcoming the "sex division" that has enslaved women to their bodies and to men for millennia. Rebarbative for many at that time, the book is being reread today with newfound interest, given the impact of forty years of technological developments that have outpaced our social theories.[14] From Firestone's perspective, Nietzsche's philosophy of male maternity may turn out to have been a timely meditation. It will at any rate continue causing mother trouble.

Preface

1. Sacks, *Shakespeare's Images of Pregnancy*, 1.
2. See Andrew Parker, "Introduction: Mimesis and the Division of Labor," in Rancière, *The Philosopher and His Poor*, ix–xx.
3. Plato, *The Symposium*, 47 (209c–d).
4. See Michel Foucault, "What Is an Author?," in *The Essential Works of Foucault*, 2:217.
5. Jacques Lacan, "The Situation of Psychoanalysis and the Training of Psychoanalysts in 1956," in *Écrits*, 397–98.
6. Kristeva, *Desire in Language*, 237.

Introduction

1. Rose, "On Knowledge and Mothers: On the Work of Christopher Bollas," in *On Not Being Able to Sleep*, 151.
2. Critchley, *Continental Philosophy*, 62. On the difficulty of representing the history of an *absence* of representation (of "woman," paradigmatically, but perhaps also of "mother"), see Deutscher, *A Politics of Impossible Difference*, esp. 26–30.
3. Beauvoir, *The Second Sex*, 63, 496.
4. Feminist theorists grasped this point long ago, under the sign of irony. See, for example, Russo, *The Female Grotesque*; and Zwinger, "Blood Relations."
5. Badiou, "Philosophy as Biography." This is the text of a talk delivered at the Miguel Abreu Gallery in New York City on 13 November 2007. All quotations are taken from this source.
6. Among other texts by Derrida on the mother as limit, see *Of Grammatology*; *Glas*; and "Circumfession" in Bennington and Derrida, *Jacques Derrida*.
7. Dick and Kofman, *Derrida*, soundtrack quoted from 64:58 to 67:05.
8. Elsewhere, complaining that Barbara Johnson turned what he had taught her back against him, Derrida adopted the persona (if this is the right term) of an aggrieved mother: "Unbeatable, I tell you: nothing to say against this plenitude, however gross it may be, since she was full *only* of all of you, *already*, and everything that all of you would have to say against it. This is what I call in English the logic of *pregnancy* and in French the fore-

closure of the name of the mother. In other words, you are all born, don't forget, and you can write only against your mother who bore within her along with you, what she has borne you to write against her, your writing with which she would be large. And full, you will never get out of it. Ah! but against whom had I written?—I would like it to have been your mother. And she above all.—Who?" ("Envois," in *The Post Card*, 150). Whatever we make of "Envois," whose referential status is anything but certain, it seems safe to say that Derrida rarely if ever *invited* his readers to treat him maternally. In this respect, at least, he may remind us of Freud: "'And—I must tell you (you were frank with me and I will be frank with you), I do *not* like to be the mother in transference—it always surprises and shocks me a little. I feel so very masculine.' I asked him if others had what he called this mother-transference on him. He said ironically and I thought a little wistfully, 'O, *very* many'" (Doolittle [H. D.], *Tribute to Freud*, 146–47).

9. Weiss, *Refiguring the Ordinary*, 183–84.

10. Ferrell, *Copula*, 2–3.

11. Ruddick, "Thinking Mothers/Conceiving Birth," 29–30.

12. Ibid., 29. I will return to Ruddick's second radical notion, already hinted at in this passage—that "maternal thinking" is independent of gender—even though she retracts this possibility in her later work. See also her *Maternal Thinking*.

13. Andrea O'Reilly and Sara Ruddick, "A Conversation about *Maternal Thinking*," in O'Reilly, *Maternal Thinking*, 18.

14. Le Dœuff, "Ants and Women," 53.

15. Ruddick, "Thinking Mothers/Conceiving Birth," 29–30. Ruddick is intriguingly close in this view to Jacques Rancière's account of Marxist orthodoxy in its inability to represent workers as thinking people; see *The Philosopher and His Poor*.

16. Ruddick refers here to Hirsch's iconic *The Mother/Daughter Plot*.

17. See Le Dœuff, *The Philosophical Imaginary*, 100, 126. See also Lloyd, *The Man of Reason*. For approaches that proceed instead from some conception of the embodied difference between women and men—often influenced by Luce Irigaray's (dis)engagement with philosophy—see Diprose, *The Bodies of Women*; Gatens, *Imaginary Bodies*; and Grosz, *Volatile Bodies*.

18. I am paraphrasing here the conclusion to Stanton, "Difference on Trial." Moreover, a woman's identity may be less temporally restricted than a mother's. Is a mother always a mother? Even, say, after the death of an only child? *When* does a person become a mother? Right-wing pronatalists across the globe assume that maternity is not only enduring but that it precedes birth. On the other hand, Condorcet described pregnancy

as a "passing" indisposition, like gout or a cold, which should not prevent women from exercising their universal rights as citizens (*Condorcet*, 98). This was, obviously, an argument in defense of women's rights, not mothers'. Appeals on behalf of the citizen-mother have since become frequent in the West wherever "separate-sphere" gender ideology makes maternity a civic obligation. See the introduction to Parker et al., *Nationalisms and Sexualities*.

19. I understand this problem to be structural. The index to Christina Howells's superb collection *French Women Philosophers* suggests that only 5 of its 453 pages bear on the topic of motherhood. On the vexed problem of the universal (particularly in French feminist thought), see Schor, "French Feminism Is a Universalism"; and Scott, "Universalism and the History of Feminism." See also Scott's later essay "French Universalism in the Nineties."

20. See Oliver, "Motherhood, Sexuality, and Pregnant Embodiment."

21. Snitow, "Feminism and Motherhood," 32.

22. Arendell, "Conceiving and Investigating Motherhood," 1192.

23. Griffin, "Feminism and Motherhood," 33, 35.

24. Rich, *Of Woman Born*, ix.

25. Bowlby, "Generations," 2.

26. Beauvoir, *The Second Sex*, 492. See also Firestone, *The Dialectic of Sex*. Jeffner Allen proceeded to argue what Beauvoir never quite did—that "motherhood is dangerous to women because it continues the structure within which females must be women and mothers and because it denies to females the creation of a subjectivity and world that is open and free" (*Sinuosities*, 28–29).

27. Dinnerstein, *The Mermaid and the Minotaur*; Chodorow, *The Reproduction of Mothering*; and Wallace, *Black Macho and the Myth of the Superwoman*. On the simultaneous rise of the "new momism" in the U.S popular media, see Douglas and Michaels, *The Mommy Myth*.

28. See, for example, Garner, Kahane, and Sprengnether, *The (M)other Tongue*; Sayers, *Mothers of Psychoanalysis*; and Doane and Hodges, *From Klein to Kristeva*. Curiously, mother–son relationships have received much less recent attention—perhaps because of the limited number of stories (all of them homophobic) that psychoanalysis *can* tell about the son's mother, held responsible for both his heterosexual and homosexual object choices (the latter often indistinguishable from psychosis). Freud's *Leonardo da Vinci and a Memory of His Childhood* remains a touchstone here (esp. 52–56), as does "On Narcissism: An Introduction," in *General Psychological Theory*, 56–82. See Barande, *Le maternel singulier*.

29. Butler, *Gender Trouble*, 84–85.

30. De Lauretis, *The Practice of Love*, 198.

31. See, for example, Schwartz, *Sexual Subjects*; Mamo, *Queering Reproduction*.

32. Kristeva, *Desire in Language*, 239. See also "Stabat Mater."

33. Kristeva, *Black Sun*, 27–28.

34. Irigaray, "And the One Doesn't Stir without the Other," 1, and *Sexes and Genealogies*, 18. Unlike Kristeva, Irigaray has never thought matricide a good idea. See also Jacobs, *On Matricide*.

35. Snitow, "Feminism and Motherhood," 42. Nancy Chodorow's *The Reproduction of Mothering* famously begins with the words "Women mother" (3). Most readers have understood this phrase to constitute a complete sentence, with *women* as the subject and *mother* as the verb. But "women mother" is also *not* a sentence but two nouns suspended in metonymic apposition. The grammatical undecidability of these alternatives allegorizes the problem that maternity poses for feminism. See Dever, *Skeptical Feminism*, 78.

36. See, for example, Irigaray, "Women-Mothers, the Silent Substratum of the Social Order," 50; and Plaza, "The Mother/the Same," 78. Plaza replies that the mother is a phantasm, not a person: "'Mom' is neither a woman nor an individual, it is someone whom I perceive as (or rather whom *I represent to myself* as) closely linked to myself, quasi-instinctively" (78). Though I will argue below from different premises, I share with Plaza the assumption that, empirically, no one has ever seen a mother.

37. See Parkin, *Kinship*, 14; and Baraitser, *Maternal Encounters*, 4.

38. Baraitser, *Maternal Encounters*, 19.

39. Rose, "Mothers and Authors," 217.

40. Baraitser, *Maternal Encounters*, 19.

41. For example, the distinction between action and identity enabled Ruddick to propose what she later retracted: that the gender of the person who mothers a child is irrelevant even as the gender of the one who gives birth is not ("Thinking Mothers/Conceiving Birth"). Whether a man can be said to mother (as opposed to *be* a mother) has been a question in social psychology at least since Chodorow's *The Reproduction of Mothering*, which promoted men's active involvement in parenting as an antidote to patriarchy. For representatively polar responses, see Balbus, *Mourning and Modernity*, and Hollway, *The Capacity to Care*. Focusing largely on the *sense* of the maternal and its limits, this question seems to me mooted in the wake of the new medical technologies, which have made the status of the maternal *referent* uniquely problematic.

42. Weiss, *Refiguring the Ordinary*, 183. Hollway, for example, distin-

guishes "actual mothers" from gender-unspecified "maternal subjectivity" in an effort to preserve motherhood as a uniquely female experience (*The Capacity to Care*, 64). But what, today, is an "actual mother"? Has there ever been one?

43. Carsten, *After Kinship*, 7.

44. Parkin, *Kinship*, 126.

45. Bartkowski, *Kissing Cousins*, 14. David Eng has suggested that we make this distinction meaningful by racializing it; see *The Feeling of Kinship*. Recent scholarship at the intersection of gender, kinship, and medical technology has been both prodigious and highly innovative. See especially Culley, Hudson, and Van Rooij, *Marginalized Reproduction*; Franklin, *Embodied Progress*; Franklin and McKinnon, *Relative Values*; Franklin and Ragoné, *Reproducing Reproduction*; Ginsburg and Rapp, *Conceiving the New World Order*; Inhorn and van Balen, *Infertility around the Globe*; Lesnik-Oberstein, *On Having an Own Child*; Mamo, *Queering Reproduction*; Parkin and Stone, *Kinship and Family*; Ragoné, *Surrogate Motherhood*; Ragoné and Twine, *Ideologies and Technologies of Motherhood*; Stanworth, *Reproductive Technologies*; Stone, *Kinship and Gender*; Strathern, *Reproducing the Future*; Strathern, *Kinship, Law, and the Unexpected*; and Thompson, *Making Parents*.

46. Spillers, *Black, White, and in Color*, 203–29. As the subtitle of this influential essay implies, Spillers is concerned with what becomes of maternity's sense (though not, I think, its referent) when the right to claim motherhood has been stolen under slavery: "For the African female, then, the various inflections of patriarchilized female gender—'mother,' 'daughter,' 'sister,' 'wife'—are not available in the historical instance" (232). On procreation in the absence of legally sanctioned kinship, see Bentley, "The Fourth Dimension."

47. Popular opinion to the contrary, genetic testing has not made paternity certain: "The modern technique of DNA or genetic fingerprinting may seem greatly to have improved accuracy in these respects, but only specialists can be directly aware of the degree and nature of proof: the courts, who have to take such decisions, and the population at large have to take this on trust, unless they are prepared to carry out the necessary experiments to prove the matter for themselves. (In fact, even genetic fingerprinting has increasingly come under legal challenge.) For the layperson in Western societies, therefore, knowledge of this sort is a matter of faith in experts, of belief engendered ultimately by an essentially socially determined attitude towards reason and science as superior to all other forms of knowledge. Elsewhere, different attitudes may prevail, and there may be no interest in, or realization of, scientific proof at all, so that kinship be-

comes even more evidently a matter of social definition, of belief. And the means of validating any belief itself constitutes a belief. Anthropologically, 'truth' is not the truth but whatever people in a particular society and/or set of circumstances decide is the truth: even in our own society, the two do not necessarily coincide. Ultimately, therefore, despite occasional scientific interventions, paternity, and kinship generally, remain matters of purely *social* definition" (Parkin, *Kinship*, 5–6).

48. Freud, "Family Romances" (1909), in *The Standard Edition* 9:239.

49. Freud, "Notes upon a Case of Obsessional Neurosis" (1909), in *The Standard Edition* 10:233n1.

50. Freud, "Moses and Monothesism" (1939), in *The Standard Edition* 23:114. In her commentary in *Ms* magazine on the historic Baby M surrogacy case, Phyllis Chesler argued (without invoking Freud as her precedent) "that motherhood is a 'fact,' an ontologically different category than 'fatherhood,' which is an 'idea'" (quoted in Laqueur, "The Facts of Fatherhood," 207). Lacan followed Freud in suggesting that "mothers are 'real,' fathers are only conceptual; to be a father is, literally, only a concept" (MacCannell, *Figuring Lacan*, 207). The notion that the mother alone is perceivable (which Freud encountered previously in J. J. Bachofen and Lewis Henry Morgan) has frequently resurfaced in anthropology. For example, "Motherhood is different. Conception is an internal and microscopic event that we laymen believe scientists have investigated, whereas gestation and birth, and with them the relation of physical motherhood, are macroscopic processes that, in principle, anyone can see for himself. Hence the descriptions of physical motherhood in diverse cultures do not vary as greatly as with fatherhood. . . . Fathers are not self-evident as mothers are" (Barnes, "Genetrix : Genitor :: Nature : Culture?," 68).

51. Derrida and Roudinesco, *For What Tomorrow*, 41. Derrida returned often in the mid- and late 1990s to the "legal fiction" of paternity in James Joyce and Freud. See, for example, *Politics of Friendship*, 168n25; *Archive Fever*, 47–48; *Deconstruction in a Nutshell*, 26–27; and *H.C. for Life, That Is to Say—*, 109. I am grateful to Jolan Bogdan for a preview of "The Uncertainty of the Mother," which concerns Derrida's little-known book *Ki az anya?*.

52. Derrida, *Deconstruction in a Nutshell*, 27.

53. Freud, "A Special Type of Object Choice Made by Men," in *Sexuality and the Psychology of Love*, 43; and Derrida and Roudinesco, *For What Tomorrow*, 41.

54. Derrida, "La veilleuse," 27–28; my translation. See also Nancy, *À plus d'un titre*.

55. Kofman, *Rue Ordener, Rue Labat*, which also reflects on Leonardo da

Vinci's "two mothers" (63–64). On Freud's differently multiple mothers, see Swan, "'Mater' and Nannie"; as well as Sprengnether, *The Spectral Mother*, 13–21. Tina Chanter reads Kofman's maternal doublings alongside Freud's in "Playing with Fire."

56. Cavarero, *In Spite of Plato*, 82.

57. Kristeva, *Hatred and Forgiveness*, 85. In describing "the mother's passion for the new subject that will be her child, provided he/she ceases to be her double" (86), Kristeva never imagines this new subject as having to reckon with multiple mothers—with kinds of doubling that fracture the mother's "side" from the start. This problem is hardly Kristeva's alone: psychoanalysis more generally has thus far resisted asking how the new family forms have affected retroactively its most cherished assumptions about the nature and genealogy of desire.

58. Derrida, *Glas*, 115–17.

59. See Walker, *Philosophy and the Maternal Body*. My thinking here again owes much to Jacqueline Rose's *On Not Being Able to Sleep*, which wonders what, in epistemological and ethical terms, the mother has been always "asked to bear" (158, 161). Kelly Oliver recently reflected on the work of "certain feminist philosophers who set out to prove themselves in the world of the father by vigorously protecting the mother from victimization by patriarchy" ("Julia Kristeva's Maternal Passions," 2). Oliver acknowledged that she had been considering her own writing "and that of others who revalorize the maternal in order to protect it from debasement within phallic culture by beating up on their philosophical fathers both to prove that they themselves are worthy of the band of brothers and to protect their mothers/themselves from victimization by those very brothers, whom they love and yet resent because they will someday become the beating, and therefore deserving to be beaten, father. This is not necessarily the agenda of feminists who revalue motherhood as a vocation for themselves, so that they can become mothers worthy of recognition by mankind. Rather, these are feminist avengers who take on the father/brothers to save the mother whom they love, as ambivalent as that love may be due to the abjection of maternity within the family of man" (2). But because these avenging philosophers are "too invested in pleasing the father with our intellectual pursuits to *be* her, yet too loyal to [the mother's] craziness, to her depression, to *be* him" (3), they preempt the mother even in the act of "protecting" her since, once more, this mother cannot be a philosopher, even an avenging one.

60. On the paradigmatic status of the mother/father opposition in Saussurean linguistics, see my "Holding the *Fort!*"

61. "Derridabase" in Bennington and Derrida, *Jacques Derrida*, 210.

Bennington adds that "this anteriority communicates with the common name of 'mother'" just as, for Derrida, "writing" communicates with its specific concept even while generalizing itself beyond its traditional limits (211). See also Lacoue-Labarthe and Nancy, *Retreating the Political*, 133–34, which makes this point in a slightly different idiom: "This is why the so-called question of the mother is, first of all, the question of a maternal retreat [*d'un retrait maternel*] —of the mother as retreat and of the retreat of the mother [*de la mère comme retrait et du retrait de la mère*]." Nancy, in *The Birth to Presence*, speaks similarly of a form of maternity "more 'maternal' than maternity, more archaic than any gestation of any genesis" (29).

62. Derrida, *Positions*, 45. Derrida observes later in this interview that "dissemination figures that which *cannot* be the father's" (86). It cannot be the mother's either, for the very same reasons.

63. Baraitser, *Maternal Encounters*, 6.

64. Mossman, *Politics and Narratives of Birth* 2, 5, 6; and Ferrell, *Copula*, x.

65. Guenther, *The Gift of the Other*, 8. But does birth occur at and as a moment? If so, which one? The question of when a fetus becomes a person has more to do with politico-religious judgments than with literality understood as the ground or condition of sensation. See Deutscher, "The Inversion of Exceptionality"; and O'Byrne, *Natality and Finitude*.

66. Guenther, "Being-from-Others," 99.

67. Huffer, *Maternal Pasts, Feminist Futures*, 7.

68. Shetty, "(Dis)figuring the Nation," 72.

69. Freud, *Introductory Lectures on Psychoanalysis*, 197.

70. Levinas, *Otherwise Than Being*, 66–71.

71. Sandford, "Masculine Mothers?," 182–83.

72. Ibid., 183. See also Bevis, "'Better than Metaphors?'"

73. Guenther, "'Like a Maternal Body,'" 131.

74. Cavarero, "Birth, Love, Politics," 19. Butler's response to Cavarero informs my own approach to the singular/general relationship; see *Giving an Account of Oneself*, 34. François Raffoul counters the notion that Heidegger neglected birth or simply opposed it to death; see *The Origins of Responsibility*, 270–72.

75. Barthes, *Camera Lucida*, 74–75.

76. Derrida, *The Work of Mourning*, 58. Of course, Barthes's mother was not his *mother* on the day the photo was taken. Barthes's recently published *Mourning Diary* has this especially moving entry for November 5: "Sad afternoon. Shopping. Purchase (frivolity) of a tea cake at the bakery. Taking care of the customer ahead of me, the girl behind the counter says *Voilà*. The expression I used when I brought *maman* something, when I was taking care of her. Once, toward the end, half-conscious, she repeated,

faintly, *Voilà* (I'm here, a word we used to each other all our lives). The word spoken by the girl at the bakery brought tears to my eyes. I kept on crying quite a while back in the silent apartment" (37). Perhaps *voilà* could have such intimate significance for Barthes and his mother only by being also, constantly, on everybody's lips.

77. Freud, "Negation" in *The Standard Edition* 19:233. I take issue, in short, with any ethics that *possesses* the mother in recalling her, as in the following instance: "For the gift of birth does not merely give me a range of possibilities; it gives me, brings me forth as an existent. To repeat this originating possibility as my own choice may be authentic; but this 'authenticity' requires the profoundly unethical erasure of the other who grants the sheer possibility of existence by giving birth to me: *my* mother" (Guenther, "Being-From-Others," 107; my emphasis). As if the possessive were not another form of the mother's erasure.

78. Pontalis, *Windows = Fenêtres*, 97.

79. What makes "Ersatz" all the more interesting is its difference from the anecdote that seems to have formed its basis:

A patient of some sixty-odd years has just gone to visit her elderly mother who, as they say, is not all there. After her visit, she comes straight to a session, still filled with an intense rage like that of a child when her mother refuses to do what she expects from her. So, somewhat foolishly I admit, but one should never be scared to admit one's own inadequacy or stupidity, I tell her: "You don't really think that at her age and in the state she's in, you have the power to cure your mother, to *change* her, do you?"

Then the idea came to me, and I'll freely confess it is not a very original one, but it had never forced itself upon me in that way before, that the desire to change one's mother comes from the fact—among others—that no matter how you qualify her—bad, good, good-enough—the mother is not interchangeable. And it is precisely because one cannot exchange her that one persists obstinately in changing her at all costs. By changing her, I mean either curing her from her depression, from her madness, or else devoting oneself to rendering her less absorbed in herself, ensuring that she attends us without watching us too closely—in other words, being present without being intrusive. We can all find father-substitutes. It is even the precondition for girls to overcome their Oedipus complex, and boys can choose their teacher or their analyst as a father-figure, not having dared to confront their own fathers directly.

However, in my opinion, there is no *ersatz* for the mother. She is irreplaceable, she is unchangeable. An analyst can try all he likes to "act the mother" (as Ferenczi was accused of doing); he is *not* the mother. ("Notable Encounters," 155)

Unlike "Ersatz," which seems to acknowledge the Derridean point that "there is no maternity that does not appear subject to substitution," Pontalis is emphatic here that the mother's true being—True Being "itself"—resists imitation . . . if anything can. See Derrida, *Monolingualism of the Other*, 88.

80. Derrida, *The Ear of the Other*, 5; and Bennington and Derrida, *Jacques Derrida*, 36n.

81. See Deutscher, *Yielding Gender*, 86–87, and "Autobiobodies." To notice life *in* the work is to work simultaneously against immanentism and psychobiography.

82. See Neppi, *Le babil et la caresse*; and O'Donohoe, "Living with Mother." For example, when Sartre objects strenuously to describing the present as "pregnant with the future [*gros de l'avenir*]," is he complaining that the present is thereby misconceived as non-self-identical, or that the present is misconceived as a mother? Perhaps these questions are the same? (*Being and Nothingness*, 124–25).

83. See, for example, Chakravorty, Milevska, and Barlow, *Conversations with Gayatri Chakravorty Spivak*, 153, 163; Guardiola-Rivera, "Interview with Gayatri Spivak"; Hayot, "'The Slightness of My Endeavor,'" 262; Spivak, *The Post-colonial Critic*, 83, 90, 93; Spivak, "Translation as Culture," 20; and Sanders, *Gayatri Chakravorty Spivak*, 122. An entire essay could be devoted to the following paragraph, which precedes a discussion of language acquisition in Melanie Klein: "I am standing with my mother in Charles de Gaulle airport in Paris. For a week we have fed our ears on academic French. Suddenly I hear an exchange in the harsh accents of upstate New York. I turn to my mother and say, in Bengali, roughly this: 'Hard to listen to this stuff.' And my mother: 'Dear, a mother tongue.' My mother, caught up as she was in the heyday of resistance to the Raj, still extended imaginative charity to English" (Spivak, "Rethinking Comparativism," 612).

84. See, for example, Safranski, *Martin Heidegger*, 144. Is this gesture simply an expression of gratitude? What other affects (aggression above all) could it be thought to convey? Oedipally playing mother off against lover (perhaps to the point of parody), Catherine Clément returns to this moment in her novel *Martin and Hannah*, 97–98: "Yes, Martin could place the book on his mother's body, over her heart. Mere printed pages, neatly bound. No conflict between that and the gift of thinking. His lover had been infused with the spirit of his work; his mother had been given the material object, as was her due. The dead woman and the absent woman were those destined to receive Martin's thinking." Heidegger kept a small

photograph of his mother on his writing desk; see Petzet, *Encounters and Dialogues with Martin Heidegger*, 121.

85. See Caputo, "The Absence of Monica," 150.

86. Heidegger, *What Is Called Thinking?*, 48. My thanks to Avital Ronell for gifting me with this passage. See Ronell, *The Telephone Book*, 20–25.

87. This scene of maternal instruction recalls another described by Freud: "When I was six years old and was given my first lessons by my mother, I was expected to believe that we were all made of earth and must therefore return to earth. This did not suit me and I expressed doubts of the doctrine. My mother thereupon rubbed the palms of her hands together—just as she did in making dumplings, except that there was no dough between them—and showed me the blackish scales of epidermis produced by the friction as a proof that we were made of earth. My astonishment at this ocular demonstration knew no bounds and I acquiesced in the belief which I was later to hear expressed in the words: *Du bist der Natur einen Tod schuldig* [Thou owest Nature a death]" (*The Interpretation of Dreams*, 238–39). Entirely silent during this "ocular demonstration," Amalia Nathanson Freud has taught her son two lessons here, one explicitly about the inevitability of death and the other implicitly about the difference between two kinds of thinking—maternal *Handwerk* and Theory proper. On the hand as an organ of thought, see Derrida, "Heidegger's Hand (Geschlecht II)," in *Psyche*, 2:37. For another reading of the Freud passage, see Kofman, *The Enigma of Woman*, 74–78.

88. Nietzsche, *Ecce Homo*, 7. I return to Nietzsche's maternity in this book's coda.

89. Foucault, "What Is an Author?," in *Essential Works of Foucault*, vol. 2, 217.

90. Ibid., 219.

91. For example, criticizing Heidegger's German-Jewish heirs for "overlooking the intellectual threads that precipitated his Nazi involvement," Richard Wolin never wonders at the mother's absence in his account of genealogical transmission: "Thus, like a Greek tragedy—though on a smaller scale—the sins of the father will be visited upon the daughters and sons" (*Heidegger's Children*, 20). Large or small, Greek tragedies never omit mothers.

1. Mom, *Encore*

1. Mitchell and Rose, *Feminine Sexuality*.

2. Lacan, *On Feminine Sexuality*, 81; *Encore*, 75. Subsequent page numbers appear in the running text and refer first to the English and then to the French edition. Unattributed translations in this chapter are my own.

3. Excellent anthologies on the topic include Price and Shildrick, *Feminist Theory and the Body*; and Fraser and Greco, *The Body*.

4. Roudinesco, *Jacques Lacan and Co.*, 689.

5. Barnard, introduction to Barnard and Fink, *Reading Seminar XX*, 1–2. In addition to contributions by the editors, this international collection includes essays by Geneviève Morel, Renata Salecl, Colette Soler, Paul Verhaeghe, and Slavoj Žižek.

6. Such claims have since become commonplace: "Since Lacan has produced a general epistemology that overcomes the opposition between the humanities and the hard sciences, his work has implications that go far beyond academia and psychoanalysis" (Leupin, *Lacan Today*, xiv). Whatever happened to the "limits of knowledge"?

7. See Sigmund Freud, "Female Sexuality" (1931) and "Femininity" (1933), in *The Standard Edition*, 21:223–43 and 22:112–135. On what a woman wants, see Jones, *The Life and Work of Sigmund Freud*, 2:468. On "the sexual researches of children," see Freud, *Three Essays on the Theory of Sexuality*, 60–63.

8. Jacqueline Rose saw this risk clearly early on: "Lacan's reference to woman as Other needs, therefore, to be seen as an attempt to hold apart two moments which are in constant danger of collapsing into each other—that which assigns woman to the negative place of its own (phallic) system, and that which asks the question as to whether women might, as a very effect of that assignation, break against and beyond that system itself" (*Feminine Sexuality*, 51–52).

9. I allude here to Kofman, *Aberrations*. Kofman, notably, seems to have had little interest in Lacan's manner of becoming-woman.

10. Lacan, *Écrits*, 582. On Lacan's mother generally, see Barzilai, *Lacan and the Matter of Origins*.

11. Soler, *What Lacan Said About Women*, 113. In similarly promoting the mother's erotic connection to the father as a condition of the child's emotional independence, Julia Kristeva's later work has been resolutely Lacanian (if not *echt*-Freudian); see, for example, "The Passion According to Motherhood," in *Hatred and Forgiveness*, 79–84, and especially 86.

12. Lacan, *The Other Side of Psychoanalysis*, 112.

13. "Mom" originally appeared in *The Oxford Literary Review* in 1985. I have redacted much of the essay rather than reproduce it here verbatim.

14. Laplanche and Pontalis, *The Language of Psycho-analysis*, 90, 423.

15. See Greco, *Illness as a Work of Thought*.

16. Freud, *The Psychopathology of Everyday Life*, in *The Standard Edition* 6:257.

17. Inside and outside become something other than opposites by the time of "Instincts and Their Vicissitudes," in Freud, *The Standard Edition*, 14:111–40; see also note 22 below.

18. Nasio, *Five Lessons on the Psychoanalytic Theory of Jacques Lacan*, 124.

19. Nasio, *Hysteria*, 49.

20. Greco, *Illness as a Work of Thought*, 87.

21. Leclaire, *Psychoanalyzing*, 46.

22. "The 'instinct [drive]' appears to us as a concept on the frontier between the mental and the somatic, as the psychical representative of the stimuli originating from within the organism and reaching the mind, as a measure of the demand made upon the mind for work in consequence of its connection with the body" (Freud, "Instincts and Their Vicissitudes," 121–22).

23. Derrida, *Psyche*, 1:123–24. My understanding of the centrality of representation to the modeling of psychosomatic illness derives in large part from Derrida's criticism in "Envoi" (124) of Laplanche's and Pontalis's suggestion that "the relation between soma and psyche . . . is to be understood by analogy with the relationship between a delegate and his mandator" (*The Language of Psycho-analysis*, 364).

24. Leclaire, *Psychoanalyzing*, 38, 44.

25. Lacan, "Seminar of 21 January 1975," in *On Feminine Sexuality*, 165.

26. Freud, "Letter to Carl Müller-Braunschweig (1935)," 329.

27. Derrida took this claim for the uniquely human nature of sexuality to be tendentious; see, in particular, his remarks on Lacan in *The Animal That Therefore I Am*, 119–40.

28. See Laplanche, *Life and Death in Psychoanalysis*.

29. David-Ménard, "Lacanians Against Lacan," 95; and Jacqueline Rose, "Introduction—II," in Mitchell and Rose, *Feminine Sexuality*, 44. This may also be why, with Lacan and after, hysteria has reclaimed its formerly paradigmatic status in psychoanalytic theory: "The hysteric has no body, for something in the history of her body could not be formulated, except in symptoms" (David-Ménard, *Hysteria from Freud to Lacan*, 66).

30. Lacan, *Écrits*, 462–63.

31. Juliet Mitchell, "Introduction—I," in Mitchell and Rose, *Feminine Sexuality*, 20.

32. David-Ménard, *Hysteria from Freud to Lacan*, 66; my emphasis.

33. Rose, "Introduction—II," 33, 35, 39.

34. Jameson, "Imaginary and Symbolic in Lacan," 352–53.

35. Lacan, *Écrits*, 581.

36. Gallop, "Penis/Phallus," 243, 247. Gallop argued further that "Lacanians might wish to polarize the two terms into a neat opposition, but it is hard to polarize synonyms" (*Thinking through the Body*, 126). Mikkel Borch-Jacobsen wondered why Lacan never got around to explaining "why a single organ should obsess both sexes. . . . But this is precisely the 'paradox' that Lacan means to found in theory. Since the privilege of the phallus cannot be that of the real organ, it *must*, he explains, be that of the phallic signifier—which puts us right back on the merry-go-round, since we do not understand why this signifier is sexual" (*Lacan*, 214–15).

37. Gallop, "Quand Nos Lèvres S'Écrivent," 78–79.

38. Kristeva, *Powers of Horror*, 2, 5, 7.

39. Melville, "Psychoanalysis and the Place of 'Jouissance,'" 349.

40. Shepherdson, "The Epoch of the Body," 188.

41. Adams, "Versions of the Body," 27.

42. Ibid., 28.

43. Ibid., 28.

44. Shepherdson, *Lacan and the Limits of Language*, 3–4; my emphases.

45. Wilson, *Psychosomatic*, 8.

46. Ibid., 5.

47. Derrida, *Glas*, 115b: "Remains—the mother."

48. *Poubellication* is Lacan's neologism, a forced coupling of "publication" and "garbage bin" (*poubelle*); see *Encore* (26/29) and "La psychanalyse: Raison d'un échec," in his *Autre écrits*, 343. On Lacan's conflicting attitudes about *Écrits*, which he finally agreed to publish when he was sixty-five years old, see Roudinesco, *Jacques Lacan*, 319–31. Melville alludes to *Encore*'s reading crisis in "Psychoanalysis and the Place of 'Jouissance,'" 367.

49. Jacques Lacan, "Radiophonie," in *Autre écrits*, 403.

50. Lacoue-Labarthe and Nancy, *The Title of the Letter*.

51. Lacan asserts that Lacoue-Labarthe and Nancy are "pawns" (65/62)—of Derrida, obviously, even though his name also goes unmentioned, given Lacan's hilarious riffing later in *Encore* on the phrase "beyond the phallus": "Why not make a book title out of it? It'll be the next book in the Galilée collection" (74/69). Derrida and Lacan started causing trouble for each other at least as early as 1967, when Lacan made fun of Derrida's neologism

différance and showed that he could deploy it just as skillfully as its coiner; see *My Teaching*, 18.

52. Jacques Lacan, "The Instance of the Letter in the Unconscious; or, Reason since Freud," in *Écrits*, 493.

53. Jacques Lacan, ". . . Ou pire," in *Autre écrits*, 550.

54. Derrida first charged Lacan with phonocentrism in *Positions*, 108.

55. Sigmund Freud, "On the Teaching of Psycho-analysis in Universities" (1919), in *The Standard Edition* 17:169, 73.

56. Freud, *The Question of Lay Analysis*, 23, 67, 93.

57. Lacan, *The Four Fundamental Concepts of Psycho-analysis*, 263.

58. Jacques Lacan, "Psychoanalysis and Its Teaching," in *Écrits*, 366.

59. Ibid., 379.

60. Lacan, *The Four Fundamental Concepts of Psycho-analysis*, 7.

61. Lacan, *My Teaching*, 93.

62. Lacan, *Television*, 3.

63. Lacan, *My Teaching*, 3.

64. Jacques Lacan, "The Situation of Psychoanalysis and the Training of Psychoanalysts in 1956," in *Écrits*, 397–98.

65. For more on "the pass," see Roudinesco, *Jacques Lacan and Co.*, 443–61.

66. Jacques Lacan, in *Lettres de l'École* (1979), cited in Borch-Jacobsen, *Lacan*, 158.

67. Roudinesco, *Jacques Lacan and Co.*, 567.

68. Leupin, *Lacan Today*, xv.

69. Lacan, "Psychoanalysis and Its Teaching," 383.

70. Jacques Lacan, "L'Étourdit," in *Autre écrits*, 472, 482–83, 475. See Roudinesco, *Jacques Lacan*, 358–84, for more on Lacan's idiosyncratic logic and topology.

71. Derrida, *Who's Afraid of Philosophy?*, 81.

72. Ibid., 91.

73. Lacan, *The Four Fundamental Concepts of Psycho-analysis*, 63.

74. Caruth, *Unclaimed Experience*, 109–10.

75. Lucey, *Gide's Bent*, 126–27.

76. Dever, *Death and the Mother from Dickens to Freud*, 48–49.

2. History, Fiction, and "The Author of *Waverley*"

1. In Freud's usage, *family romance* describes a narrative fantasy in which a child, imagining itself to have been adopted, replaces its own parents with "others of better birth" (Sigmund Freud, "Family Romances," in *The*

Sexual Enlightenment of Children, 41–45). On how this fantasy may have influenced the development of the European novel, see Robert, *Origins of the Novel*; Boheemen, *The Novel as Family Romance*.

2. Eleanor Marx and Paul Lafargue as quoted in Prawer, *Karl Marx and World Literature*, 255n, 386, 396. On the Scottish connection, see Raddatz, *Karl Marx*, 21–22.

3. Raddatz, indeed, underscores the "romance" character of this trans-ference of familial affections: "The dedication [to Ludwig von Westphalen] with which Marx, then aged twenty-three, headed his doctoral disserta-tion—which would normally have been dedicated to his father or his par-ents—has a ring of veneration about it: 'To his dear fatherly friend . . . as a token of filial love'" (*Karl Marx*, 22).

4. Fredric Jameson, introduction to Lukács, *The Historical Novel*, 1. All further citations will be given parenthetically in the running text. "Com-posed during the winter of 1936/7 and published in Russian soon after its completion" (13), *The Historical Novel* first appeared in English translation in 1962. According to Perry Anderson, it "is still probably the best known of all works of Marxist literary theory" ("From Progress to Catastrophe," 24).

5. Elsewhere Jameson defines this linkage—loose enough, in the version quoted above, to cover any form of "sociological" criticism—more pre-cisely as a *mediation*, "the classical dialectical term for the establishment of relationships between, say, the formal analysis of a work of art and its social ground, or between the internal dynamics of the political state and its economic base. . . . the analysis of mediations aims to demonstrate what is not evident in the appearance of things, but rather in their underlying reality, namely that *the same* essence is at work in the specific languages of culture as in the organization of the relations of production" (*The Political Unconscious*, 39–40). "*The same* essence," we will see, should also be com-mon to father and son—even (or especially) if they happen not to resemble each other.

6. Foucault, *The Order of Things*, 221. See also Terdiman, "Deconstruct-ing Memory," 14: "The nineteenth century became a present—perhaps the first present—whose self-conception was defined by a disciplined obses-sion with the past."

7. Claire Lamont, introduction to Scott, *Waverley*, xxxvi.

8. G. M. Trevelyan as quoted in Bliss, *Sir Walter Scott and the Visual Arts*, 28; Kroeber, *Romantic Narrative Art*, 180.

9. Shaw, *The Forms of Historical Fiction*, 22; and Andrew Hook, intro-duction to Scott, *Waverley*, 10. For Hook, indeed, these were not unre-lated outcomes, Scott's virile historicism having rescued the novel from

its early gender troubles: "After Scott the novel was no longer in danger of becoming the preserve of the woman writer and the woman reader. Instead it became the appropriate form for writers' richest and deepest imaginative explorations of human experience" (10). As if being female prevented one from undertaking the richest and deepest explorations of human experience. On Scott's complex debts to his female predecessors, see especially Ferris, *The Achievement of Literary Authority*; and Trumpener, *Bardic Nationalism*. Further references will be to the Penguin edition of *Waverley*, which contains in an appendix the full prefatory apparatus of the 1829 text, with citations or page numbers appearing parenthetically in the running text.

10. Chandler, *England in 1819*, 136. Chandler suggests, moreover, that Scott was crucial for Lukács's development of "what might be properly called a 'Marxist criticism'" (256).

11. Baxandall and Morawski, *Marx and Engels on Literature and Art*, 116.

12. Jameson, *Postmodernism*, 404–5; and Meek, *Social Science and the Ignoble Savage*, 219–21.

13. See, for example, Elam, *Romancing the Postmodern*; Ferris, *The Achievement of Literary Authority*; Welsh, *The Hero of the Waverley Novels*; and Wilt, *Secret Leaves*.

14. See Sedgwick, *Between Men*. See also her "Gender Criticism," in Greenblatt and Gunn, *Redrawing the Boundaries*, 293: "Making heterosexuality historically visible is difficult because, under its institutional pseudonyms such as Inheritance, Marriage, Dynasty, Domesticity, and Population, heterosexuality has been permitted to masquerade so fully as History itself—when it has not been busy impersonating Romance."

15. "'That man,' said Flora, 'will find an inestimable treasure in the affections of Rose Bradwardine who shall be so fortunate as to become their object. Her very soul is in the home, and in the discharge of all those quiet virtues of which home is the centre. Her husband will be to her what her father now is—the object of all her care, solicitude, and affection. She will see nothing, and connect herself with nothing, but by him and through him'" (183).

16. Jameson, *Postmodernism*, 380. Marx is savage, however, on the transformation of the Highlands into sheep-walks and deer preserves: "What 'clearing of estates' really and properly signifies, we learn only in the promised land of modern romance, the Highlands of Scotland. There the process is distinguished by its systematic character, by the magnitude of the scale on which it is carried out at one blow (in Ireland landlords have gone to the length of sweeping away several villages at one blow; in Scotland areas as large as German principalities are dealt with)" (*Capital* 1:728).

17. See Nairn, *The Break-Up of Britain*, 111, 146–48; Eric Richards, "Scotland and the Uses of the Atlantic Empire," in Bailyn and Morgan, *Strangers within the Realm*, 67–114; and Hugh Trevor-Roper, "The Invention of Tradition: The Highland Tradition of Scotland," in Hobsbawm and Ranger, *The Invention of Tradition*, 15–41. For a hard assessment of Lukács's role in the Popular Front, see Deutscher, *Marxism in Our Time*, 290–92. Judith Wilt points out that "the Waverley Novels still await a full-scale treatment of their Orientalist impulse and of the ways in which this enables (and disables) Scott's vision of race in Universal History" ("Walter Scott," 303). For an important start on this project, see Makdisi, *Romantic Imperialism*, esp. 70–99. Given that *Waverley* says little about the Highlands' fate after the Union, Makdisi can cast Scott as the author of much more than a series of novels: "What happens to a people, a history, a culture, that falls victim to a colonial project whose objective is not only to exploit its victims, but to dispossess them and claim all of their land in order to re-encode it, re-name it, to literally re-write it and re-invent it? What happens to the history of such a dispossessed people?" (71).

18. Hegel, *Aesthetics*, 1:68, 55. On the "concrete universal" in Western Marxist criticism, see Demetz, *Marx, Engels, and the Poets*. That types, however, function iteratively (the word derives from *tupos*, meaning "impression," "image," "model")—and thus can always disrupt the dialectical consolidation they were designed specifically to foster—is a point made pervasively by Philippe Lacoue-Labarthe; see especially his *Typography*.

19. Hegel, *The Logic of Hegel*, 352.

20. The reference, of course, is to "The Creative Writers and Daydreaming" (rpt. in Freud, *The Uncanny*), where Freud entertains the hypothesis that "the literary work, like the daydream, is a continuation of, and substitute for, the earlier play of childhood" (32). See Kofman, *The Childhood of Art*. Marx's meditation on the "timelessness" of classical Greek art rests on a similar conceit: "A man cannot become a child again, or he becomes childish. But does he not find joy in the child's naïveté, and must he himself not strive to reproduce its truth at a higher stage?" (*Grundrisse*, 111).

21. Charles Karelis, "Hegel's Concept of Art: An Interpretive Essay," in Hegel, *Hegel's Introduction to Aesthetics*, xlv.

22. Hook, introduction, 14–15.

23. Sroka, "Fact, Fiction, and the Introductions to the Waverley Novels," 142.

24. Hook, introduction, 12.

25. Fleishman, *The English Historical Novel*, 10.

26. Derrida, *The Post Card*, 467–68.

27. Derrida, *Positions*, 45. See also Derrida, *Dissemination*, 36: "Fiction is

in the service of meaning, truth is (the truth of) fiction, the fictive arranges itself on a hierarchy, it negates itself and dissipates itself as the accessory to the concept."

28. Brooks, *Reading for the Plot*, 28.

29. Derrida, *Dissemination*, 45. See also Derrida, "Psyche: Inventions of the Other," trans. Catherine Porter, in *Psyche* 1:5: "There is no natural invention—and yet invention also presupposes originality, originarity, generation, engendering, genealogy, that is to say, a set of values often associated with genius or geniality, thus with naturality. Hence the question of the son, of the signature, and of the name. . . . Who finds himself excluded from this scene of invention? What other of invention? Father, son, daughter, wife, brother, or sister?" Not to mention, again, the mother.

30. Brooks, *Reading for the Plot*, 63. See also Beizer, *Family Plots*, which similarly links the narrative structures of nineteenth-century fiction "to themes of the father and the family line and to related issues of authority, subordination and insubordination, legitimacy, genealogy, heredity, and transmission. A chain of associations further attaches this tradition to formal principles of mimesis, order, coherence, linearity, unity, closure, and totalization" (3).

31. Jon Elster, *An Introduction to Karl Marx*, 4; my emphasis.

32. P. Zajotti as quoted in Sandra L. Bermann, introduction to Manzoni, *On the Historical Novel*, 30.

33. Manzoni, *On the Historical Novel*, 72–73, 63, 65. Among those taking the other side was Thomas Babington Macaulay, who applauded Scott's "use of those fragments of truth which historians have scornfully thrown behind them in a manner which may well excite their envy" (quoted in Hayden, *Scott*, 309). When Gustave Flaubert's Bouvard and Pécuchet weighed in finally with *their* opinion, it was a sign that the debate had grown quite stale: "External facts are not everything. They must be completed by psychology. Without imagination history is defective.—'Let's send for some historical novels!'" (*Bouvard and Pécuchet*, 129). Naturally, the next chapter opens with "First they read Walter Scott."

34. Sir Walter Scott, "An Essay on Romance," in *The Miscellaneous Prose Works of Sir Walter Scott, Bart.*, 6:103, 104, 107, 117. Scott may have learned this game of "telephone" from Voltaire: "The first foundations of every history are the narratives, of fathers to their children, transmitted then from one generation to another. They are at most only probable at their origin, when they do not shock common sense, and they lose a degree of probability at each generation" ("Dictionnaire philosophique [III]," in *Oeuvres complètes*, 19:347–49).

35. Derrida's paraphrase of Hegel in *Who's Afraid of Philosophy?* 122. See

also Lacoue-Labarthe, *The Subject of Philosophy*, 15: "There are two kinds of fiction, the 'good' one, obviously, and the 'bad' one; the one that leads to truth, effaces itself before truth or even heightens it—and the other one, the one that resists, that does not efface itself, does not lift [*ne se (re)lève pas*], the aberrant one."

36. Scott, *Sir Walter Scott on Novelists and Fiction*, 54.

37. Ibid., 260; and Scott, *The Prefaces to the Waverley Novels*, 16.

38. Hayden, *Scott*, 284.

39. Homer Obed Brown points out that the Waverley novels include multitudes of fathers and uncles "but almost no mothers, no major ones anyway" (*Institutions of the English Novel from Defoe to Scott*, 155), which raises the question of how mothers are counted and classified: for whom would a mother *not* be major? On deceased or otherwise absent mothers in nineteenth-century fiction, see Bronfen, *Over Her Dead Body*; Dever, *Death and the Mother from Dickens to Freud*; and Thaden, *The Maternal Voice in Victorian Fiction*.

40. Raleigh, "'Waverley' as History," 29.

41. On the Jacobite Rebellion's impact on the formal structure of the English novel, see Brown, *Institutions of the English Novel from Defoe to Scott*.

42. Hook, introduction, 25, 26. On the dialectical *Aufhebung* as a form of magic, see also Hegel, *Phenomenology of Spirit*, 19: "This tarrying with the negative is the magical power that converts [Spirit] into being."

43. Derrida, *The Post Card*, 318.

44. On critical discourse as an "acting out" of the dynamics internal to its objects, see Shoshana Felman, "Turning the Screw of Interpretation," in Felman, *Literature and Psychoanalysis*, 94–207. On transference in the practice of historiography, see also LaCapra, *History and Criticism*, 11: "All history, moreover, must more or less blindly encounter the problem of a transferential relation to the past whereby the processes at work in the object of study acquire their displaced analogues in the historians account."

45. Wilt, *Secret Leaves*, 28. Wilt's is the first extended treatment of *Waverley* to pursue the highly un-Lukácsian argument that Scott's origins are contaminated from the outset, that "the easy connection of open eyes, awakening, with 'reality' or 'real history,' and of closed eyes, 'the dream,' with romance, breaks down over and over again in the novel" (35). My reading of *Waverley* also draws on Dryden, *The Form of American Romance*; Elam, *Romancing the Postmodern*; Valente, "Upon the Braes."

46. F. A. Pottle, "The Power of Memory in Boswell and Scott," in Jeffares, ed., *Scott's Mind and Art*, 250.

47. See Levine, *The Realistic Imagination*, 101. Where Levine contends that "Scott misses what later novelists would see as opportunities to make the problem of fiction itself one of the novel's major preoccupations" (90), I am proposing that *Waverley* succeeds in doing just that.

48. See Dryden, *The Form of American Romance*, 13–15; Garside, "Waverley's Pictures of the Past"; Meltzer, *Salome and the Dance of Writing*, 204–13.

49. Hegel, *Aesthetics*, 2:865, 1:155–56. Naomi Schor discusses "the extraordinary fascination exerted over Hegel by the very details" this passage would suppress: "Hegel succeeds in embodying the most natural, not to say naturalistic details, even as he consigns them to erasure" (*Reading in Detail*, 26).

50. It is only fair to record here Hegel's own antipathy to Scott. When, in fact, he wishes to rebuke certain historians for being so distracted by particulars that they are "incapable [of recognizing] a whole, a general design," Hegel singles out Scott's "portraiture" as the prime example of this tendency: "A series of individual characteristics—as in one of Walter Scott's novels—collected from every quarter, *painstakingly* and *laboriously* assembled,—characteristics drawn from historical writings, correspondence and chronicles,—such a procedure involves us in numerous fortuitous details, [which are] historically *no doubt authentic*; yet the *main interest* [is] in no way clarified [by them], but rather confused,—and thus [it is] immaterial whether such and such a soldier—, precisely the same effect. [They ought to] leave this sort of thing to Walter Scott's novels, this detailed *portraiture* incorporating all the minutiae of the age" (*Lectures on the Philosophy of World History*, 19).

51. Levine, *The Realistic Imagination*, 104–5.

52. Sroka, "Fact, Fiction, and the Introductions to the Waverley Novels," 152. See also Iser, *The Implied Reader*, 95: "Imagination and reality interact upon one another, so that in the reality of the novel, neither history nor imagination can assume a completely dominant role."

53. Scott, *The Prefaces to the Waverley Novels*, 59–60.

54. Derrida, *Dissemination*, 36. See also Cottom, *The Civilized Imagination*, 134–35: "There is always the tendency in [Scott's] novels for elements that are apparently defined with the utmost clarity to drift beyond borderlines toward a general condition of disorder and confusion."

55. As Wilt confirms, Scott's prefatory apparatus "has often seemed just an inert barrier to the story, so that in this century it became a commonplace warning, reader to reader, especially teacher to student, to start Scott novels at chapter 2" (*Secret Leaves*, 185–86).

56. Derrida, *Writing and Difference*, 212; and Derrida, *Dissemination*, 27n.

57. Derrida, *Dissemination*, 44–45.

58. Foucault, "What Is an Author?," in *Essential Works of Foucault, 1954–1984*, 2:214–15, 213. See also Kamuf, *Signature Pieces*. On the legal construction of authorship in a variety of national contexts, see McGill, *American Literature and the Culture of Reprinting, 1834–1853*; Rose, *Authors and Owners*; Saunders, *Authorship and Copyright*; Saint-Amour, *The Copywrights*; Woodmansee and Jaszi, *The Construction of Authorship*.

59. See also Ferris, *The Achievement of Literary Authority*, 6: "The Author of Waverley is neither exactly the author of *Waverley* nor exactly the author of the collectivity known as the Waverley Novels" (6). Using one of Scott's prefatory pseudonyms to demonstrate the complexity of the act of avowing an anonymous novel as one's own, Gérard Genette explains why "effecting a fiction is not just a matter of stating it in a sentence of the type 'I, Marivaux, am not the author of the memoirs that follow' or 'I, [Laurence] Templeton, am the author of the novel that follows'" (*Paratexts*, 279).

60. See Bertrand Russell, "On Denoting," in *Logic and Knowledge*, 41–56.

61. Scott as quoted in Abrams, *The Mirror and the Lamp*, 214.

62. Scott, *The Prefaces to the Waverley Novels*, 49. See also Freud, *The Origins of Psycho-analysis*, 296–97: "I was quite unable to express myself with noble simplicity, but lapsed into a facetious, circumlocutory straining after the picturesque. I know that, but the part of me that knows it and appraises it is unfortunately not the part that is productive."

63. Freud again will admit as much in suggesting a highly improbable precedent—Empedocles—for his dualist theory of the instincts: "My delight was proportionately great when I recently discovered that that theory was held by one of the great thinkers of ancient Greece. For the sake of this confirmation I am happy to sacrifice the prestige of originality, especially as I read so widely in earlier years that I can never be quite certain that what I thought was a creation of my own mind may not have been an outcome of cryptomnesia" ("Analysis Terminable and Interminable," in *Therapy and Technique*, 263).

64. Wilt, *Secret Leaves*, 27.

65. Barthes, moreover, simply transfers *to the reader* the (otherwise intact) functions of authorship: "The reader is the space on which all the quotations that make up a writing are inscribed without any of them being lost; a text's unity lies not in its origin but in its destination" ("The Death of the Author," in *Image, Music, Text*, 148).

66. Foucault, "What Is an Author?," 211–12. On another of Scott's contemporaries—a writer who similarly wrestled with Hegel, preoccupied himself with the relationship between fathers and sons, generated a profusion of

wayward prefaces, and turned pseudonymity into a kind of art form—see Agacinski, *Aparté*, 119–20: "Kierkegaard himself identified the question of the name [of the author] with that of the work's paternity, regardless of whether he lay claim to this paternity retrospectively or whether, on the contrary, he marked out its irrevocable ambiguity, designating himself sometimes as the author of an operation strategically calculated from the outside, sometimes as the victim of an operation of pure loss, as though in the end he had been the sacrificial victim of his writing."

67. Lukács, *Theory of the Novel*, 14, 16–17.

68. Ibid., 18.

69. Ibid., 20, 17.

70. As Marx would acknowledge in his analysis of capital formation: "[Value] differentiates itself as original value from itself as surplus-value; as the father differentiates himself quâ the son, yet both are one and of one age: for only by the surplus-value of £10 does the £100 originally advanced become capital, and so soon as this takes place, so soon as the son, and by the son, the father, is begotten, so soon does their difference vanish, and they again become one, £110" (*Capital* 1:154).

71. Delphy, *Close to Home*, 15.

72. Quoted in Seigel, *Marx's Fate*, 50. See also Lukács, *Record of a Life*, 35: "I was completely estranged from my family, or at least from a part of it. . . . My mother was a shrewd woman who soon saw what was happening. She fell seriously ill and died of cancer of the breast. Under pressure from other members of the family I wrote her a letter. When she received it she said, 'I must be very ill for Dr. Georg to write me a letter.'" As Lee Congdon laconically confirms, "Lukács developed, from his earliest years, an intense dislike for his mother" (*The Young Lukács*, 4).

73. Lukács, *Record of a Life*, 145.

74. Derrida, *Glas*, 28a. See also Hartmann, "The Unhappy Marriage of Marxism and Feminism," 2: "The 'marriage' of marxism and feminism has been like the marriage of husband and wife in English common law: marxism and feminism are one, and that one is marxism."

3. Translating Revolution

First presented at a panel organized by Barbara Johnson at the English Institute, Harvard University, in September 2003, this chapter owes everything to Johnson's *Mother Tongues*. I am grateful as well to Judith Butler, James Chandler, Penelope Deutscher, Jay Grossman, Claudia Johnson,

Tina Lupton, Jeffrey Masten, Meredith McGill, Françoise Meltzer, Yopie Prins, Joshua Scodel, Silke Weineck, and Elizabeth Wingrove for their various forms of commentary and material assistance, and to audiences at the University of Chicago, Rutgers University, the University of Michigan, and Northwestern University for their engaged responses.

1. Heidegger, "Letter on Humanism," in *Pathmarks*, 272.

2. Derrida, "The *Retrait* of Metaphor," trans. Peggy Kamuf, in *Psyche*, 1:69. All further citations will be made parenthetically in the running text.

3. If only because we know what Freud would have said about the house as a maternal symbol; see my discussion in the introduction to the present book (19–20).

4. Derrida cites this passage again in *Given Time*, 80. The full text runs as follows: "Im Dialekt wunelt das Sprachwesen. In ihm wurzelt auch, wenn die Mundart die Sprache der Mutter ist, das Heimische des Zuhaus, die Heimat. Die Mundart ist nicht nur die Sprache der Mutter, sondern zugleich und zuvor die Mutter der Sprache" (Martin Heidegger, "Sprache und Heimat," *Gesamtausgabe*, 13:156).

5. Ibid., 13:155. On the distinction between *Mundart* and *Sprache*, see Sallis, *Echoes*, 208. See also Phillips, *Heidegger's Volk*, 204–5: "It is the untransmittable that, for Heidegger, constitutes the *Heimat* of Dasein, since transmission is the substance of the 'they,' of the everyone that is everywhere. . . . What a dialect has to say is less important than the manner in which it says it, *in which it does not say it*. The content of an utterance in dialect is its point of weakness regarding a universally comprehensible language, since it is the content that admits of transmission and that is consequently the promise of a global language. The dialect in its secrecy stands opposed to reification and in place of an extralingual object, it harbors *Heimat* as the originary idiocy of Dasein."

6. Merkin, "The Literary Freud." See also Boynton, "The Other Freud (the Wild One)."

7. Bettelheim, *Freud and Man's Soul*. Ernest Jones's winning argument for adopting "the classical nomenclature" recalls nothing so much as the medieval church's insistence on a standardized Latin Mass: "There is no other way of securing terms free from the numerous accessory connotations and associations inevitable in a spoken language, and hence of escaping possibilities of misunderstanding. . . . It is much easier to confine a new classical term to one definite meaning. The fact that this meaning may not at first sight be obvious, particularly to the uneducated, is a further notable advantage for it replaces the temptation to a casual and vague apprehension by the necessity of serious and precise study" (Darius Gray Ornston, "Alternatives to a Standard Edition," in *Translating Freud*, 107).

8. See the entry "Instinct (or Drive)" in Laplanche and Pontalis, *The Language of Psycho-analysis*, 214–17; see also Laplanche, *Life and Death in Psychoanalysis*, 9–10, and my discussion of Freud's treatment of sexuality in chapter 1 of the present book (31–33). As early as 1966 Strachey was having to defend his decision to translate *Trieb* as "instinct" rather than import a term like *drive* which, "in this [nominative] sense, is not an English word" (James Strachey, "Notes on Some Technical Terms Whose Translation Calls for Comment," in Freud, *The Standard Edition*, 1:xxv).

9. See Laplanche, *Essays on Otherness*, 260–65.

10. Phillips, *Promises, Promises*, 364; and Merkin, "The Literary Freud," 43. See also Phillips, "Making the Case."

11. "Phillips is an odd choice to edit the Freud translation on many counts, not least because he doesn't know German, the language in which Freud wrote. When I mention this fact to the eminent literary critic Frank Kermode, who is a Phillips enthusiast, he is somewhat taken aback. 'That's a tremendous bit of cheek, isn't it?' he says, half-admiringly" (Merkin, "The Literary Freud," 42). Phillips had in fact *argued* "that the general editor should not read German" so that a single editorial vision would not be imposed on the series (Phillips, "After Strachey"). All sixteen volumes have yet to be released in the United States.

12. James Strachey, "Notes," in Freud, *The Standard Edition* 1:xviii; and Phillips, "After Strachey." Geoffrey Hartman scoffed at the Penguin program as a "free love approach to translation"; see "Freud for Everyman (and Everywoman)," 155. As it happened, only ten translators could commit to the project, which meant that several had to take on more than one text. Each volume in the series is also introduced by an academic humanist known for his or her readings of Freud.

13. Adam Phillips, "A Note on the Texts," in Phillips, *The Penguin Freud Reader*, xvii. Penguin applied similar editorial principles to its multivolume retranslation of Marcel Proust's *In Search of Lost Time*, with Christopher Prendergast serving as the general editor. Introducing the series in her superb new version of *Swann's Way*, Lydia Davis explains why Penguin decided to engage "a group of translators, each of whom would take on one of the seven volumes": "At the initial meeting of the Penguin Classics project, those present had acknowledged that a degree of heterogeneity across the volumes was inevitable and perhaps even desirable, and that philosophical differences would exist among the translators. As they proceeded, therefore, the translators worked fairly independently, and decided for themselves how close their translations should be to the original—how many liberties, for example, might be taken with the sanctity of Proust's long sentences. And Christopher Prendergast, as he reviewed all

the translations, kept his editorial hand relatively light" (Proust, *Swann's Way*, xxi–xxii).

14. Wood, "There Is No Cure." One of the translators also admits to being "struck by the great number of similarities [to the *Standard Edition*] that remained, even where I had agonized over multiple alternatives" (Graham Frankland, "Translator's Preface," in Freud, *The Unconscious*, xxv).

15. Shaun Whiteside, "Translator's Preface," in Freud, *On Murder, Mourning, and Melancholia*, xxxii.

16. Nicola Luckhurst, "Translator's Introduction," in Freud and Breuer, *Studies in Hysteria*, xxxviii.

17. See Alan Bance, "Translator's Preface," in Freud, *Wild Analysis*, xxvii; Helena Ragg-Kirkby, "Translator's Preface," in Freud, *Outline of Psychoanalysis*, xxiv; Shaun Whiteside, "Translator's Preface," in Freud, *The Psychology of Love*, xxvii; and Frankland, "Translator's Preface," xxii.

18. Meanwhile, a *Revised Standard Edition* (RSE) has been in the works for years under the single-handed editorship of Mark Solms, the South African neuro-psychoanalyst who previously translated and edited Freud's pre-psychoanalytic papers. The RSE will include new annotations, a glossary, updated bibliographic materials, and previously unpublished writings by Freud that surfaced after Strachey completed his work. Delayed for labyrinthine legal reasons, the RSE will, whenever it finally appears, staunchly defend Strachey's established lexicon with one notable exception: *drive* will be officially admitted into the fold. For more on the project, see Solms, "Controversies in Freud Translation"; and Jones, "An Interview with Mark Solms."

19. As Whiteside put it, "our brief as translators was to approach Freud's writings as 'literary' texts, in other words, to bring as few preconceptions as possible to the task at hand" (Freud, *On Murder, Mourning, and Melancholia*, xxx). Has the "literary" ever been free of preconceptions?

20. Marx and Engels, *Collected Works*; hereafter cited as *CW*.

21. Draper, *The Marx-Engels Register*, 292–13. See also the entry "Marx" in France, *The Oxford Guide to Literature in English Translation*, 325–27.

22. Of course, the question of what constitutes the "complete" writings of Marx and Engels is no simple one, as the publication history of the various major German editions makes clear. The first attempt, the Moscow-based *Marx-Engels Gesamtausgabe* (1927–35), abbreviated as MEGA, was terminated during Stalin's purges; it included writings up to 1848 when it ceased publication. The East German *Marx-Engels Werke* (1956–68), or MEW, ran to forty-three volumes but omitted the recently discovered *Grundrisse*, the later economic manuscripts, as well as the notebooks. The

new *Marx-Engels Gesamtausgabe*, known as MEGA2, began in Berlin in 1975 and continues today in Amsterdam under the auspices of the Internationale Marx-Engels-Stiftung. The most ambitious scholarly edition to date, MEGA2 was originally to include some 164 volumes, but that figure has been scaled back to 114, roughly half of which have appeared as of September 2011. Its goal is to produce nothing less than a "complete works" of Marx and Engels that would incorporate, using the best current bibliographic methods, all published and unpublished books, articles, reviews, letters, notebooks, marginal notes, and commonplace books—everything, in short, that might qualify *as* a work, and then some. Foucault's questions in "What Is an Author?" thus retain their pertinence here: "Even when an individual has been accepted as an author, we must still ask if everything that he wrote, said, or left behind is part of his work. The problem is both theoretical and practical. When undertaking the publication of Nietzsche's works, for example, where should one stop? Surely everything must be published, but what is 'everything'?" (*Essential Works of Foucault*, 2:207). On the vicissitudes of the MEGA and the MEW, see Draper, *The Marx-Engels Register*, 202–13. Jürgen Rojahn, the executive director of MEGA2, surveys the state of the undertaking in "Publishing Marx and Engels after 1989." For a list of all extant MEGA2 volumes and those still projected, see http://www.bbaw.de/bbaw/Forschung/Forschungsprojekte/mega/en/Startseite (accessed 25 August 2011). Rojahn and others discuss what MEGA2 can offer a contemporary reassessment of Marxism in "The Emergence of a Theory," 29–46. See also Brophy, "Recent Publications of the Marx-Engels Gesamtausgabe (MEGA)."

23. Rancière, *The Names of History*, 8. See also Parker, "Re-Marx: Prehistory."

24. See Eric J. Hobsbawm, "The Fortunes of Marx's and Engels's Writings," in Hobsbawm, *Marxism in Marx's Day*, 328, 341–43; and Derrida, "Geopsychoanalysis: '. . . and the Rest of the World.'" For more on the territories of psychoanalysis, see Parker, "Modeling Freud and Fundamentalism."

25. See Draper, *The Marx-Engels Register*, 202: "The ongoing English-language edition . . . is by no means simply an English version of the [*Marx-Engels Werke*]; it is more like an English-language version of a revised MEW that has not yet appeared in German." See also Grubrich-Simitis, *Back to Freud's Texts*, 53: "All concerned were constantly aware of the paradox of our position, that the first comprehensive critical *German-language* edition of Freud was substantially based on the achievements of *English-speaking* editors."

26. Derrida, *The Ear of the Other*, 119–20.

27. Derrida, *Resistances of Psychoanalysis*, 10.

28. Alan Bass, "On the History of a Mistranslation and the Psychoanalytic Movement," in Graham, *Difference in Translation*, 137. On the impertinence of distinguishing between "right" and "wrong" interpretations in the analytic process, see Freud's "Constructions in Analysis," in Freud, *Therapy and Technique*, 273–86.

29. Marx to Engels, 11 December 1858, *CW* 40:360.

30. This paradox lends itself easily to license: "I think that ideally a psychoanalytic translation should be distinct from any other translation. It should identify in footnotes the meaning of words in the original text that might have escaped the conscious awareness of the author" (Patrick J. Mahony, "A Psychoanalytic Theory of Translation," in Ornston, *Translating Freud*, 46). See also Mahony, "Freud and Translation."

31. Abraham and Torok, *The Shell and the Kernel*, 83, 86; and Jacques Derrida, "Me—Psychoanalysis: An Introduction to the Translation of 'The Shell and the Kernel' by Nicolas Abraham," trans. Richard Klein, in Derrida, *Psyche*, 1:131.

32. Thus, says Abraham, "psychoanalysis cannot be allotted a determined place in the order of the sciences," given its propensity to collapse subject and object even while increasing the space between "I" and "me" (*The Shell and the Kernel*, 83–84). Deconstruction's reception of Freud has understood this anomalousness as an axiom—and largely as a form of praise. See, for example, Prokhoris, *The Witch's Kitchen*, 4–5: "It follows that the science of the unconscious cannot be conceptualized on the model of the other sciences. For its method puts into practice a paradox still without parallel: the method is traversed, invested, even constituted by the very object it seeks to construct." Classic statements of this conception include Bersani, *The Freudian Body*, 4: "Psychoanalysis is an unprecedented attempt to give a theoretical account of precisely those forces which obstruct, undermine, play havoc with theoretical accounts themselves"; and Weber, *The Legend of Freud*, xvi: "Must not psychoanalytical thinking itself partake of—repeat—the dislocations it seeks to describe?"

33. Freud, "Observations on 'Wild' Psycho-analysis," in *The Standard Edition* 11:222.

34. I allude here in turn to Balibar, *The Philosophy of Marx*; Rancière, *The Philosopher and His Poor*; and Gayatri Chakravorty Spivak, "Scattered Speculations on the Question of Value," in Landry and MacLean, eds., *The Spivak Reader*, 107–40.

35. See Foucault, "What Is an Author?," in *Essential Works of Foucault*, 2:216–20.

36. Derrida, *The Ear of the Other*, 71. Derrida may have been meditating here on the degree to which "inheritance" translates translation.

37. He also might have recalled here that the privilege of inheritance is far from universal. He nearly did so in "Marx and Sons," in Sprinker, *Ghostly Demarcations*, 213–66. For more on the gender of inheritance, see chapter 2 of the present work.

38. De Man, *Aesthetic Ideology*, 38. See also Sallis, *On Translation*, 23–24.

39. Freud, *The Interpretation of Dreams*, 339–40.

40. Patrick J. Mahony, "Transformations and Patricidal Deconstruction," in Derrida, *The Ear of the Other*, 96–97. See also Mahony, "Towards the Understanding of Translation in Psychoanalysis."

41. Freud, *The Complete Letters of Sigmund Freud to Wilhelm Fliess, 1877–1904*, 208. See also Laplanche, *New Foundations for Psychoanalysis*; and Fletcher and Stanton, eds., *Laplanche: Seduction, Translation, Drives*.

42. Phillips, *Promises, Promises*, 129. See also Bourguignon et al., *Traduire Freud*; and the special issue of *L'écrit du temps*, "La décision de traduire: L'exemple Freud."

43. Frankland, *Freud's Literary Culture*, 6–7. Wilhelm Liebknecht recounts how Marx "scolded me one day because I did not know . . . Spanish! He snatched up *Don Quixote* out of a pile of books and gave me a lesson immediately" (quoted in Prawer, *Karl Marx and World Literature*, 208).

44. Marx and Engels, *The German Ideology*, in *CW* 5:36.

45. On this point, see Jean-Jacques Lecercle, "Marxism and Language," in Bidet and Kouvelakis, *Critical Companion to Contemporary Marxism*, 471–85.

46. Marx, *The Eighteenth Brumaire of Louis Bonaparte*, 15–16.

47. Jacques Derrida, "Living On/Border Lines," in Bloom et al., *Deconstruction and Criticism*, 102. Commenting elsewhere on this passage from the *Brumaire*, Derrida underscores the peculiar nature of the forgetting that Marx took to be the precondition for revolution: "For what one must forget will have been indispensable. . . . One must forget the specter and the parody, Marx seems to say, so that history can continue. But if one is content to forget it, then the result is bourgeois platitude: life, that's all. So one must not forget it, one must remember it but while forgetting it enough, in this very memory, in order to find again the *spirit* of the revolution without making its *specter* return [*den* Geist *der Revolution wiederzufinden, nicht ihr* Gespenst *wieder umgehen machen*]" (Derrida, *Specters of Marx*, 110). Remembrance *and/as* forgetting: would the mother tongue then be a spirit or a specter?

48. Marx, *Grundrisse*, 162–63; translation modified.

49. Marx, *Capital*, 1:188.

50. Wolfson, *Le schizo et les langues.*

51. Gilles Deleuze, "Louis Wolfson; or, The Procedure," in *Essays Critical and Clinical*, 9.

52. Daniel Heller-Roazen, "Schizophonetics," in *Echolalias*, 186.

53. Freud, *Jokes and Their Relation to the Unconscious*, 81.

54. Derrida, "What Is a 'Relevant' Translation?," 176. This tradition would presumably include Walter Benjamin's understanding that translation, of all literary forms, "is the one charged with the special mission of watching over the maturing process of the original language and the birth pangs of its own [*die Wehen des eigenen*]" ("The Task of the Translator," in *Illuminations*, 73). Paul de Man takes issue with Harry Zohn's rendering of *Wehen* here "as 'birth pangs,' as being particularly about the pains of childbirth," insisting instead that *Wehen* "can mean birth pangs, but it does mean any kind of suffering, without necessarily the connection of birth and rebirth." (Native German speakers inform me that, in the plural, *Wehen* refers *only* to labor pains—which underscores the strangeness of de Man's objection to Zohn.) For de Man, translation is "not a natural process" and thus should not be figured in terms of birth: "The translation does not resemble the original in the way that the child resembles the parent" (*The Resistance to Theory*, 85, 83). Where de Man may have assumed that family resemblance falls squarely on the side of nature, Benjamin recalled that "kinship does not necessarily involve likeness" (74). Tracking *Wehen*'s "illegitimate" associations in de Man's text, Barbara Johnson returns to these passages in *Mother Tongues*, 59–61.

55. See Kofman, *Pourquoi rit-on?* 186–87.

56. Freud, *The Joke and Its Relation to the Unconscious*, 68.

57. Judith Butler hears an echo of the Yiddish *Oy vey* in the German *Wehen*; see "Betrayal's Felicity."

58. Birnbaum, *Yiddish*, 37. According to Franz Kafka, Yiddish "consists solely of foreign words" ("An Introductory Talk on the Yiddish Language," in Anderson, *Reading Kafka*, 264).

59. Grossman, *The Discourse on Yiddish in Germany from the Enlightenment to the Second Empire*, 88; and Traverso, *The Marxists and the Jewish Question*, 6.

60. Yosef Hayim Yerushalmi recalls Theodor Reik's testimony that "Freud's mother did not speak to him in High German but in Galician Yiddish. If this be so, even though Amalie Freud had grown up in Vienna, what shall we say of Jakob Freud, who grew up in Galicia? Even granting that German was spoken in the home that Freud did not leave until he was twenty-seven, is it not reasonable to suppose that Yiddish was a lin-

gua franca alongside it and that he could speak or at least understand it as well?" (*Freud's Moses*, 69).

61. Harshav, *The Meaning of Yiddish*, 4. An analogy with medieval Latin may again suggest itself: "The vernacular, and sites of vernacular education, were associated with ideas of the female, while Latin, taught by men whether in aristocratic households or Church for grammar schools, was associated with ideas of the male" (Ferguson, *Dido's Daughters*, 107).

62. Seidman, *A Marriage Made in Heaven*, 16. This gender dimorphism extended even to typography: "Yiddish texts were printed in a different typeface (called *Vaybertaytsh*, 'women's German'), to separate them from the holy, 'square letters' of the holy texts (much as women were separated in the synagogue)" (Harshav, *Language in Time of Revolution*, 116).

63. Gilman, *Jewish Self-Hatred*, 199. By the middle of the century, Yiddish had lost all its former standing within the Dutch Jewish community; see Wallet, "End of the Jargon-Scandal." Years later, Eleanor Marx would reverse this process by learning enough Yiddish to address Jewish immigrants in London's East End; see Kapp, *Eleanor Marx*, 2:521.

64. Marx to Arnold Ruge, 25 Jan 1843, in *CW* 1:397.

65. Marx to Engels, 8 January 1863, in *CW* 41:442.

66. In addition to Gilman, see Künzli, *Karl Marx*; and Seigel, *Marx's Fate*.

67. Derrida, *Glas*, 116b.

68. Marx, *Capital*, 1:52.

69. Derrida, *Points . . .* , 374.

70. Traverso, *The Marxists and the Jewish Question*, 110. See also Mufti, *Enlightenment in the Colony*.

71. Levin, *While Messiah Tarried*, 292. Medem tells this story in detail in his memoir *Vladimir Medem*, 1–5. See also Frankel, *Prophecy and Politics*; Gitelman, *The Emergence of Modern Jewish Politics*; Jacobs, *Jewish Politics in Eastern Europe*; Minczeles, *Histoire générale du Bund*; and Tobias, *The Jewish Bund in Russia from Its Origins to 1905*.

Coda

1. Michel Foucault, "What Is an Author?," in *Essential Works of Foucault*, 2:217.

2. Michel Foucault, "Nietzsche, Freud, Marx," in *Essential Works of Foucault*, 2:272.

3. Michel Foucault, "The Return of Morality," in *Politics, Philosophy, Culture*, 251.

4. Nietzsche, *Ecce Homo*, 10, 7. In Derrida's gloss, "the mother is living on, and this living on is the name of the mother" ("Otobiographies," in *The Ear of the Other*, 16).

5. Nietzsche, *The Gay Science*, 6.

6. Ibid., 75.

7. Plato, *The Symposium*, 44; Sidney, "Astrophil and Stella," in *The Major Works*, 153; and Balzac, *Cousin Bette*, 218–19. See also Pender, "Spiritual Pregnancy in Plato's Symposium"; Sandford, *Plato and Sex*; and Sheffield, "Psychic Pregnancy and Platonic Epistemology." On male pregnancy in Western folklore, see Zapperi, *The Pregnant Man*; and Legman, *Rationale of the Dirty Joke*.

8. Oliver, *Womanizing Nietzsche*, 147–48.

9. Schotten, *Nietzsche's Revolution*, 157, 159. Nietzsche's defenders on this score include Ainley, "'Ideal Selfishness'"; and Patton, "Nietzsche and the Body of the Philosopher."

10. Gatens, *Imaginary Bodies*, 55.

11. Witt, "Babies and Books," 185.

12. Friedman, "Creativity and the Childbirth Metaphor," 55, 56.

13. "Male Pregnancy," *Wikipedia* (accessed 18 August 2011). On Thomas Beatie's pregnancies, see Trebay, "He's Pregnant. You're Speechless," which features commentary by Eve Kosofsky Sedgwick: "He's pregnant, he seems happy. It's not happening in any kind of a judicial, let alone criminal, context so it's not a matter of claiming a right. It's a matter of exercising one." See also Currah, "Expecting Bodies."

14. Firestone, *The Dialectic of Sex*. For a range of contemporary responses see Merck and Sandford, *Further Adventures of "The Dialectic of Sex."*

Abraham, Nicolas, and Maria Torok. *The Shell and the Kernel: Renewals of Psychoanalysis*. Ed. and trans. Nicholas T. Rand. Chicago: University of Chicago Press, 1994.

Abrams, M. H. *The Mirror and the Lamp: Romantic Theory and the Critical Tradition*. New York: Oxford University Press, 1953.

Adams, Parveen. "Versions of the Body." *m/f: a feminist journal*, nos. 11–12 (1986), 27–34.

Agacinski, Sylviane. *Aparté: Conceptions and Deaths of Søren Kierkegaard*. Trans. Kevin Newmark. Tallahassee: Florida State University Press, 1988.

Ainley, Alison. "'Ideal Selfishness': Nietzsche's Metaphor of Maternity." *Exceedingly Nietzsche*, ed. David Farrell Krell and David Wood, 116–30. New York: Routledge, 1988.

Allen, Jeffner. *Sinuosities: Lesbian Poetic Politics*. Bloomington: Indiana University Press, 1996.

Althusser, Louis. *Lenin and Philosophy, and Other Essays*. Trans. Ben Brewster. New York: Monthly Review Press, 1972.

Anderson, Mark, ed. *Reading Kafka: Prague, Politics, and the Fin de Siècle*. New York: Schocken Books, 1989.

Anderson, Perry. "From Progress to Catastrophe." *London Review of Books*, 28 July 2011, 24–28.

Arendell, Terry. "Conceiving and Investigating Motherhood: The Decade's Scholarship." *Journal of Marriage and Family* 62, no. 4 (2000), 1192–207.

Badiou, Alain. "Philosophy as Biography." *The Symptom*, no. 9, 13 November 2007, http://www.lacan.com/symptom.

Bailyn, Bernard, and Philip D. Morgan, eds. *Strangers within the Realm: Cultural Margins of the First British Empire*. Chapel Hill: University of North Carolina Press, 1991.

Balbus, Isaac D. *Mourning and Modernity: Essays in the Psychoanalysis of Contemporary Society*. New York: Other Press, 2005.

Balibar, Étienne. *The Philosophy of Marx*. Trans. Chris Turner. London: Verso, 1995.

Balzac, Honoré de. *Cousin Bette*. Trans. Sylvia Raphael. Oxford: Oxford University Press, 1992.

Baraitser, Lisa. *Maternal Encounters: The Ethics of Interruption*. London: Routledge, 2009.

Barande, Ilse. *Le maternel singulier: Freud et Léonard de Vinci*. Paris: Aubier Montaigne, 1977.

Barnard, Suzanne, and Bruce Fink, eds. *Reading Seminar XX: Lacan's Major Work on Love, Knowledge, and Feminine Sexuality.* Albany: State University of New York Press, 2002.

Barnes, J. A. "Genetrix : Genitor :: Nature : Culture?" *The Character of Kinship,* ed. Jack Goody, 61–74. Cambridge: Cambridge University Press, 1974.

Barthes, Roland. *Camera Lucida: Reflections on Photography.* Trans. Richard Howard. New York: Hill and Wang, 1981.

———. *Image, Music, Text.* Trans. Stephen Heath. New York: Hill and Wang, 1978.

———. *Mourning Diary.* Trans. Richard Howard. New York: Hill and Wang, 2010.

———. *S/Z.* Trans. Richard Miller. New York: Hill and Wang, 1974.

———. *S-Z.* Paris: Éditions du Seuil, 1970.

Bartkowski, Frances. *Kissing Cousins: A New Kinship Bestiary.* New York: Columbia University Press, 2008.

Barzilai, Shuli. *Lacan and the Matter of Origins.* Stanford: Stanford University Press, 1999.

Bass, Alan. "On the History of a Mistranslation and the Psychoanalytic Movement." *Difference in Translation,* ed. Joseph F. Graham, 102–41. Ithaca: Cornell University Press, 1985.

Bassin, Donna, Margaret Honey, and Meryle Mahrer Kaplan, eds. *Representations of Motherhood.* New Haven: Yale University Press, 1994.

Baxandall, Lee, and Stefan Morawski, eds. *Marx and Engels on Literature and Art: A Selection of Writings.* St. Louis: Telos Press, 1973.

Beauvoir, Simone de. *The Second Sex.* Trans. H. M. Parshley. 1st edn. New York: Alfred A. Knopf, 1953.

Beizer, Janet L. *Family Plots: Balzac's Narrative Generations.* New Haven: Yale University Press, 1986.

Benjamin, Walter. *Illuminations.* Ed. Hannah Arendt. Trans. Harry Zohn. New York: Schocken Books, 1969.

Bennington, Geoffrey, and Jacques Derrida. *Jacques Derrida.* Trans. Bennington. Chicago: University of Chicago Press, 1993.

Bentley, Nancy. "The Fourth Dimension: Kinlessness and African American Narrative." *Critical Inquiry* 35, no. 2 (2009), 270–92.

Bersani, Leo. *The Freudian Body: Psychoanalysis and Art.* New York: Columbia University Press, 1986.

Bettelheim, Bruno. *Freud and Man's Soul.* New York: Alfred A. Knopf, 1983.

Bevis, Kathryn. "'Better Than Metaphors'? Dwelling and the Maternal Body in Emmanuel Levinas." *Literature and Theology* 21, no. 3 (2007), 317–29.

Bidet, Jacques, and Stathis Kouvelakis, eds. *Critical Companion to Contemporary Marxism*. Leiden: Brill, 2008.

Birnbaum, Solomon A. *Yiddish: A Survey and a Grammar*. Toronto: University of Toronto Press, 1979.

Bliss, Douglas Percy. *Sir Walter Scott and the Visual Arts*. Glasgow: Foulis Archive Press, 1971.

Bloom, Harold, Paul de Man, Jacques Derrida, Geoffrey H. Hartman, and J. Hillis Miller. *Deconstruction and Criticism*. New York: Continuum, 1979.

Bogdan, Jolan. "The Uncertainty of the Mother: Derrida and the Deconstruction of Genealogy." Unpublished manuscript, 2010.

Boheemen, Christine van. *The Novel as Family Romance: Language, Gender, and Authority from Fielding to Joyce*. Ithaca: Cornell University Press, 1987.

Borch-Jacobsen, Mikkel. *Lacan: The Absolute Master*. Stanford: Stanford University Press, 1991.

Bourguignon, André, Pierre Cotet, Jean Laplanche, and François Robert. *Traduire Freud*. Paris: Presses Universitaires de France, 1989.

Bowlby, Rachel. "Generations." *Textual Practice* 21, no. 1 (2007), 1–16.

Boynton, Robert S. "The Other Freud (the Wild One): New Translation Aims to Free the Master from His Disciples' Obsessions." *New York Times*, 10 June 2000.

Bronfen, Elisabeth. *Over Her Dead Body: Death, Femininity, and the Aesthetic*. New York: Routledge, 1992.

Brooks, Peter. *Reading for the Plot: Design and Intention in Narrative*. New York: Alfred A. Knopf, 1984.

Brophy, James M. "Recent Publications of the Marx-Engels *Gesamtausgabe* (MEGA)." *Central European History* 40, no. 3 (2007), 523–37.

Brown, Homer Obed. *Institutions of the English Novel from Defoe to Scott*. Philadelphia: University of Pennsylvania Press, 1997.

Butler, Judith. "Betrayal's Felicity." *Diacritics* 34, no. 1 (2004), 82–87.

———. *Gender Trouble: Feminism and the Subversion of Identity*. 10th anniversary edn. New York: Routledge, 1999.

———. *Giving an Account of Oneself*. New York: Fordham University Press, 2005.

Caputo, John D. "The Absence of Monica: Heidegger, Derrida, and Augustine's Confessions." *Feminist Interpretations of Martin Heidegger*, ed. Nancy J. Holland and Patricia J. Huntington, 149–64. University Park: Pennsylvania State University Press, 2001.

Carsten, Janet. *After Kinship*. Cambridge: Cambridge University Press, 2004.

Caruth, Cathy. *Unclaimed Experience: Trauma, Narrative, and History*. Baltimore: Johns Hopkins University Press, 1996.

Cavarero, Adriana. "Birth, Love, Politics." Trans. Isabella Bertoletti and Miguel Vatter. *Radical Philosophy*, no. 86 (1997), 19–23.

———. *In Spite of Plato: A Feminist Rewriting of Ancient Philosophy*. Trans. Serena Anderlini-D'Onofrio and Aine O'Healy. New York: Routledge, 1995.

Chakravorty, Swapan, Suzana Milevska, and Tani E. Barlow. *Conversations with Gayatri Chakravorty Spivak*. London: Seagull Books, 2006.

Chandler, James K. *England in 1819: The Politics of Literary Culture and the Case of Romantic Historicism*. Chicago: University of Chicago Press, 1998.

Chanter, Tina. "Playing with Fire: Kofman and Freud on Being Feminine, Jewish, and Homosexual." *Sarah Kofman's Corpus*, ed. Tina Chanter and Pleshette DeArmitt, 91–121. Albany: State University of New York Press, 2008.

Chanter, Tina, ed. *Feminist Interpretations of Emmanuel Levinas*. University Park: Pennsylvania State University Press, 2001.

Chanter, Tina, and Pleshette DeArmitt, eds. *Sarah Kofman's Corpus*. Albany: State University of New York Press, 2008.

Chodorow, Nancy. *The Reproduction of Mothering: Psychoanalysis and the Sociology of Gender*. Berkeley: University of California Press, 1978.

Cixous, Hélène. *Stigmata: Escaping Texts*. Trans. Keith Cohen, Catherine A. F. MacGillivray, and Eric Prenowitz. London: Routledge, 1998.

Clément, Catherine. *Martin and Hannah: A Novel*. Trans. Julia Shirek Smith. Amherst, N.Y.: Prometheus Books, 2001.

Condorcet, Jean-Antoine-Nicolas de Caritat. *Condorcet: Selected Writings*. Ed. Keith Michael Baker. Indianapolis: Bobbs-Merrill, 1976.

Congdon, Lee. *The Young Lukács*. Chapel Hill: University of North Carolina Press, 1983.

Cottom, Daniel. *The Civilized Imagination: A Study of Ann Radcliffe, Jane Austen, and Sir Walter Scott*. Cambridge: Cambridge University Press, 1985.

Critchley, Simon. *Continental Philosophy: A Very Short Introduction*. Oxford: Oxford University Press, 2001.

Culley, Lorraine, Nicky Hudson, and Floor Van Rooij, eds. *Marginalized Reproduction: Ethnicity, Infertility, and Reproductive Technologies*. London: Earthscan, 2009.

Currah, Paisley. "Expecting Bodies: The Pregnant Man and Transgender Exclusion from the Employment Non-discrimination Act." *Women's Studies Quarterly* 36, nos. 3–4 (2008), 330–36.

Davey, Moyra, ed. *Mother Reader: Essential Writings on Motherhood*. New York: Seven Stories Press, 2001.

David-Ménard, Monique. *Hysteria from Freud to Lacan: Body and Language in Psychoanalysis*. Trans. Catherine Porter. Ithaca: Cornell University Press, 1989.

———. "Lacanians Against Lacan." Trans. Brian Massumi. *Social Text*, no. 6 (1982), 86–111.

De Lauretis, Teresa. *The Practice of Love: Lesbian Sexuality and Perverse Desire*. Bloomington: Indiana University Press, 1994.

Deleuze, Gilles. *Essays Critical and Clinical*. Trans. Daniel W. Smith and Michael A. Greco. Minneapolis: University of Minnesota Press, 1997.

Delphy, Christine. *Close to Home: A Materialist Analysis of Women's Oppression*. Trans. Diana Leonard. Amherst: University of Massachusetts Press, 1984.

De Man, Paul. *Aesthetic Ideology*. Ed. Andrzej Warminski. Minneapolis: University of Minnesota Press, 1996.

———. *The Resistance to Theory*. Minneapolis: University of Minnesota Press, 1986.

Demetz, Peter. *Marx, Engels, and the Poets: Origins of Marxist Literary Criticism*. Trans. Jeffrey L. Sammons. Chicago: University of Chicago Press, 1967.

Derrida, Jacques. *The Animal That Therefore I Am*. Ed. Marie-Louise Mallet. Trans. David Wills. New York: Fordham University Press, 2008.

———. *Archive Fever: A Freudian Impression*. Trans. Eric Prenowitz. Chicago: University of Chicago Press, 1996.

———. *Deconstruction in a Nutshell: A Conversation with Jacques Derrida*. Ed. John D. Caputo. New York: Fordham University Press, 1997.

———. *Dissemination*. Trans. Barbara Johnson. Chicago: University of Chicago Press, 1981.

———. *The Ear of the Other: Otobiography, Transference, Translation: Texts and Discussions with Jacques Derrida*. Ed. Christie V. McDonald. Trans. Avital Ronell and Peggy Kamuf. Lincoln: University of Nebraska Press, 1988.

———. "Geopsychoanalysis: '. . . and the Rest of the World.'" Trans. Donald Nicholson-Smith. *The Psychoanalysis of Race*, ed. Christopher Lane, 65–90. New York: Columbia University Press, 1998.

———. *Given Time: 1; Counterfeit Money*. Trans. Peggy Kamuf. Chicago: University of Chicago Press, 1992.

———. *Glas*. Trans. John P. Leavey Jr. and Richard Rand. Lincoln: University of Nebraska Press, 1986.

———. *H. C. for Life, That Is to Say—*. Trans. Laurent Milesi and Stefan Herbrechter. Stanford: Stanford University Press, 2006.

———. *Ki az anya? Szuletes, termeszet, nemzet*. Trans. Janos Boros, Gabor Csordas, and Jolan Orban. Budapest: Jelenkor, 1997.

———. *Monolingualism of the Other; or, The Prosthesis of Origin*. Trans. Patrick Mensah. Stanford: Stanford University Press, 1998.

———. *Of Grammatology*. Trans. Gayatri Chakravorty Spivak. Baltimore: Johns Hopkins University Press, 1976.

———. *Points . . . : Interviews, 1974–1994*. Ed. Elisabeth Weber. Trans. Peggy Kamuf and others. Stanford: Stanford University Press, 1995.

———. *Politics of Friendship*. Trans. George Collins. London: Verso, 1997.

———. *Positions*. Trans. Alan Bass. Chicago: University of Chicago Press, 1981.

———. *The Post Card: From Socrates to Freud and Beyond*. Trans. Alan Bass. Chicago: University of Chicago Press, 1987.

———. *Psyche: Inventions of the Other*. Vol. 1. Ed. Peggy Kamuf and Elizabeth Rottenberg. Stanford: Stanford University Press, 2007.

———. *Psyche: Inventions of the Other*. Vol. 2. Ed. Peggy Kamuf and Elizabeth Rottenberg. Stanford: Stanford University Press, 2008.

———. *Resistances of Psychoanalysis*. Trans. Peggy Kamuf, Pascale-Anne Brault, and Michael Naas. Stanford: Stanford University Press, 1998.

———. *Specters of Marx: The State of the Debt, the Work of Mourning, and the New International*. Trans. Peggy Kamuf. New York: Routledge, 1994.

———. "La veilleuse." *James Joyce ou l'écriture matricide*, by Jacques Trilling, 7–32. Belfort: Circé, 2001.

———. "What Is a 'Relevant' Translation?" Trans. Lawrence Venuti. *Critical Inquiry* 27, no. 2 (2001), 174–200.

———. *Who's Afraid of Philosophy? Right to Philosophy 1*. Trans. Jan Plug. Stanford: Stanford University Press, 2002.

———. *The Work of Mourning*. Trans. Pascale-Anne Brault and Michael Naas. Chicago: University of Chicago Press, 2001.

———. *Writing and Difference*. Trans. Alan Bass. Chicago: University of Chicago Press, 1978.

Derrida, Jacques, and Elisabeth Roudinesco. *For What Tomorrow: A Dialogue*. Trans. Jeff Fort. Stanford: Stanford University Press, 2004.

Deutscher, Isaac. *Marxism in Our Time*. Ed. Tamara Deutscher. Berkeley: Ramparts Press, 1971.

Deutscher, Penelope. "Autobiobodies: Nietzsche and the Life-Blood of the Philosopher." *Parallax* 11, no. 3 (2005), 28–39.

———. "The Inversion of Exceptionality: Foucault, Agamben, and 'Reproductive Rights.'" *South Atlantic Quarterly* 107, no. 1 (2008), 55–70.

———. *A Politics of Impossible Difference: The Later Work of Luce Irigaray*. Ithaca: Cornell University Press, 2002.

———. *Yielding Gender: Feminism, Deconstruction, and the History of Philosophy*. London: Routledge, 1997.

Dever, Carolyn. *Death and the Mother from Dickens to Freud: Victorian Fiction and the Anxiety of Origins*. Cambridge: Cambridge University Press, 1998.

———. *Skeptical Feminism: Activist Theory, Activist Practice*. Minneapolis: University of Minnesota Press, 2004.

Dick, Kirby, and Amy Ziering Kofman. *Derrida*. Jane Doe Films, 2003.

Dinnerstein, Dorothy. *The Mermaid and the Minotaur: Sexual Arrangements and Human Malaise*. New York: Harper and Row, 1976.

Diprose, Rosalyn. *The Bodies of Women: Ethics, Embodiment, and Sexual Difference*. London: Routledge, 1994.

Diprose, Rosalyn, and Robyn Ferrell, eds. *Cartographies: Poststructuralism and the Mapping of the Body*. Sydney: Allen and Unwin, 1991.

Doane, Janice L., and Devon L. Hodges. *From Klein to Kristeva: Psychoanalytic Feminism and the Search for the "Good Enough" Mother*. Ann Arbor: University of Michigan Press, 1992.

Doolittle, Hilda (H. D.). *Tribute to Freud*. 2nd edn. New York: New Directions, 2009.

Douglas, Susan J., and Meredith W. Michaels. *The Mommy Myth: The Idealization of Motherhood and How It Has Undermined Women*. New York: Free Press, 2004.

Draper, Hal. *The Marx-Engels Register: A Complete Bibliography of Marx and Engels' Individual Writings*. New York: Schocken Books, 1985.

Dryden, Edgar A. *The Form of American Romance*. Baltimore: Johns Hopkins University Press, 1988.

Elam, Diane. *Romancing the Postmodern*. London: Routledge, 1992.

Elster, Jon. *An Introduction to Karl Marx*. Cambridge: Cambridge University Press, 1986.

Eng, David L. *The Feeling of Kinship: Queer Liberalism and the Racialization of Intimacy*. Durham: Duke University Press, 2010.

Felman, Shoshana, ed. *Literature and Psychoanalysis: The Question of Reading, Otherwise*. Baltimore: Johns Hopkins University Press, 1982.

Ferguson, Margaret W. *Dido's Daughters: Literacy, Gender, and Empire in Early Modern England and France*. Chicago: University of Chicago Press, 2003.

Ferrell, Robyn. *Copula: Sexual Technologies, Reproductive Powers*. Albany: State University of New York Press, 2006.

Ferris, Ina. *The Achievement of Literary Authority: Gender, History, and the Waverley Novels.* Ithaca: Cornell University Press, 1991.

Firestone, Shulamith. *The Dialectic of Sex: The Case for Feminist Revolution.* New York: Bantam, 1971.

Flaubert, Gustave. *Bouvard and Pécuchet.* Trans. A. J. Krailsheimer. Harmondsworth: Penguin, 1976.

Fleishman, Avrom. *The English Historical Novel: Walter Scott to Virginia Woolf.* Baltimore: Johns Hopkins Press, 1971.

Fletcher, John, and Martin Stanton, eds. *Jean Laplanche: Seduction, Translation, Drives: A Dossier.* Trans. Stanton. London: Psychoanalytic Forum, Institute of Contemporary Arts, 1992.

Foucault, Michel. *Essential Works of Foucault, 1954–1984,* vol. 2, *Aesthetics, Method, and Epistemology.* Ed. James D. Faubion. Trans. Robert Hurley and others. New York: New Press, 1998.

———. *The Order of Things: An Archaeology of the Human Sciences.* Trans. Alan Sheridan. New York: Vintage, 1973.

———. *Politics, Philosophy, Culture: Interviews and Other Writings, 1977–1984.* Ed. Lawrence D. Kritzman. Trans. Alan Sheridan and others. New York: Routledge, 1988.

France, Peter, ed. *The Oxford Guide to Literature in English Translation.* Oxford: Oxford University Press, 2000.

Frankel, Jonathan. *Prophecy and Politics: Socialism, Nationalism, and the Russian Jews, 1862–1917.* Cambridge: Cambridge University Press, 1981.

Frankland, Graham. *Freud's Literary Culture.* Cambridge: Cambridge University Press, 2000.

Franklin, Sarah. *Embodied Progress: A Cultural Account of Assisted Conception.* London: Routledge, 1997.

Franklin, Sarah, and Susan McKinnon, eds. *Relative Values: Reconfiguring Kinship Studies.* Durham: Duke University Press, 2001.

Franklin, Sarah, and Helena Ragoné, eds. *Reproducing Reproduction: Kinship, Power, and Technological Innovation.* Philadelphia: University of Pennsylvania Press, 1998.

Fraser, Mariam, and Monica Greco, eds. *The Body: A Reader.* London: Routledge, 2005.

Freud, Sigmund. *The Complete Letters of Sigmund Freud to Wilhelm Fliess, 1877–1904.* Ed. and trans. J. Moussaieff Masson. Cambridge: Belknap, 1985.

———. *General Psychological Theory: Papers on Metapsychology.* Ed. Philip Rieff. Trans. Cecil M. Baines, Joan Riviere, M. N. Searl, and James Strachey. New York: Touchstone Books, 1997.

———. *The Interpretation of Dreams*. Trans. James Strachey. 3rd edn. New York: Avon, 1965.

———. *Introductory Lectures on Psychoanalysis*. Ed. and trans. James Strachey. New York: W. W. Norton, 1989.

———. *The Joke and Its Relation to the Unconscious*. Trans. Joyce Crick. New York: Penguin, 2003.

———. *Jokes and Their Relation to the Unconscious*. Ed. and trans. James Strachey. New York: W. W. Norton, 1963.

———. *Leonardo da Vinci and a Memory of His Childhood*. Trans. James Strachey. New York: W. W. Norton, 1964.

———. "Letter to Carl Müller-Braunschweig (1935)." *Psychiatry*, vol. 34 (1971), 328–29.

———. *On Murder, Mourning, and Melancholia*. Trans. Saun Whiteside. London: Penguin, 2005.

———. *The Origins of Psycho-analysis: Letters to Wilhelm Fliess, Drafts, and Notes, 1887–1902*. Ed. Marie Bonaparte, Anna Freud, and Ernst Kris. Trans. Eric Mosbacher and James Strachey. New York: Basic Books, 1954.

———. *Outline of Psychoanalysis*. Trans. Helena Ragg-Kirkby. London: Penguin, 2003.

———. *The Psychology of Love*. Trans. Shaun Whiteside. New York: Penguin, 2007.

———. *The Question of Lay Analysis: Conversations with an Impartial Person*. Ed. and trans. James Strachey. New York: W. W. Norton, 1969.

———. *The Sexual Enlightenment of Children*. Ed. Philip Rieff. Trans. Douglas Bryan, E. B. M. Herford, E. Colburn Mayne, and James Strachey, New York: Collier Books, 1963.

———. *Sexuality and the Psychology of Love*. Ed. Philip Rieff. Trans. J. Bernays, R. Gabler, E. B. M. Herford, Barbara Low, E. Colburn Mayne, Joan Riviere, Alix Strachey, and James Strachey. New York: Collier Books, 1963.

———. *The Standard Edition of the Complete Psychological Works of Sigmund Freud*. 24 vols. Ed. and trans. James Strachey. London: Hogarth Press, 1953.

———. *Therapy and Technique*. Ed. Philip Rieff. Trans. J. Bernays, Edward Glover, Joan Riviere, and James Strachey. New York: Collier Books, 1963.

———. *Three Essays on the Theory of Sexuality*. Ed. and trans. James Strachey. New York: Basic Books, 1962.

———. *The Uncanny*. Trans. Hugh Haughton. New York: Penguin, 2003.

————. *The Unconscious*. Trans. Graham Frankland. London: Penguin, 2005.

————. *Wild Analysis*. Trans. Alan Bance. London: Penguin, 2002.

Freud, Sigmund, and Josef Breuer. *Studies in Hysteria*. Trans. Nicola Luckhurst. London: Penguin, 2004.

Friedman, Susan Stanford. "Creativity and the Childbirth Metaphor: Gender Difference in Literary Discourse." *Feminist Studies* 13, no. 1 (1987), 49–82.

Gallop, Jane. "Penis/Phallus: Same Difference." *Men by Women*, ed. Janet M. Todd, 243–51. New York: Holmes and Meier, 1981.

————. "Quand Nos Lèvres S'Écrivent: Irigaray's Body Politic." *Romanic Review* 74, no. 1 (1983), 77–83.

————. *Thinking through the Body*. New York: Columbia University Press, 1988.

Garner, Shirley Nelson, Claire Kahane, and Madelon Sprengnether, eds. *The (M)other Tongue: Essays in Feminist Psychoanalytic Interpretation*. Ithaca: Cornell University Press, 1985.

Garside, P. D. "*Waverley*'s Pictures of the Past." *ELH: English Literary History* 44, no. 4 (1977), 659–82.

Gatens, Moira. *Imaginary Bodies: Ethics, Power, and Corporeality*. London: Routledge, 1996.

Genette, Gérard. *Paratexts: Thresholds of Interpretation*. Trans. Jane E. Lewin. Cambridge: Cambridge University Press, 1997.

Gilman, Sander L. *Jewish Self-Hatred: Anti-Semitism and the Hidden Language of the Jews*. Baltimore: Johns Hopkins University Press, 1986.

Ginsburg, Faye D., and Rayna Rapp, eds. *Conceiving the New World Order: The Global Politics of Reproduction*. Berkeley: University of California Press, 1995.

Gitelman, Zvi, ed. *The Emergence of Modern Jewish Politics: Bundism and Zionism in Eastern Europe*. Pittsburgh: University of Pittsburgh Press, 2003.

Goody, Jack, ed. *The Character of Kinship*. Cambridge: Cambridge University Press, 1974.

Gourgouris, Stathis, ed. *Freud and Fundamentalism: The Psychical Politics of Knowledge*. New York: Fordham University Press, 2010.

Graham, Joseph F., ed. *Difference in Translation*. Ithaca: Cornell University Press, 1985.

Greco, Monica. *Illness as a Work of Thought: A Foucauldian Perspective on Psychosomatics*. London: Routledge, 1998.

Greenblatt, Stephen Jay, and Giles B. Gunn, eds. *Redrawing the Boundaries:*

The Transformation of English and American Literary Studies. New York: Modern Language Association of America, 1992.

Griffin, Susan. "Feminism and Motherhood." *Mother Reader: Essential Writings on Motherhood*, ed. Moyra Davey, 33–45. New York: Seven Stories Press, 2001.

Griffiths, A. Phillips, ed. *Contemporary French Philosophy.* Cambridge: Cambridge University Press, 1987.

Grossman, Jeffrey A. *The Discourse on Yiddish in Germany from the Enlightenment to the Second Empire.* Rochester, N.Y.: Camden House, 2000.

Grosz, E. A. *Volatile Bodies: Toward a Corporeal Feminism.* Bloomington: Indiana University Press, 1994.

Grubrich-Simitis, Ilse. *Back to Freud's Texts: Making Silent Documents Speak.* Trans. Philip Slotkin. New Haven: Yale University Press, 1996.

Guardiola-Rivera, Oscar. "Interview with Gayatri Spivak." *Naked Punch*, 29 August 2009, http://www.nakedpunch.com.

Guenther, Lisa. "Being-from-Others: Reading Heidegger after Cavarero." *Hypatia* 23, no. 1 (2008), 99–118.

———. *The Gift of the Other: Levinas and the Politics of Reproduction.* Albany: State University of New York Press, 2006.

———. " 'Like a Maternal Body': Emmanuel Levinas and the Motherhood of Moses." *Hypatia* 21, no. 1 (2006), 119–36.

Harshav, Benjamin. *Language in Time of Revolution.* Berkeley: University of California Press, 1993.

———. *The Meaning of Yiddish.* Berkeley: University of California Press, 1990.

Hartman, Geoffrey. "Freud for Everyman (and Everywoman)." *Raritan* 25, no. 1 (2005), 150–64.

Hartmann, Heidi. "The Unhappy Marriage of Marxism and Feminism: Towards a More Progressive Union." *Women and Revolution: A Discussion of the Unhappy Marriage of Marxism and Feminism*, ed. Lydia Sargent, 1–42. Boston: South End Press, 1981.

Hayden, John O., ed. *Scott: The Critical Heritage.* New York: Barnes and Noble, 1970.

Hayot, Eric. " 'The Slightness of My Endeavor': An Interview with Gayatri Chakravorty Spivak." *Comparative Literature* 57, no. 3 (2005), 256–72.

Hegel, Georg Wilhelm Friedrich. *Aesthetics: Lectures on Fine Art.* Trans. T. M. Knox. 2 vols. Oxford: Clarendon, 1974.

———. *Hegel's Introduction to Aesthetics: Being the Introduction to the Berlin Aesthetics Lectures of the 1820s.* Trans. T. M. Knox. Oxford: Clarendon, 1979.

————. *Lectures on the Philosophy of World History: Introduction, Reason in History*. Trans. H. B. Nisbet. Cambridge: Cambridge University Press, 1975.

————. *The Logic of Hegel: Translated from the Encyclopaedia of the Philosophical Sciences*. Trans. William Wallace. 2nd ed. Oxford: Clarendon, 1892.

————. *Phenomenology of Spirit*. Trans. A. V. Miller. Oxford: Clarendon, 1977.

Heidegger, Martin. *Gesamtausgabe*, vol. 13, *Veröffentlichte Schriften 1910–1976*, part 1, *Aus der Erfahrung des Denkens 1910–1976*. Ed. Hermann Heidegger. Frankfurt am Main: Vittorio Klostermann, 2002.

————. *Pathmarks*. Ed. William McNeill. Cambridge: Cambridge University Press, 1998.

————. *What Is Called Thinking?* Trans. J. Glenn Gray. New York: Harper and Row, 1968.

Heller-Roazen, Daniel. *Echolalias: On the Forgetting of Language*. New York: Zone, 2005.

Hirsch, Marianne. *The Mother/Daughter Plot: Narrative, Psychoanalysis, Feminism*. Bloomington: Indiana University Press, 1989.

Hirsch, Marianne, and Evelyn Fox Keller, eds. *Conflicts in Feminism*. New York: Routledge, 1990.

Hobsbawm, Eric J., ed. *Marxism in Marx's Day*. Bloomington: Indiana University Press, 1982.

Hobsbawm, Eric, and Terence Ranger, eds. *The Invention of Tradition*. Cambridge: Cambridge University Press, 1983.

Holland, Nancy J., and Patricia J. Huntington, eds. *Feminist Interpretations of Martin Heidegger*. University Park: Pennsylvania State University Press, 2001.

Hollway, Wendy. *The Capacity to Care: Gender and Ethical Subjectivity*. London: Routledge, 2006.

Howells, Christina, ed. *French Women Philosophers: A Contemporary Reader*. London: Routledge, 2004.

Huffer, Lynne. *Maternal Pasts, Feminist Futures: Nostalgia, Ethics, and the Question of Difference*. Stanford: Stanford University Press, 1998.

Inhorn, Marcia Claire, and Frank van Balen, eds. *Infertility around the Globe: New Thinking on Childlessness, Gender, and Reproductive Technologies*. Berkeley: University of California Press, 2002.

Irigaray, Luce. "And the One Doesn't Stir without the Other." Trans. Hélène Vivienne Wenzel. *Signs* 7, no. 1 (1981), 60–67.

————. *Sexes and Genealogies*. Trans. Gillian C. Gill. New York: Columbia University Press, 1993.

———. "Women-Mothers, the Silent Substratum of the Social Order." *The Irigaray Reader*, ed. Margaret Whitford, 47–53. Cambridge, Mass.: Basil Blackwell, 1991.

Iser, Wolfgang. *The Implied Reader: Patterns of Communication in Prose Fiction from Bunyan to Beckett*. Baltimore: Johns Hopkins University Press, 1974.

Jacobs, Amber. *On Matricide: Myth, Psychoanalysis, and the Law of the Mother*. New York: Columbia University Press, 2007.

Jacobs, Jack Lester, ed. *Jewish Politics in Eastern Europe: The Bund at One Hundred*. New York: New York University Press, 2001.

Jameson, Fredric. "Imaginary and Symbolic in Lacan." *Yale French Studies*, nos. 56–57 (1977), 338–95.

———. *The Political Unconscious: Narrative as a Socially Symbolic Act*. Ithaca: Cornell University Press, 1981.

———. *Postmodernism; or, The Cultural Logic of Late Capitalism*. Durham: Duke University Press, 1991.

Jeffares, A. Norman, ed. *Scott's Mind and Art*. New York: Barnes and Noble, 1969.

Johnson, Barbara. *Mother Tongues: Sexuality, Trials, Motherhood, Translation*. Cambridge: Harvard University Press, 2003.

Jones, Ernest. *The Life and Work of Sigmund Freud*. 3 vols. New York: Basic Books, 1953.

Jones, Jason B. "An Interview with Mark Solms." *Bookslut*, May 2007, http://www.bookslut.com.

Kamuf, Peggy. *Signature Pieces: On the Institution of Authorship*. Ithaca: Cornell University Press, 1988.

Kapp, Yvonne. *Eleanor Marx*. 2 vols. New York: Pantheon Books, 1977.

Kofman, Sarah. *Aberrations: Le devenir-femme d'Auguste Comte*. Paris: Aubier, 1978.

———. *The Childhood of Art: An Interpretation of Freud's Aesthetics*. Trans. Winifred Woodhull. New York: Columbia University Press, 1988.

———. *The Enigma of Woman: Woman in Freud's Writings*. Trans. Catherine Porter. Ithaca: Cornell University Press, 1985.

———. *Pourquoi rit-on? Freud et le mot d'esprit*. Paris: Éditions Galilée, 1986.

———. *Rue Ordener, Rue Labat*. Trans. Ann Smock. Lincoln: University of Nebraska Press, 1996.

Krell, David Farrell, and David Wood, eds. *Exceedingly Nietzsche*. New York: Routledge, 1988.

Kristeva, Julia. *Black Sun: Depression and Melancholia*. Trans. Leon S. Roudiez. New York: Columbia University Press, 1989.

———. *Desire in Language: A Semiotic Approach to Literature and Art.* Ed. Leon S. Roudiez. Trans. Thomas Gora, Alice Jardine, and Roudiez. New York: Columbia University Press, 1980.

———. *Hatred and Forgiveness.* Trans. Jeanine Herman. New York: Columbia University Press, 2010.

———. *Powers of Horror: An Essay on Abjection.* Trans. Leon S. Roudiez. New York: Columbia University Press, 1982.

———. "Stabat Mater." Trans. Leon S. Roudiez. *The Portable Kristeva,* ed. Kelly Oliver, 310–33. New York: Columbia University Press, 2002.

Kroeber, Karl. *Romantic Narrative Art.* Madison: University of Wisconsin Press, 1966.

Künzli, Arnold. *Karl Marx: Eine Psychographie.* Vienna: Europa Verlag, 1966.

Lacan, Jacques. *Autre écrits.* Paris: Éditions du Seuil, 2001.

———. *Écrits: The First Complete Edition in English.* Trans. Bruce Fink. New York: W. W. Norton, 2006.

———. *Encore [Le séminaire livre XX, 1972–1973].* Ed. Jacques-Alain Miller. Paris: Éditions du Seuil, 1975.

———. *The Four Fundamental Concepts of Psycho-analysis.* Trans. Alan Sheridan. New York: W. W. Norton, 1981.

———. *My Teaching.* Trans. David Macey. London: Verso, 2008.

———. *On Feminine Sexuality: The Limits of Love and Knowledge [Book XX, Encore, 1972–1973].* Trans. Bruce Fink. New York: W. W. Norton, 1998.

———. *The Other Side of Psychoanalysis,* 1969–70. Trans. Russell Grigg. The Seminar of Jacques Lacan, Book XVII. New York: W. W. Norton, 2006.

———. *Television.* Trans. Denis Hollier, Rosalind Krauss, and Annette Michelson. New York: W. W. Norton, 1990.

LaCapra, Dominick. *History and Criticism.* Ithaca: Cornell University Press, 1985.

Lacoue-Labarthe, Philippe. *The Subject of Philosophy.* Trans. Thomas Trezise. Minneapolis: University of Minnesota Press, 1993.

———. *Typography: Mimesis, Philosophy, Politics.* Ed. Christopher Fynsk. Cambridge: Harvard University Press, 1989.

Lacoue-Labarthe, Philippe, and Jean-Luc Nancy. *Retreating the Political.* Ed. Simon Sparks. Trans. Christopher Fynsk, Simon Sparks, Richard Stamp, and Céline Surprenant. London: Routledge, 1997.

———. *The Title of the Letter: A Reading of Lacan.* Trans. François Raffoul and David Pettigrew. Albany: State University of New York Press, 1992.

"La décision de traduire: L'exemple Freud." *L'écrit du temps,* no. 7 (1984).

Landry, Donna, and Gerald M. MacLean, eds. *The Spivak Reader: Selected Works of Gayatri Chakravorty Spivak.* New York: Routledge, 1996.

Lane, Christopher, ed. *The Psychoanalysis of Race.* New York: Columbia University Press, 1998.

Laplanche, Jean. *Essays on Otherness.* Ed. John Fletcher. New York: Routledge, 1999.

———. *Life and Death in Psychoanalysis.* Trans. Jeffrey Mehlman. Baltimore: Johns Hopkins University Press, 1976.

———. *New Foundations for Psychoanalysis.* Trans. David Macey. Oxford: Basil Blackwell, 1989.

Laplanche, Jean, and J.-B. Pontalis. *The Language of Psycho-analysis.* Trans. Donald Nicholson-Smith. New York: W. W. Norton, 1974.

Laqueur, Thomas W. "The Facts of Fatherhood." *Conflicts in Feminism,* ed. Marianne Hirsch and Evelyn Fox Keller, 205–21. New York: Routledge, 1990.

Lecercle, Jean-Jacques. "Marxism and Language." *Critical Companion to Contemporary Marxism,* ed. Jacques Bidet and Stathis Kouvelakis, 471–85. Leiden: Brill, 2008.

Leclaire, Serge. *Psychoanalyzing: On the Order of the Unconscious and the Practice of the Letter.* Trans. Peggy Kamuf. Stanford: Stanford University Press, 1998.

Le Dœuff, Michèle. "Ants and Women; or, Philosophy without Borders." *Contemporary French Philosophy,* ed. A. Phillips Griffiths, 41–54. Cambridge: Cambridge University Press, 1987.

———. *The Philosophical Imaginary.* Trans. Colin Gordon. London: Athlone Press, 1989.

Legman, Gershon. *Rationale of the Dirty Joke: An Analysis of Sexual Humor.* New York: Grove, 1968.

Lesnik-Oberstein, Karín. *On Having an Own Child: Reproductive Technologies and the Cultural Construction of Childhood.* London: Karnac Books, 2008.

Leupin, Alexandre. *Lacan Today: Psychoanalysis, Science, Religion.* New York: Other Press, 2004.

Levin, Nora. *While Messiah Tarried: Jewish Socialist Movements, 1871–1917.* New York: Schocken Books, 1977.

Levinas, Emmanuel. *Otherwise Than Being; or, Beyond Essence.* Trans. Alphonso Lingis. Dordrecht: Kluwer Academic, 1991.

Levine, George. *The Realistic Imagination: English Fiction from Frankenstein to Lady Chatterley.* Chicago: University of Chicago Press, 1981.

Lloyd, Genevieve. *The Man of Reason: "Male" and "Female" in Western Philosophy.* Minneapolis: University of Minnesota Press, 1984.

Lucey, Michael. *Gide's Bent: Sexuality, Politics, Writing*. New York: Oxford University Press, 1995.

Lukács, György. *The Historical Novel*. Trans. Hannah Mitchell and Stanley Mitchell. Lincoln: University of Nebraska Press, 1983.

———. *Record of a Life: An Autobiographical Sketch*. Ed. István Eörsi. Trans. Rodney Livingstone. London: Verso, 1983.

———. *The Theory of the Novel: A Historico-Philosophical Essay on the Forms of Great Epic Literature*. Trans. Anna Bostock. Cambridge: MIT Press, 1971.

MacCannell, Juliet Flower. *Figuring Lacan: Criticism and the Cultural Unconscious*. Lincoln: University of Nebraska Press, 1986.

Mahony, Patrick J. "Freud and Translation." *American Imago* 58, no. 4 (2001), 837–40.

———. "A Psychoanalytic Theory of Translation." *Translating Freud*, ed. Darius Gray Ornston, 24–47. New Haven: Yale University Press, 1992.

———. "Towards the Understanding of Translation in Psychoanalysis." *Meta* 27, no. 1 (1982), 63–71.

Makdisi, Saree. *Romantic Imperialism: Universal Empire and the Culture of Modernity*. Cambridge: Cambridge University Press, 1998.

Mamo, Laura. *Queering Reproduction: Achieving Pregnancy in the Age of Technoscience*. Durham: Duke University Press, 2007.

Manzoni, Alessandro. *On the Historical Novel*. Trans. Sandra Bermann. Lincoln: University of Nebraska Press, 1984.

Marder, Elissa. *The Mother in the Age of Mechanical Reproduction: Psychoanalysis, Photography, Deconstruction*. New York: Fordham University Press, 2011.

Marx, Karl. *Capital: A Critique of Political Economy*. Ed. Friedrich Engels. Trans. Samuel Moore and Edward Aveling. 3 vols. New York: International Publishers, 1967.

———. *The Eighteenth Brumaire of Louis Bonaparte*. Ed. C. P. Dutt. Trans. anonymous. New York: International Publishers, 1935.

———. *Grundrisse: Foundations of the Critique of Political Economy (Rough Draft)*. Ed. and trans. Martin Nicolaus. Harmondsworth: Penguin, 1973.

Marx, Karl, and Frederick Engels. *Collected Works*. 50 vols. New York: International Publishers, 1975.

McGill, Meredith L. *American Literature and the Culture of Reprinting, 1834–1853*. Philadelphia: University of Pennsylvania Press, 2003.

Medem, Vladimir. *Vladimir Medem, the Life and Soul of a Legendary Jewish Socialist*. Trans. Samuel A. Portnoy. New York: Ktav, 1979.

Meek, Ronald L. *Social Science and the Ignoble Savage*. Cambridge: Cambridge University Press, 1976.

Meisel, Perry, and Walter M Kendrick, eds. *Bloomsbury/Freud: The Letters of James and Alix Strachey, 1924–1925*. New York: Basic Books, 1985.

Meltzer, Françoise. *Salome and the Dance of Writing: Portraits of Mimesis in Literature*. Chicago: University of Chicago Press, 1987.

Melville, Stephen. "Psychoanalysis and the Place of 'Jouissance.'" *Critical Inquiry* 13, no. 2 (1987), 349–70.

Merck, Mandy, and Stella Sandford, eds. *Further Adventures of "The Dialectic of Sex": Critical Essays on Shulamith Firestone*. New York: Palgrave Macmillan, 2010.

Merkin, Daphne. "The Literary Freud." *New York Times Magazine*, 13 July 2003, 40–44.

Miller, Nancy K., ed. *The Poetics of Gender*. New York: Columbia University Press, 1986.

Minczeles, Henri. *Histoire générale du Bund: Un mouvement révolutionnaire juif*. Paris: Éditions Austral, 1995.

Mitchell, Juliet, and Jacqueline Rose, eds. *Feminine Sexuality: Jacques Lacan and the École Freudienne*. Trans. Jacqueline Rose. New York: W. W. Norton, 1982.

Mossman, Carol A. *Politics and Narratives of Birth: Gynocolonization from Rousseau to Zola*. Cambridge: Cambridge University Press, 1993.

Mufti, Aamir. *Enlightenment in the Colony: The Jewish Question and the Crisis of Postcolonial Culture*. Princeton: Princeton University Press, 2007.

Nairn, Tom. *The Break-Up of Britain: Crisis and Neonationalism*. 2nd exp. edn. London: NLB and Verso, 1981.

Nancy, Jean-Luc. *À plus d'un titre: Jacques Derrida*. Paris: Galilée, 2007.

———. *The Birth to Presence*. Trans. Brian Holmes. Stanford: Stanford University Press, 1993.

Nasio, Juan-David. *Five Lessons on the Psychoanalytic Theory of Jacques Lacan*. Trans. David Pettigrew and François Raffoul. Albany: State University of New York Press, 1998.

———. *Hysteria: The Splendid Child of Psychoanalysis*. Ed. Judith Feher Gurewich and Susan Fairfield. Trans. Fairfield. Northvale, N.J.: J. Aronson, 1997.

Neppi, Enzo. *Le babil et la caresse: Pensée du maternel chez Sartre*. New York: Peter Lang, 1995.

Nietzsche, Friedrich Wilhelm. *Ecce Homo: How to Become What You Are*. Trans. Duncan Large. Oxford: Oxford University Press, 2007.

———. *The Gay Science: With a Prelude in German Rhymes and an Appendix of Songs*. Ed. Bernard Arthur Owen Williams. Trans. Josefine Nauckhoff and Adrian Del Caro. Cambridge: Cambridge University Press, 2001.

O'Byrne, Anne E. *Natality and Finitude.* Bloomington: Indiana University Press, 2010.

O'Donohoe, Benedict. "Living with Mother: Sartre and the Problem of Maternity." *Sens Public*, 14 July 2006, http://www.sens-public.org.

Oliver, Kelly. "Julia Kristeva's Maternal Passions." *Journal of French and Francophone Philosophy* 18, no. 1 (2008–10), 1–8.

———. "Motherhood, Sexuality, and Pregnant Embodiment: Twenty-Five Years of Gestation." *Hypatia* 25, no. 4 (2010), 760–77.

———. *Womanizing Nietzsche: Philosophy's Relation to the "Feminine."* New York: Routledge, 1995.

Oliver, Kelly, ed. *The Portable Kristeva.* New York: Columbia University Press, 2002.

O'Reilly, Andrea, ed. *Maternal Thinking: Philosophy, Politics, Practice.* Toronto: Demeter Press, 2009.

Ornston, Darius Gray, ed. *Translating Freud.* New Haven: Yale University Press, 1992.

Parker, Andrew. "Holding the *Fort!* Instituting Gender, Engendering Institutions." *Genders*, no. 1 (1988), 75–82.

———. "Modeling Freud and Fundamentalism." *Freud and Fundamentalism: The Psychical Politics of Knowledge*, ed. Stathis Gourgouris, 17–25. New York: Fordham University Press, 2010.

———. "Mom." *Oxford Literary Review* 8, nos. 1–2 (1985), 96–104.

———. "Re-Marx: Prehistory." *Rethinking Marxism: A Journal of Economics, Culture, and Society* 9, no. 4 (1996), 1–15.

Parker, Andrew, Mary Russo, Doris Sommer, and Patricia Yaeger, eds. *Nationalisms and Sexualities.* New York: Routledge, 1992.

Parkin, Robert. *Kinship: An Introduction to Basic Concepts.* Oxford: Basil Blackwell, 1997.

Parkin, Robert, and Linda Stone, eds. *Kinship and Family: An Anthropological Reader.* Malden, Mass.: Basil Blackwell, 2004.

Patton, Paul. "Nietzsche and the Body of the Philosopher." *Cartographies: Poststructuralism and the Mapping of the Body*, ed. Rosalyn Diprose and Robyn Ferrell, 43–54. Sydney: Allen and Unwin, 1991.

Pender, E. E. "Spiritual Pregnancy in Plato's Symposium." *Classical Quarterly* 42, no. 1, n.s. (1992), 72–86.

Petzet, Heinrich Wiegand. *Encounters and Dialogues with Martin Heidegger, 1929–1976.* Trans. Parvis Emad and Kenneth Maly. Chicago: University of Chicago Press, 1993.

Phillips, Adam. "After Strachey." *London Review of Books*, 4 October 2007, 36–38.

———. "Making the Case: Freud's Literary Engagements." *Profession 2003*, ed. Modern Language Association of America, 10–20. New York: Modern Language Association of America, 2003.

———. *Promises, Promises: Essays on Literature and Psychoanalysis*. New York: Basic Books, 2001.

Phillips, Adam, ed. *The Penguin Freud Reader*. London: Penguin, 2006.

Phillips, James. *Heidegger's Volk: Between National Socialism and Poetry*. Stanford: Stanford University Press, 2005.

Plato. *The Symposium*. Ed. M. C. Howatson and Frisbee C. C. Sheffield. Trans. M. C. Howatson. Cambridge: Cambridge University Press, 2008.

Plaza, Monique. "The Mother/the Same: Hatred of the Mother in Psychoanalysis." *Feminist Issues* 2, no. 1 (1982), 75–99.

Pontalis, J.-B. "Notable Encounters." Trans. Christine Irizarry. *American Imago* 63, no. 2 (2006), 145–57.

———. *Windows = Fenêtres*. Trans. Anne Quinney. Lincoln: University of Nebraska Press, 2003.

Prawer, S. S. *Karl Marx and World Literature*. Oxford: Clarendon, 1976.

Price, Janet, and Margrit Shildrick, eds. *Feminist Theory and the Body: A Reader*. New York: Routledge, 1999.

Prokhoris, Sabine. *The Witch's Kitchen: Freud, Faust, and the Transference*. Trans. G. M. Goshgarian. Ithaca: Cornell University Press, 1995.

Proust, Marcel. *Swann's Way*. Trans. Lydia Davis. New York: Penguin, 2004.

Raddatz, Fritz Joachim. *Karl Marx: A Political Biography*. Trans. Richard Barry. Boston: Little, Brown, 1978.

Raffoul, François. *The Origins of Responsibility*. Bloomington: Indiana University Press, 2010.

Ragoné, Helena. *Surrogate Motherhood: Conception in the Heart*. Boulder: Westview, 1994.

Ragoné, Heléna, and France Winddance Twine, eds. *Ideologies and Technologies of Motherhood: Race, Class, Sexuality, Nationalism*. New York: Routledge, 2000.

Raleigh, John Henry. "'Waverley' as History; or, 'Tis One Hundred and Fifty-Six Years Since." *Novel: A Forum on Fiction* 4, no. 1 (1970), 14–29.

Rancière, Jacques. *The Names of History: On the Poetics of Knowledge*. Trans. Hassan Melehy. Minneapolis: University of Minnesota Press, 1994.

———. *The Philosopher and His Poor*. Ed. Andrew Parker. Trans. John Drury, Corinne Oster, and Andrew Parker. Durham: Duke University Press, 2004.

Rich, Adrienne. *Of Woman Born: Motherhood as Experience and Institution*. 10th anniversary edn. New York: W. W. Norton, 1986.

Richetti, John, ed. *The Columbia History of the British Novel*. New York: Columbia University Press, 1994.

Robert, Marthe. *Origins of the Novel*. Trans. Sacha Rabinovitch. Bloomington: Indiana University Press, 1980.

Rojahn, Jürgen. "The Emergence of a Theory: The Importance of Marx's
Notebooks Exemplified by Those from 1844." *Rethinking Marxism: A
Journal of Economics, Culture, and Society* 14, no. 4 (2002), 29–46.

———."Publishing Marx and Engels after 1989: The Fate of the MEGA."
Internationale Marx-Engels-Stiftung, 1998, http://www.iisg.nl/imes.

Ronell, Avital. *The Telephone Book: Technology, Schizophrenia, Electric
Speech*. Lincoln: University of Nebraska Press, 1989.

Rose, Jacqueline. *On Not Being Able to Sleep: Psychoanalysis and the Modern
World*. Princeton: Princeton University Press, 2003.

Rose, Mark. *Authors and Owners: The Invention of Copyright*. Cambridge:
Harvard University Press, 1993.

———. "Mothers and Authors: Johnson v. Calvert and the New Children
of Our Imagination." *The Visible Woman: Imaging Technologies, Gender,
and Science*, ed. Paula Treichler, Lisa Cartwright, and Constance Penley,
217–39. New York: New York University Press, 1998.

Roudinesco, Elisabeth. *Jacques Lacan*. Trans. Barbara Bray. New York:
Columbia University Press, 1997.

———. *Jacques Lacan and Co.: A History of Psychoanalysis in France, 1925–
1985*. Trans. Jeffrey Mehlman. Chicago: University of Chicago Press,
1990.

Ruddick, Sara. *Maternal Thinking: Toward a Politics of Peace, with a New
Preface*. 2nd edn. Boston: Beacon Press, 1995.

———. "Thinking Mothers/Conceiving Birth." *Representations of Motherhood*, ed. Donna Bassin, Margaret Honey, and Meryle Mahrer Kaplan,
29–45. New Haven: Yale University Press, 1994.

Russell, Bertrand. *Logic and Knowledge: Essays, 1901–1950*. Ed. Robert
Charles Marsh. London: Allen and Unwin, 1956.

Russo, Mary J. *The Female Grotesque: Risk, Excess, and Modernity*. New
York: Routledge, 1995.

Sacks, Elizabeth. *Shakespeare's Images of Pregnancy*. New York: St. Martin's
Press, 1980.

Safranski, Rüdiger. *Martin Heidegger: Between Good and Evil*. Trans. Ewald
Osers. Cambridge: Harvard University Press, 1998.

Saint-Amour, Paul K. *The Copywrights: Intellectual Property and the Literary
Imagination*. Ithaca: Cornell University Press, 2003.

Sallis, John. *Echoes: After Heidegger*. Bloomington: Indiana University
Press, 1990.

———. *On Translation*. Bloomington: Indiana University Press, 2002.

Sanders, Mark. *Gayatri Chakravorty Spivak: Live Theory*. London: Continuum, 2006.

Sandford, Stella. "Masculine Mothers? Maternity in Levinas and Plato." *Feminist Interpretations of Emmanuel Levinas*, ed. Tina Chanter, 180–202. University Park: Pennsylvania State University Press, 2001.

———. *Plato and Sex*. Cambridge: Polity Press, 2010.

Sargent, Lydia, ed. *Women and Revolution: A Discussion of the Unhappy Marriage of Marxism and Feminism*. Boston: South End Press, 1981.

Sartre, Jean-Paul. *Being and Nothingness: An Essay on Phenomenological Ontology*. Trans. Hazel E. Barnes. New York: Philosophical Library, 1956.

Saunders, David. *Authorship and Copyright*. London: Routledge, 1992.

Sayers, Janet. *Mothers of Psychoanalysis: Helene Deutsch, Karen Horney, Anna Freud, Melanie Klein*. New York: W. W. Norton, 1991.

Schor, Naomi. "French Feminism Is a Universalism." *differences: A Journal of Feminist Cultural Studies* 7, no. 1 (1995), 15–47.

———. *Reading in Detail: Aesthetics and the Feminine*. New York: Methuen, 1987.

Schotten, C. Heike. *Nietzsche's Revolution: Décadence, Politics, and Sexuality*. New York: Palgrave Macmillan, 2009.

Schwartz, Adria E. *Sexual Subjects: Lesbians, Gender, and Psychoanalysis*. New York: Routledge, 1998.

Scott, Joan Wallach. "French Universalism in the Nineties." *differences: A Journal of Feminist Cultural Studies* 15, no. 2 (2004), 32–53.

———. "Universalism and the History of Feminism." *differences: A Journal of Feminist Cultural Studies* 7, no. 1 (1995), 1–14.

Scott, Walter. *The Miscellaneous Prose Works of Sir Walter Scott, Bart*. 6 vols. Boston: Wells and Lilly, 1829.

———. *The Prefaces to the Waverley Novels*. Ed. Mark A. Weinstein. Lincoln: University of Nebraska Press, 1978.

———. *Sir Walter Scott on Novelists and Fiction*. Ed. Ioan Williams. London: Routledge and Kegan Paul, 1968.

———. *Waverley*. Ed. Andrew Hook. Harmondsworth: Penguin, 1972.

———. *Waverley; or, 'Tis Sixty Years Since*. Ed. Claire Lamont. Oxford: Clarendon, 1981.

Sedgwick, Eve Kosofsky. *Between Men: English Literature and Male Homosocial Desire*. New York: Columbia University Press, 1985.

———. "Gender Criticism." *Redrawing the Boundaries: The Transformation of English and American Literary Studies*, ed. Stephen Jay Greenblatt and Giles B. Gunn, 271–302. New York: Modern Language Association of America, 1992.

Seidman, Naomi. *A Marriage Made in Heaven: The Sexual Politics of Hebrew and Yiddish*. Berkeley: University of California Press, 1997.

Seigel, Jerrold E. *Marx's Fate: The Shape of a Life*. Princeton: Princeton University Press, 1978.

Shaw, Harry E. *The Forms of Historical Fiction: Sir Walter Scott and His Successors*. Ithaca: Cornell University Press, 1983.

Sheffield, Frisbee C. C. "Psychic Pregnancy and Platonic Epistemology." *Oxford Studies in Ancient Philosophy*, vol. 20 (2001), 1–33.

Shepherdson, Charles. "The Epoch of the Body: Need and Demand in Kojève and Lacan." *Perspectives on Embodiment*, ed. Gail Weiss and Honi Fern Haber, 183–212. New York: Routledge, 1988.

——. *Lacan and the Limits of Language*. New York: Fordham University Press, 2008.

Shetty, Sandhya. "(Dis)figuring the Nation: Mother, Metaphor, Metonymy." *differences: A Journal of Feminist Cultural Studies* 7, no. 3 (1995), 50–79.

Sidney, Sir Philip. *The Major Works*. Ed. Katherine Duncan-Jones. Oxford: Oxford University Press, 2002.

Snitow, Ann. "Feminism and Motherhood: An American Reading." *Feminist Review*, no. 40 (1992), 32–51.

Soler, Colette. *What Lacan Said About Women: A Psychoanalytic Study*. Trans. John Holland. New York: Other Press, 2006.

Solms, Mark. "Controversies in Freud Translation." *Psychoanalysis and History* 1, no. 1 (1999), 28–43.

Spillers, Hortense J. *Black, White, and in Color: Essays on American Literature and Culture*. Chicago: University of Chicago Press, 2003.

Spivak, Gayatri Chakravorty. *The Post-colonial Critic: Interviews, Strategies, Dialogues*. Ed. Sarah Harasym. New York: Routledge, 1990.

——. "Rethinking Comparativism." *New Literary History* 40, no. 3 (2009), 609–26.

——. "Translation as Culture." *Parallax* 6, no. 1 (2000), 13–24.

Sprengnether, Madelon. *The Spectral Mother: Freud, Feminism, and Psychoanalysis*. Ithaca: Cornell University Press, 1990.

Sprinker, Michael, ed. *Ghostly Demarcations: A Symposium on Jacques Derrida's "Spectres of Marx."* London: Verso, 1999.

Sroka, Kenneth M. "Fact, Fiction, and the Introductions to the Waverley Novels." *Wordsworth Circle* 2, no. 4 (1971), 142–52.

Stanton, Domna A. "Difference on Trial: A Critique of the Maternal Metaphor in Cixous, Irigaray, and Kristeva." *The Poetics of Gender*, ed. Nancy K. Miller, 157–82. New York: Columbia University Press, 1986.

Stanworth, Michelle, ed. *Reproductive Technologies: Gender, Motherhood, and Medicine*. Minneapolis: University of Minnesota Press, 1987.

Stone, Linda. *Kinship and Gender: An Introduction*. Boulder: Westview, 1997.

Strathern, Marilyn. *Kinship, Law, and the Unexpected: Relatives Are Always a Surprise*. Cambridge: Cambridge University Press, 2005.

———. *Reproducing the Future: Essays on Anthropology, Kinship, and the New Reproductive Technologies*. Manchester: Manchester University Press, 1992.

Swan, Jim. "'Mater' and Nannie: Freud's Two Mothers and the Discovery of the Oedipus Complex." *American Imago* 31, no. 1 (1974), 1–64.

Terdiman, Richard. "Deconstructing Memory: On Representing the Past and Theorizing Culture in France since the Revolution." *Diacritics* 15, no. 4 (1985), 13–36.

Thaden, Barbara Z. *The Maternal Voice in Victorian Fiction: Rewriting the Patriarchal Family*. New York: Garland, 1997.

Thompson, Charis. *Making Parents: The Ontological Choreography of Reproductive Technologies*. Cambridge: MIT Press, 2005.

Tobias, Henry Jack. *The Jewish Bund in Russia from Its Origins to 1905*. Stanford: Stanford University Press, 1972.

Todd, Janet M., ed. *Men by Women*. New York: Holmes and Meier, 1981.

Traverso, Enzo. *The Marxists and the Jewish Question: The History of a Debate, 1843–1943*. Trans. Bernard Gibbons. Atlantic Highlands, N.J.: Humanities Press, 1994.

Trebay, Guy. "He's Pregnant. You're Speechless." *New York Times*, 22 June 2008.

Treichler, Paula, Lisa Cartwright, and Constance Penley, eds. *The Visible Woman: Imaging Technologies, Gender, and Science*. New York: New York University Press, 1998.

Trumpener, Katie. *Bardic Nationalism: The Romantic Novel and the British Empire*. Princeton: Princeton University Press, 1997.

Valente, Joseph. "Upon the Braes: History and Hermeneutics in 'Waverley.'" *Studies in Romanticism* 25, no. 2 (1986), 251–76.

Voltaire, François-Marie Arouet. *Oeuvres complètes*. Vol. 19. Paris: Garnier Frères, 1879.

Walker, Michelle Boulous. *Philosophy and the Maternal Body: Reading Silence*. New York: Routledge, 1998.

Wallace, Michele. *Black Macho and the Myth of the Superwoman*. New York: Dial Press, 1979.

Wallet, Bart. "'End of the Jargon-Scandal': The Decline and Fall of Yiddish in the Netherlands (1796–1886)." *Jewish History* 20, nos. 3–4 (2006), 333–48.

Weber, Samuel M. *The Legend of Freud*. Minneapolis: University of Minnesota Press, 1982.

Weiss, Gail. *Refiguring the Ordinary*. Bloomington: Indiana University Press, 2008.

Weiss, Gail, and Honi Fern Haber, eds. *Perspectives on Embodiment: The Intersections of Nature and Culture*. New York: Routledge, 1999.

Welsh, Alexander. *The Hero of the Waverley Novels: With New Essays on Scott*. Exp. edn. Princeton: Princeton University Press, 1992.

Whitford, Margaret, ed. *The Irigaray Reader*. Cambridge, Mass.: Basil Blackwell, 1991.

Wilson, Elizabeth A. *Psychosomatic: Feminism and the Neurological Body*. Durham: Duke University Press, 2004.

Wilt, Judith. *Secret Leaves: The Novels of Walter Scott*. Chicago: University of Chicago Press, 1985.

———. "Walter Scott: Narrative, History, Synthesis." *The Columbia History of the British Novel*, ed. John Richetti, 300–326. New York: Columbia University Press, 1994.

Witt, Mary Ann Frese. "Babies and Books: Birth as Metaphor in Nietzsche and Pirandello." *Comparative Critical Studies* 6, no. 2 (2009), 183–200.

Wolfson, Louis. *Le schizo et les langues*. Paris: Gallimard, 1970.

Wolin, Richard. *Heidegger's Children: Hannah Arendt, Karl Löwith, Hans Jonas, and Herbert Marcuse*. Princeton: Princeton University Press, 2001.

Wood, Michael. "There Is No Cure." *London Review of Books*, 6 July 2006, 3–7.

Woodmansee, Martha, and Peter Jaszi, eds. *The Construction of Authorship: Textual Appropriation in Law and Literature*. Durham: Duke University Press, 1994.

Yerushalmi, Yosef Hayim. *Freud's Moses: Judaism Terminable and Interminable*. New Haven: Yale University Press, 1991.

Zapperi, Roberto. *The Pregnant Man*. Trans. Brian Williams. Rev. and updated 4th edn. Chur, Switz.: Harwood Academic, 1991.

Zwinger, Lynda. "Blood Relations: Feminist Theory Meets the Uncanny Alien Bug Mother." *Hypatia* 7, no. 2 (1992), 74–90.

ANDREW PARKER is a professor of English at Amherst College. He is the editor of Jacques Rancière's *The Philosopher and His Poor*, which he translated with John Drury and Corinne Oster (Duke, 2004), and the coeditor of six other books, most recently *After Sex?: On Writing since Queer Theory* (Duke, 2011).

Library of Congress Cataloging-in-Publication Data

Parker, Andrew, 1953–
The theorist's mother / Andrew Parker.
p. cm.
Includes bibliographical references and index.
ISBN 978-0-8223-5218-1 (cloth : alk. paper)
ISBN 978-0-8223-5232-7 (pbk. : alk. paper)
1. Motherhood—Philosophy. I. Title.
HQ759.P27 2012
306.874′3—dc23
2011041910